REGIS

On the Crest of the West

Charlie & M.J.,

    I hope that this book revives some memories and may they be pleasant. God bless you.

        Harry Stansell S.J.

Dedication

John J. Brown, President, 1899-1903 and 1906-1920.
To the Jesuits of the New Mexico-Colorado Mission

REGIS
On the Crest of the West

Harold L. Stansell, S. J.

REGIS
EDUCATIONAL
CORPORATION

Imprimatur: James Vincent Casey, Archbishop of Denver

Typography & Design/Graphic Impressions, Inc./Denver

Photographs/Regis files and friends

*Printed in the United States of America
by Pruett Press, Boulder, Colorado*

© *Copyright 1977 by Regis Educational Corporation*

Library of Congress card catalog number 77-088130

International Standard Book Number 09601460-1-6

*Published by Regis Educational Corporation
Denver, Colorado*

Contents

Presidents vi

Preface... vii

Acknowledgements... ix

The Las Vegas Phase.. 1

The Morrison Experience 23

Denver — A Self Contained Operation... 41

Unfulfilled Dreams 77

Stabilization and Growth... 147

Expansion and Modernization.. 175

Transition to the Second Hundred Years....................................... 205

Alumni 227

Bibliographical Notes.. 233

Index 235

Abbreviations 238

Presidents

LAS VEGAS COLLEGE
1. Salvatore Personè — October 1, 1878
2. Dominic Pantanella — January 4, 1883
3. Salvatore Personè — August 10, 1884

MORRISON
4. Dominic Pantanella — August 10, 1884
   (Sacred Heart College, Morrison)

DENVER
   Salvatore Personè — 1888
5. Joseph M. Marra — January 19, 1892
6. John B. Guida — July 29, 1896
7. John J. Brown — September 1, 1899
8. Anthony J. Schuler — September 1, 1903
9. John J. Brown — August 15, 1906
10. Robert M. Kelley — August 15, 1920
11. Aloysius A. Breen — September 20, 1926
12. Gerald P. Walsh — July 31, 1931
13. John J. Driscoll (Acting President) — September 23, 1931
14. Joseph A. Herbers — January 6, 1932
15. Robert M. Kelley — February 21, 1935
16. John J. Flanagan — March 19, 1942
17. Raphael C. McCarthy — June 10, 1947
18. Richard F. Ryan — July 1, 1953
19. Frederick T. Daly (Acting President) — October 24-December 18, 1967
20. Louis G. Mattione — March 1, 1968
21. Thomas James Casey (Acting President) — July 1, 1971
22. David M. Clarke — August 1, 1972

Preface

We experience no rarer moment in life than that moment suspended between what is past and what is prologue. What has passed before us and the potential that awaits us can either be man's most trying moment or his richest. It is for such a moment that this book has become reality. And for Regis it is our richest.

At moments like this I am often reminded of the poignant and enduring words of Ecclesiastes:

> For everything there is a season,
> and a time for every matter under heaven;
> a time to be born, and a time to die;
> a time to plant, and a time to pluck up
>   what is planted;
> a time to kill, and a time to heal;
> a time to break down, and a time to build up;
> a time to weep, and a time to laugh;
> a time to mourn, and a time to dance;
> a time to cast away stones, and a time
>   to gather stones together;
> a time to embrace, and a time to refrain
>   from embracing;
> a time to seek, and a time to lose;
> a time to keep, and a time to cast away;
> a time to rend, and a time to sew;
> a time to keep silence, and a time to speak;
> a time to love, and a time to hate;
> a time for war, and a time for peace.

This year, as Regis enters its century mark, we pass into that special moment of inbetween—a time to celebrate and a time to reflect, a time to reminisce and a time to renew our vision.

At such a time of reflection we once again are reminded of the men and the forces that brought us to this moment. Regis' 100th anniversary is a direct reflection of the Jesuit presence in education.

The Society of Jesus (Jesuits) came into existence as a community of companions, united in understanding and affection, resolved to serve their fellowmen, and in the very act of so doing, to further their own growth in the Christian life.

The Jesuit presence in education is a direct result of St. Ignatius Loyola's determination to meet the needs of his age. That concern and commitment has continued through the ages and was carried to Las Vegas, New Mexico, where, 100 years ago, a band of Jesuit missionaries carved out a college in the desert.

Ever since Ignatius shaped the Jesuit mission, high schools, colleges and universities have flourished around the world because they met the needs of the times. Their curriculums suited and continue to suit the times and thus have been particular to them. Their goal has been more general and less bound to a place and a time. They brought themselves and their students to experience this world physically, socially, intellectually and spiritually. They have brought themselves and their students to reflect on that experience, to come to a self-understanding, and a life of choice and action most in accord with the best in themselves and in their world.

That spirit continues at Regis today. Having served more than 15,000 students in its history, Regis still is determined to teach its students to think critically, to introduce them to beauty and order, to free them from blind prejudices and mindlessness, to free them from fear of the world order man has created or blundered into, and to help them mature their conscience and their faith.

The direction Regis must take is reasonably clear. We are continuing to meet the needs of our students and are committed to instilling a sense of values upon which they can base decisions for tomorrow. Ahead there are literally tens of thousands of decisions yet to be made, and often the facts pertinent to a particular decision will not be made clear. Nevertheless, Regis is determined to face each decision as it occurs and to maintain its tradition of quality, for Regis is committed to the future as it enters its second hundred years of education and service to the people of Denver, the state and the nation.

Father David M. Clarke, S.J.
President

Acknowledgements

This book has been written because Francis J. Malecek, Professor of Philosophy, made the timely suggestion to President David M. Clarke that an effort be made to record the history of the school for the first hundred years. Regrettably, the author did not achieve a better balance in his narration between the college and the high school. I am indebted to many people who have made this book possible. In the first place I am most grateful to David M. Clarke and the Board of Trustees who were most generous in providing the necessary funds for this project. Thanks are due to William J. Hannon, Director of Corporate Services, for his patience and assistance in making arrangements for the disbursement of money when it was needed and to Mrs. Bernice Fisher in supplying some necessary equipment. The following members of the administrative staff have been helpful: Lawrence W. Durance, A. Thomas Elliot, Thomas A. Emmet, Mary O'Donnell, Paul Q. Riederer and Paul Max. The president's secretaries, Rexonna Burch and Paula Chambers, graciously provided materials from the files. Eleanor M. Kelly, the Dean's secretary, gave the author access to some helpful documents filed in the office of the Dean. Tim Willard and Arthur O. Verdieck, S.J., of the high school staff were cooperative. Special gratitude is due Phillip E. Gauthier, former director of public information, who willingly supplied data and refreshed the memory of the author about many events. The author is mindful of the debt he owes to John Francis Bannon, S.J., who encouraged him to continue the study of history, and to Lowrie J. Daly, S.J., of St. Louis University who facilitated his access to materials in the Pius XII Library. Thanks are due to Joseph P. Donnelly, S.J., who read the first draft of some of the chapters and offered helpful suggestions. Over the years the author has been fortunate in having colleagues in the department of history who have stimulated his interest in the study of history and he is grateful for his association with the following: Fred R. Van Valkenburg, Bernard W. Sheehan, Gordon D. Ross, Walker Edwards, Donald L. Salmon, Ronald D. Brockway, Peter M. Wright, and his former students and colleagues James D. Wright and James B. Guyer, S.J. William B. Faherty, S.J., noted author, has given more assistance than he suspects. Dr. James M. Erdmann and Dr. Allen du Pont Breck of the University of Denver offered helpful suggestions. Frederick T. Daly, S.J., Robert L. Kraus, S.J., and Jeanette

Ryan made notable contributions, as did James J. Hennesey, S.J.

Archivists and librarians have been very cooperative, especially Edmond Lamalle, S.J., and József Fejér, S.J., in charge of the archives of the Society of Jesus in Rome; Francesco Meduri, S.J., Naples; Sister Elizabeth Skiff, Archdiocese of Denver; Catherine Weidle, St. Louis Room, Pius XII Library, St. Louis; Dennis D. North and David A. Farr, Dayton Memorial Library; Ann West of Regis High School; Mrs. Larry Steele of the State Historical Society of Colorado; and the staff of the Western History Section, Denver Public Library.

Mrs. Joseph Gargaro, who typed the manuscript, has been a model of patience and perseverance, and Mrs. William Popick, who did the proofreading, saved the author from many pitfalls. I am indebted to them and will cherish the memory of our association. Howard Harms of Pruett Press, a true gentleman, has facilitated my task and has given generously of his time and effort to see the book through the press. I am grateful to John V. Coyne for recommending Mr. Harms and Pruett Press.

My fellow Jesuits have made the task of writing this history much more pleasant than it might have been. Provincial Leo F. Weber gave me free access to correspondence on file in his office and offered sage advice on some delicate matters. Paul F. Distler most generously supplied copies of pertinent documents. John P. Teeling, former rector of the Jesuit community, made funds available for a trip to Rome and Naples, and his successor, William S. Udick, was a constant source of encouragement. Special thanks are due to the members of the Jesuit community for their patience, especially to Joseph V. Downey, who gave assistance in matters related to the seismograph station. Robert J. O'Sullivan read the typescript and offered helpful suggestions. Thomas J. Steele also read the typescript and was exacting in his recommendations for improvements in the text. Sister Eustacia Stansell, C.PP.S., merits my gratitude for her moral support. Finally, words cannot express my appreciation for the assistance and inspiration I derived from Raymond Corrigan, S.J., who introduced me to the study of history, Thomas P. Neill, who directed my graduate studies, and Edward R. Vollmar, S.J., an authority on the work of the Jesuits in the New Mexico-Colorado Mission. They have departed this life but they live on in the work they had accomplished.

Chapter 1

The Las Vegas Phase

1877-1888

On August 15, 1867, five Jesuits, members of the Dispersed Province of Naples, arrived in Santa Fe. They had traveled with a caravan that left Leavenworth, Kansas, on June 14th in the company of Jean Baptiste Lamy, Bishop of Santa Fe. Their journey had been adventurous and sometimes dangerous, covering thousands of miles since the departure from Le Havre on May 9.[1] These men formed part of a group of religious that had been recruited by the dedicated bishop; among others making up the band that traveled across the Santa Fe Trail were three Sisters of Loretto, two of Charity of Cincinnati, and two Brothers of the Christian Schools. The Sisters and Brothers came to join small communities of their orders which by 1867 were already reasonably well established in the diocese which had been formed in 1850. The Jesuits, the first members of their order to reach the vast American Southwest over the Santa Fe Trail, arrived to minister to the religious needs of the Spanish-speaking people of the Territory of New Mexico and eventually to found an institution of higher learning which was to serve the needs of the Catholic Church in the Rocky Mountain Region.

Four of the Jesuits were newcomers to the United States, and the fifth, Father Livio Vigilante, the oldest at forty-eight, had been teaching in Worcester, Massachusetts, where he learned English; his services would be needed to help his brethren when they started their work in New Mexico. He was also the logical choice as religious superior of the group. Of the other four two were lay brothers and two priests. Of the former Prisco Caso, who had been in Naples at the time he received his assignment, was a cook, and as such was to prove himself indispensable to the well-being of his companions. The other lay brother, Raphael Vezza, was a carpenter. Of the two priests, Raphael Bianchi, thirty-one-years old, was not destined to survive for long; he died on December 28, 1868. The fifth member of the group, Donato M.

---

[1] Sister M. Lilliana Owens, S.L., published two accounts of the journey; one, ''Account of the Journey of Reverend Donato M. Gasparri, S.J., to New Mexico in 1867''; the other, ''Diary of the Mission of New Mexico May 27, 1867-October 18, 1874.'' The latter account is attributed to Livio Vigilante the only one of the five who had some knowledge of English. *Jesuit Beginnings in New Mexico 1867-1882* (El Paso, Texas, Revista Catolica Press, 1950), pp. 86-94; 95-108.

Gasparri, must be considered the real founder of the Mission. Dynamic, forceful, untiring, he made the Jesuit presence felt in New Mexico.

How does the historian account for this new chapter in the history of the diocese of Santa Fe? Why were these men available in 1867 for apostolic work in the United States? One explanation is found in the fact that the Neapolitans had been looking for places in which the members of the Province could find work and a home. In the 1860's the Italian patriot, Giuseppe Garibaldi, had made an essential contribution to the unification of Italy when he conquered the Kingdom of Naples and expelled the ruling family. The new government followed a vigorous anticlerical policy which resulted in the confiscation of religious houses in southern Italy. This was not a new experience for the members of the Society of Jesus. During the nineteenth century they had to make adjustments from time to time when they were expelled from their homelands. Somehow they managed to maintain their identity and their loyalty to the order under the jurisdiction of their elected Superior General. When the Neapolitans were expelled from their houses in Southern Italy, they continued as a juridical entity which termed itself The Dispersed Province of Naples. Their religious brothers in Europe offered them hospitality and many found opportunities to continue their work. To cite but one example, there were thirty-two Neapolitan Jesuits in the Spanish Province of Aragon in 1867.[2]

The situation seemed to be propitious when Jean Baptiste Lamy[3] petitioned authorities in Rome for some Jesuits to work in his diocese. In 1866 he approached Alessandro Cardinal Barnabo, Prefect of the Sacred Congregation of the *Propaganda Fidei,* who referred the request to Pieter Beckx, Superior General of the Society of Jesus, who in turn passed it on to Francisco Ferrante, Provincial of the Dispersed Province of Naples. Ferrante and his consultors decided that the Neapolitan Jesuits should establish a mission in New Mexico and he assigned the five men to go to the Territory and assist Bishop Lamy. The Jesuits began pastoral work in Bernalillo, New Mexico. Since there was difficulty in obtaining a clear title to the property there, they moved to Albuquerque, which became the main center of their activities. Besides doing pastoral work in the Albuquerque area they began to preach missions in other parishes in the diocese. In due time more men were assigned to the mission, and by 1873 Jesuits extended their activities to the territory of Colorado. In 1875 a total of thirty-five Jesuits were engaged in parochial work and the preaching of missions; in New Mexico there were

_____

[2]CDPN, 1867, pp. 9-10.

[3]The story of Archbishop Lamy is a fascinating one. It has been told a number of times. A recent biography of the Archbishop is that of Paul Horgan, *Lamy of Santa Fe: His Life and Times* (New York Farrar, Straus and Giroux, 1975).

fourteen in Albuquerque, five in La Junta (Tiptonville), and six in Las Vegas. Ten men were working in Southern Colorado, six in Conejos and four in Pueblo.

It is the primary objective of this history to relate the development of the college which was established in Las Vegas, New Mexico, in 1877. Consequently, the history of the mission, fascinating as it is, must be left to some future historian who will expand the basic work written by Giuseppe M. Sorrentino.[4]

True to the enduring tradition of the order in the field of education, the Jesuits in New Mexico were not content with working in parishes and preaching missions. They wanted to teach. Education in New Mexico had been sadly neglected for almost two and one-half centuries, during which the territory was claimed by Spain, and, since 1821, Mexico. True, the people had developed a rich culture made up of Spanish and Indian ingredients, a culture that was new Mexican and Catholic. However, the people were too poor to afford the luxury of formal education. About the only school that could claim to be an institution of higher education was that of Padre Antonio Jose Martinez in Taos. After the United States acquired the territory efforts were made to improve the educational situation. It was, however, to take time to overcome past deficiencies. As late as 1870, some twenty years after the Americans took over, the census revealed that of a population of 51,000 over ten years of age, 49,000 could not write and 48,000 could not read. Out of 30,000 of school age, there were only 5,000 pupils.[5] It is to the credit of Bishop Lamy that he recruited Sisters of Loretto and Sisters of Charity of Cincinnati as well as Brothers of the Christian Schools to work in his diocese. The Sisters and Brothers opened schools in the more populated towns, especially in Santa Fe where the Sisters of Loretto taught young girls and the Christian Brothers founded St. Michael's College (The College of Santa Fe). Certainly the Bishop had education in mind when he enlisted the help of the Jesuits, and his hopes were fulfilled when the sons of Ignatius began to educate young people in their parishes.

An engaging story is related by Sister Blandina Segale in her book *At the End of the Santa Fe Trail.* In 1876 Sister Blandina and Sister Martha were told to leave Trinidad, Colorado, and proceed to Santa Fe. Father Charles M. Pinto, S.J., the pastor of the church in Trinidad, volunteered to accompany the Sisters on their journey to their new assignment. As they approached Tiptonville, New Mexico, Father Pinto suggested that they stop at the parish

---

[4]Giuseppe M. Sorrentino, S.J., *Dalle Montagne Rocciose al Rio Bravo* (Naples, Casa Editrice Federico and Andria, n.d.).

[5]Porter A. Stratton, *The Territorial Press of New Mexico 1834-1912* (Albuquerque, University of New Mexico Press, 1969), p. 136.

and visit the Jesuits stationed there; he informed them that they would meet a Jesuit who was considered one of the best mathematicians in the order and a linguist. Sister Blandina continued:

> My curiosity was raised many degrees to see who the man might be who was consigned, with his knowledge of mathematics and languages, to a map-forgotten place. We stopped at the schoolroom door. A boy about eight years old heard the footsteps and at once opened the door. This is the scene my glance took in: 20 pupils from the ages of 7 to 13 years, in their seats, and the man of high attainments demonstrating that 2 plus 3 equals 5 plus 5 equals 10![6]

It was obvious to the Jesuits that there could not be any ambitious undertaking with regard to education until more men were available. The number of men assigned to the mission from the Province of Naples was not significantly increased until 1871 when a total of fifteen is listed in the catalogue;[7] by 1877 there were thirty-six men assigned to New Mexico and Colorado.

Although it is not our intention to get deeply involved in the history of the New Mexico-Colorado Mission, a few words should be said about those activities which, in one way or another, were related to the efforts of the Jesuits to establish a college. The administrative structure was relatively simple, especially during the first three years; that structure called for a Superior whose duty it was, among other things, to make reports to the Provincial of the Naples Province. Livio Vigilante was appointed Superior of the pioneer group but it would seem that the rigors of life on the frontier were too much for him and he returned to Maryland in 1868. His successor in the office was Donato M. Gasparri, who at age thirty-five took over the tasks of laying a solid foundation for the mission. His experience in Spain, where he was working when he received word of his assignment to New Mexico, fitted him perfectly for that territory. He understood his people and loved them; he was also determined to help them to remain loyal to their Catholic heritage. He was indefatigable in his work for his people and his church. He adjusted well to his new homeland and showed a surprising ability to understand the danger that was latent in the anti-Catholic prejudice of a number of Americans who were moving into the territory.

To combat hostile forces and to keep his people informed he saw the need for a printing press. Somehow he was able to obtain one. After Gasparri's

---

[6]Sister Blandina Segale, *At The End of the Santa Fe Trail* (Columbus, Ohio, The Columbian Press, 1932), p. 88.

[7]CDPN, 1871, p. 16.

persistent efforts to raise the necessary funds, Father Joseph Marra, of whom much will be said later, recorded of him:

> He was entirely without the means for such a gigantic task; but his daring soul did not become discouraged. He began to beg the necessary money, especially from the clergy of New Mexico and elsewhere, who received this idea with enthusiasm. The contributions were so generous he soon had sufficient money to make his project a reality.[8]

The press was delivered in 1872 and assembled in Albuquerque the next year. Fortunately Gasparri found a fellow Jesuit who volunteered to become the printer, The Reverend Enrique Ferrari.[9] Soon books of instruction and piety were being published. The press was destined to be moved to Las Vegas where it began to publish the weekly *Revista Catolica,* the first number of which appeared on January 2, 1875. This paper was the Jesuit answer to other publications in the territory; it was published in Spanish, the language of the majority of the New Mexican Catholic people and was to prove a powerful instrument in the defense of the Church in New Mexico.

As the small group of Jesuits was augmented by new arrivals from Italy, Gasparri, with customary energy, began to plan for a college. There was a two-fold concern for an educational institution in which more advanced courses could be taught than those which were available in the parish or the newly developing public schools. The first concern was associated with the aspiration to have a school in which candidates for the priesthood could find the opportunity to gain the basic skills which would enable them to pursue the higher studies of philosophy and theology. The second concern was to have a school in which, hopefully, students could work for the bachelor's degree. Given the condition of education in New Mexico at the time, both objectives were rather ambitious.

Difficulties never deterred Gasparri from making an effort. A second building was acquired in Albuquerque in 1872, and the Jesuits announced that they would open Holy Family College. The beginning was far from impressive since the first notice carried in the Province Catalogue of 1873 does not list anyone as teaching any subjects.[10] In the following year, 1874, three teachers are recorded: Vitus Carrozzini for English, Enrique Ferrari for English and Music, and Vitus Tromby for Spanish.[11] Evidently the response was less than enthusiastic, for in the following year, 1875, there is no entry concerning such a college. One of the earlier historians of the Mission, Ferdinand Troy (who for some reason had converted his family name from

---

[8]Sister M. Lilliana Owens, S.L., *op. cit.,* p. 66.
[9]*Ibid.*
[10]CDPN, 1873, pp. 18-19.
[11]CDPN, 1874, pp. 20-21.

Trojanech to Troy), wrote a letter to the Reverend Edward R. Vollmar in 1936 which included this comment:

The so-called Holy Family College was nothing but an attempt poorly executed of [a] school for the Albuquerqeans. It has a big title to interest Superiors and the population. The Superiors had too many other problems to solve and the inhabitants after the first flare did not care much for the institution. It was closed in time and the remnants handed over to the Sisters of Charity.[12]

The fortunes of the Jesuits in Albuquerque were not propitious in the earlier years. They had to close a college which hardly had a decent beginning; an attempt to establish a novitate in which candidates for acceptance into the Society of Jesus could begin their training had to be discontinued; and in 1873 when a flood threatened the valuable printing press, the machine was transferred further north to Las Vegas, New Mexico. The citizens of that town had been eager to have the Jesuits establish a house in their town ever since some Jesuits had preached a mission there. Some of the citizens were so impressed that they asked the Jesuits to establish a college.

Before considering the foundation of Las Vegas College, it is well to note that there had been some changes in the Jesuit administration. Following a standard practice, major superiors were changed after they held office for six or seven years. Consequently, Gasparri was replaced on June 23, 1876, and Raphael A. Baldassarre was appointed Superior of the Mission. Gasparri was assigned to the residence in Las Vegas. He assumed the duties of directing *Revista Catolica* and also labored as a writer for the paper. When he was not too busy with these duties he would resume the work of preaching missions. During the period of his regime as Superior, the number of men working in the territories of New Mexico and Colorado had increased from five to thirty-six. The church had an organ for defense of Catholic causes in the *Revista*. The failures in Albuquerque did not dampen the zeal of this Italian priest and the territory would hear much more from him.

The new Superior, forty-six-years old and destined to hold office for only four years, was a shadowy figure, not nearly as flamboyant as his predecessor. It was during his regime that Las Vegas College was established. Baldassare had an advantage in assessing the state of the mission when he assumed the duties of the office, an advantage deriving from the practice of the Superiors of the Jesuits sending official visitors from outside the province or mission to investigate all the houses under the care of the Society to find out what major problems needed attention as well as what projects were envisioned for the future. The offical visitor then reported to the Provincial

---

[12]R.C.A.

of the Province of Naples and to the General of the Order. The superiors deemed it wise to send someone who knew something about the United States to carry out this assignment and they were fortunate to have a capable man who was a member of the Province of Naples with considerable contact with Americans and American ways. That man was Camillus Mazzella, lecturer in dogmatic theology in Woodstock, Maryland. He was to prove himself a true friend of the Mission and, in time, would be in a position as a cardinal to present the case of the Mission in Rome based on a good knowledge of the men and the territory. Visitors were obliged to draw up a Memorial, basically a report on the visitation which called to the mind of Superiors and all members of the mission points which needed attention and which, if attended to, would revitalize the religious spirit of all of the members in the territory.

The time of visitation offered an opportunity for superiors to make proposals for other undertakings in the mission. One such project that was uppermost in the minds of Baldassarre and Gasparri was the foundation of a college in Las Vegas. The visitor concluded that from his assessment of the state of the mission the time was not ripe for such a venture. Mazzella reminded the Superior that he had limited manpower and slender resources; consequently, he recommended postponement of the project.[13]

Mazzella's report to the General included mention of the proposal for a college; the General, Pieter Beckx, wrote to Baldassare regarding the matter informing him that the proposal to open a college in Las Vegas was under consideration, but more information was needed from the Provincial of Naples. Pieter Beckx was cautious; he indicated that the Superior of the Mission should not be rash in starting something that might have to be abandoned with embarrassment (*cum dedecore*).[14]

Far from being discouraged by this directive from Rome, Baldassare continued to search for the necessary means to build a college. He urged the superior of the Jesuit residence in Las Vegas, Salvatore Personè, to undertake the task. Personè was a kind and sympathetic man; some considered him the most popular man in the Mission. He had no illusions about the magnitude of the project to which he was assigned. Later he recorded his thoughts in a letter to his brethren in Naples:

 . . . the very thought of a college would strike me with fear because of various reasons. For I would say ''Who will teach? Whom will he teach? What will he teach?'' The personnel was lacking because it

---

[13]Ferdinand M. Troy, S.J., *Historia Missionis Novi Mexici et Coloradi,* (type script copy, archives of Regis College, p. 74).

[14]*Mission, Assist. Ital. a die 18 Aug., 1873 ad diem 15 Maii, 1906,* vol. II, p. 34. S.J. Arch.

required someone who knew English well and there were few in the mission and they could not leave their work.[15]

He was even less sanguine about the ability of prospective students and confessed in his letter his worry about choosing a curriculum for students whose parents "care nothing else than that their sons be taught to read, write, figure, as they themselves, and to pronounce a few English words."[16]

Difficulties notwithstanding, Baldassare proceeded with his planning. He chose Personè as the chief officer of the college-to-be and discussed with him the most pressing problem—finances. Personè recalled an incident reminiscent of the stories found in pious legends of the Ages of Faith. He wrote that when Baldassare prepared to leave him to go in search of a loan, he received a letter from a religious (a certain Mexican woman of the Loretto Sisters) in which she offered three thousand dollars for the needs of the mission. We gladly accepted this unexpected aid of Divine Providence and said: "God wills it."[17]

With money and property, Personè took steps to start building as well as to assemble a faculty. He was fortunate to have the help of Gasparri, a member of the Jesuit Community in Las Vegas, who welcomed the challenge of helping to found a college. Gasparri hired laborers, collected the required materials and supervised the necessary preparations.

Personè did not want to lose momentum; he realized that even Gasparri could not have the building ready in time for the opening of classes. Temporary quarters were needed; fortunately a generous citizen of Las Vegas, Francisco Lopez, was willing to offer a building which, though hardly adequate, could serve the purpose. Personè accepted the offer and classes began on November 5, 1877.

Why did the Jesuits choose Las Vegas? It was a small town, some forty miles east and south of the capital; and though Santa Fe was hardly a thriving metropolis, it already had a college. The Brothers of the Christian Schools had opened a school in 1860 at the request of Archbishop Lamy, one that is still operating under the name of the College of Santa Fe. With the capital eliminated, another plausible choice would have been Albuquerque, but the memories of the previous failures in that town deterred the superior from undertaking another educational venture there. One other possibility might have been Colorado; some consideration had been given to the San Luis Valley, but that territory was not yet well developed. So Las Vegas was the

---

[15]Troy, *op cit.,* p. 80.

[16]*Ibid.*

[17]Troy, *op. cit.,* p. 81. A reference concerning the source of the $3,000 is in *Storia Annuale Della Missione.* N.M.E. Colorado 1867-1919, P.N. Arch.

logical choice; it was a growing center of Jesuit activities. The press was there and the people were enthusiastic and eager to have a school. It is just possible that Baldassare and his consultors, one of whom was Gasparri, had hopes that Las Vegas might develop into one of the greater cities of the Southwest. Las Vegas had been, moreover, an important transshipment point to Taos, Santa Fe, Albuquerque and the rest of the Rio Abajo (Down-river) area during the Santa Fe Trail period and during the approach of the railroad. Because of its strategic location it enjoyed a reasonable amount of prosperity. When the railhead passed on to Albuquerque after 1880, Las Vegas lost out economically. In 1877, however, the future looked promising.

During the summer of 1877 Personè succeeded in lining up the following faculty: Personè, president,[18] and treasurer; Alphonsus M. Rossi, who had recently finished his training as a Jesuit, was prefect of studies and professor of Latin; Lawrence Fede, first prefect of discipline and professor of Spanish; Anthony Minasi, professor of higher arithmetic; Enrique M. Ferrari, professor of music. Two laymen completed the roster: H. D. M'Ilhenney, professor of English, and W. Adamson, teacher of rudiments.[19] During the first year this faculty taught some one hundred thirty-two students.[20] Twenty-five of the total were boarding students; four were half-boarders (a curious category; they were students who took all their meals at the school but returned to their homes in the evening); and one hundred three were day-scholars. Seven youngsters were entrusted to the care of the Jesuits by Archbishop Lamy who hoped that they might go on to study for the priesthood.

It was a well-established tradition to give a name to a new institution of learning. The Jesuits chose to name the new school in honor of the Blessed Virgin; they called it St. Mary's. Before long, however, they realized that a certain amount of confusion might arise from the fact that the Christian Brothers had established a school in the neighboring town of Mora with that

---

[18]It is well to note what Edward Power wrote about the choice of presidents for Catholic Colleges in the nineteenth-century America, "To begin with, the qualifications for a president were nonacademic; his scholarly pedigree was unimportant; but his standing as a sound and solid cleric mattered, and we have no right to suppose that any priest ever occupying a presidential chair had anything less than unblemished moral and sacerdotal credentials." Edward J. Power, *Catholic Higher Education in America a History* (New York, Appleton-Century-Crofts, 1972. Reprinted by permission of Prentice-Hall, Inc.), p. 71.

[19]L.V.C., Cat., 1877-1878, p. 7.

[20]An exact accounting of the number of students in any given year is next to impossible. Students came and left during the school year; frequently parents called their sons home to work on the ranch or their place of business. The first catalogue of Las Vegas College lists 132 for the academic year 1877-78.

name. Finally the Jesuits decided to choose the designation of Las Vegas College.[21]

Before proceeding with the history of Las Vegas College, it may be helpful to call to mind that the meaning of the word "college" in 1877 was not as standard as it was to become in later times. Professor Power, who spent a great deal of time and effort studying the question of Catholic higher education, reached the conclusion:

> It was hard for Catholic colleges of the formative period to state the objectives of their courses, whatever may have been their own institutional hopes or those for higher education in general. In this respect they shared a common disadvantage that time alone could not erode. Prior to 1870 all Catholic colleges began their academic history as combinations of elementary and secondary schools. And even when upgrading added a college course of studies to a secondary-school foundation, the elementary side of teaching was difficult to abandon.[22]

It must be admitted that this conclusion applies to the educational venture of the Jesuits in Las Vegas. The best available evidence was reported by the first American Jesuit assigned to the faculty of the college three years after it was inaugurated; namely, Michael J. Hughes. Hughes was a member of the Province of Maryland-New York established in 1879. He arrived in Las Vegas in 1880 as a scholastic to help with the teaching of English in the school. He wrote to his colleagues in the East about his impressions of the Southwest. Writing about the quality of the students he reported:

> . . . teachers had very rough, though good material to work on. As the boys were not very far advanced, they were obliged to begin at the lowest rudiments with some, and the teachers who came immediately afterwards can tell what rapid progress was made. Many of those first engaged in the work were men capable of teaching philosophy and theology, and yet they labored hard and earnestly in their humble position, knowing that all they did was for God.[23]

Before proceeding to other details about that first academic year 1877-1878, it is well to take a look at the catalogue which was published at the end of the year. After an introductory statement of purpose printed in English and Spanish, there follows a listing of the faculty, a roster of students, and a program of the closing exercises with the names of the students who won prizes. In the initial statement it is noted that ". . . the course of studies will

---

[21]Troy, *op. cit.*, p. 84. The name appears for the first time in the Province Catalogue of 1878 as Veganum Collegium Inchoatum, p. 20.

[22]Power, *op. cit.*, p. 122.

[23]W.L., vol. 12, 1883, p. 301.

be gradually completed in accordance with the progressive development of students and the special requirements of this part of the country."[24]

It is somewhat surprising to find the following statement in the same source indicating that non-Catholics would be welcome:

The moral and religious culture of youth being an indispensable element of true Christian education, the Faculty of Las Vegas College deemed it their imperious duty to direct their utmost attention to the formation of both heart and mind in training the students committed to their care, and although the College be conducted on strictly Catholic principles, no undue influence will be used to make a pupil depart from his religious belief.[25]

The charges for board and tuition, then as always, constituted a problem for Personè and his colleagues. As Jesuits they were bound to follow the spirit of the Society which demanded that they make their services available without charge beyond what was necessary to meet essential expenses. It was, however, inevitable that some charge be made for housing and feeding the boarders at the school. The charges published in the catalogue of 1877-1878 seem reasonable enough: $200.00 for board and tuition for a year, $100.00 for half-boarders. Day-scholars were asked to pay from $1.00 to $3.00 monthly, but if they could not afford this minimal cost they could be "admitted gratuitously if desired."[26] Such an arrangement must have constituted a challenge for the treasurer who kept the records. This challenge was complicated by the practice of some of the parents who preferred to pay the tuition in kind. Mr. Hughes reported on this practice of the Mexicans when he wrote in 1880, ". . . the greatest difficulty is experienced by Superiors in keeping it [the college] up, because they receive so little money for the boys' tuition. The Mexicans hate to part with their 'dinero' and pay for their boys' tuition with '*oves et boves et pecora campi*' (flocks, cattle and beasts of the field)."[27]

In spite of the many difficulties such as the cramped quarters and the lack of finances, the first year came to a close that was impressive for those times. The program for the closing exercises of August 16, 1878, was published as part of the first catalogue of the college and filled seven pages. There was a musical program in which there were performances at the piano, guitar, and organ. Following the program, prizes were awarded for achievements in Christian doctrine, Latin, Spanish, English, higher arithmetic and elements

---

[24]L.V.C., Cat., 1877-1878, p. 4.
[25]*Op. cit.*, p. 4.
[26]*Ibid.*
[27]W.L., vol. IX, 1880, p. 135.

of algebra, geography and history, and music. It is worthy of passing note
that the first half of the program was written in Spanish and the second part in
English.[28]

One of the guests at the closing exercises was the Rev. Camillus Mazzella,
the official visitor of the Mission, whose responsibility it was to report to the
Provincial of the Province of Naples on the condition of the Mission.
Mazzella, who also had been Visitor in 1875, was destined for higher things;
he was recalled from Maryland where he had been teaching dogmatic
theology and in 1886 was created a cardinal of the Church. The authorities of
the Province of Naples were not happy with a Mission that did not fit their
ideas of what a Mission should be, and it was their opinion that the Mission
was hardly viable. They asked Mazzella while he was still in the United
States to keep an eye on the Mission. The cardinal-to-be liked what he saw
and was more optimistic than his superiors, and consequently he befriended
the whole New Mexico-Colorado venture.[29] He would soon see to it that
more help for the Las Vegas venture would be forthcoming. The visitor was
pleased at what he witnessed at the closing exercises. His reaction was
recorded by Troy in his history of the Mission as follows:

> Father Visitor especially could not conceal his admiration. Using many
> beautiful words, he congratulated the students on their eloquence not
> only in their mother tongue but in English as well, and he offered them
> his congratulations too for their marvelous knowledge of physics,
> chemistry, and mathematics.[30]

In the meantime while Personè and his faculty were doing their best to
bring a college into existence, Gasparri was supervising the building of
suitable quarters for the institution. His task was Herculean. Money was in
short supply and labor most unpredictable. The available workmen could not
be hurried nor entirely relied upon to do a day's work. Hughes, writing in
1883, reported:

> Fr. Gasparri was pushing on the work on the new building, in order to
> have it ready by the opening of the second year. At that time, the country
> was in a backward state, and competent and expeditious workmen were
> difficult to find so that it required constant watching to see that the work
> was done.[31]

Since the first academic year was terminated on August 16, 1878, little
time was allowed Gasparri and the workers to finish the new building in time

---

[28]L.V.C., Cat., 1877-1878, pp. 10-16.
[29]Conversation with Edward R. Vollmar, S.J., one of the more knowledgeable historians of
the Mission, 1976.
[30]Troy, *op. cit.*, p. 82.
[31]W.L., vol. XII, 1883, p. 301.

for the beginning of classes scheduled for the first Monday of November, 1878. Nature intervened to compound all the other difficulties that plagued faculty and students. In November only the classrooms and the dormitory for the boys were ready; they would have relieved the pressure if the house of Francessco Lopez could still be used. Unfortunately, unseasonable rains came and continued to such an extent that the older building became uninhabitable. The memory of those times made an indelible impression on the minds of those who lived through those troublesome days. When Michael Hughes came to Las Vegas in 1880 he heard the whole dismal story and recorded it in his communication to his colleagues in Maryland. Hughes informs his readers that the New Mexican adobe houses had advantages under normal circumstances; they were warm in winter and cool in summer. The roofs, however, were not meant to withstand heavy rains since they were in no way watertight. If the rains persisted for any length of time the water soaked through and eventually made the rooms unfit for anything else but shower baths. Hughes continued:

> The rain spared nothing, and so even at night they could take no rest. Only one room in the house was habitable, and that one was reserved for a sick Father, but all who could be accommodated went there to rest at nighttime, while the others wrapped themselves in blankets and tried to sleep sitting in their chairs. . . . They never repined, but cheerfully awaited the time when they could find better accommodations.[32]

The superiors finally decided that it would be better to make the most of the space in the unfinished building; at least the men would remain dry. After the rain had ceased the faculty returned to work and the school year got under way. Hughes reflected the sentiments of those courageous men who had lived through the beginning of the college when he wrote:

> They had begun with nothing the stupendous task of establishing a college in a poor country, they had labored with more than ordinary courage to fulfill their purpose, suffering more than the usual share of miseries, and now after two years their object was fulfilled, the college was a fact, nay more, it was a success.[33]

It is evident from Hughes' communications that he had a great admiration for the accomplishments of the Jesuits in New Mexico; he praised Gasparri, Personè and their colleagues and expressed a sympathetic understanding of the difficulties they had faced and overcome. He was carried away and used some hyperbole in the accolade he bestowed on the school when he wrote: "The college had a severe struggle for existence, but it came forth victori-

---

[32]*Op. cit.*, p. 303.
[33]*Op. cit.*, p. 304.

ous, and from that period it has been growing in strength and favor until today it stands unrivalled as the educational institution of the great south-west.''[34]

Rain and the inconveniences of moving into an unfinished building were not the only problems that had to be faced. The Neapolitans had learned much about the new country where they had been laboring for ten years. Baldassare and his consultors were aware of the need to assure stability by establishing a firm legal right for the existence of the Society in the Territory. To achieve this the superior of the Mission commissioned Gasparri, who by this time was well known throughout New Mexico, to bring before the Territorial Legislature an act to incorporate the Jesuit Fathers in New Mexico. There was good precedent for this procedure since the Sisters of Loretto and the Brothers of the Christian Schools had been incorporated in 1874, and the action of the legislature was approved by the Congress of the United States.[35]

Unfortunately for the Jesuits their request for incorporation came at a time when the whole school question in New Mexico was reaching a critical state in the political history of the territory. It was a singularly unpropitious time for the Jesuits to get involved in the political arena. But Gasparri was a fighter and he plunged into that arena with his usual energy and found himself in direct and bitter conflict with two very hostile men, Territorial Governor Samuel B. Axtell, who held that office from 1875 to 1878, and Secretary William G. Ritch who served from 1876 to 1884. This opposition was formidable enough on the surface but since the two officials were involved with the Santa Fe Ring, Gasparri was in fact challenging the whole American establishment. The ''Anglos'' or ''Gringos'' had control of the government; the extent of that control has been described by the very able historian of the Southwest, Howard R. Lamar, when he called attention to the land-hungry Americans who came to New Mexico and soon realized the usefulness of a machine to settle land questions. Lamar summed the matter up as follows:

> Out of such a need grew the first so-called Santa Fe Ring. Many legends surround its purpose and its membership, but it was essentially a set of lawyers, politicians, and businessmen who united to run the territory and to make money out of this particular region. . . . the ring reflected the corporative, monopolistic, and multiple enterprise tendencies of all American business after the Civil War. Its uniqueness lay in the fact

---

[34]*Op. cit.,* p. 305.
[35]*Op. cit.,* vol. VII, 1878, p. 132.

that, rather than dealing in some manufactured item, they regarded land
as their first medium of currency.[36]
Axtell and Ritch were not important members of the Ring but they did
cooperate with it.

It is beyond the province of this history to investigate the machinations of
the members of the Ring, but it must be noted that they were ready to exploit
the Spanish-speaking natives and hoped to secularize and Americanize
them. Both Axtell and Ritch were hostile to the Catholic Church and shared
the opinion of many non-Catholics of the nineteenth century who considered
the Jesuits the worst of the lot of Catholics. Lamar concluded that Axtell's
hatred for the Jesuits in general and Gasparri in particular "exceeded even
that of Ritch's."[37]

Given such a bias, it is easy to understand the governor's reaction to
Gasparri's activities in lobbying for the passage of the act to incorporate the
Jesuits in New Mexico. The first effort to get the bill for incorporation
through the legislature failed. Two years later it was brought before the
assembly the second time and was passed. Axtell vetoed the act; he considered the matter of sufficient importance that he appeared personally before
the lawmakers to deliver his veto message. He informed his listeners that the
bill was clearly in violation of the law of the United States. The governor
attacked the Society of Jesus and reminded the members of the legislature
that it had been denounced time and again by the head of the Catholic Church
and expelled from the most enlightened countries of Europe. He reserved his
more caustic remarks for Gasparri whom he called "This Neapolitan adven-
turer," and continued,

He comes here while the legislative assembly is in session and lobbies,
in the most brazen and shameless manner, to defeat needed and whole-
some laws, and to force through bills antagonistic to the laws of the
United States. Two years ago he intruded himself in the lower house,
and remained within the bar, and by the speaker's side, till he *forced* the
passage of this bill; but at that session it was defeated by an honest
legislative council. He now presents himself again, and, being fully
informed that what he asks is contrary to the laws of the United States,
urges you to violate your oaths and pass the bill.[38]
It is easy to predict Axtell's reaction when on January 18, 1878, the

---

[36]Howard Roberts Lamar, *The Far Southwest 1846-1912* (New York, W. W. Norton and
Company, Inc., 1970), p. 146.

[37]Lamar, *op. cit.*, p. 168.

[38]W.L., vol. VII, no. 1, 1878, pp. 42-43.

legislature voted to override the veto with a majority exceeding the required two-thirds.

The governor had one more card to play and he played it with relish. The matter was taken up in the Congress of the United States. In the third session of the Forty-fifth Congress on January 24, 1879:

Mr. Frye, from the Committee on the Judiciary, reported back with a favorable recommendation, the bill (S. No. 878) to disapprove and annul an act of the Legislative Assembly of the Territory of New Mexico, passed on the 18th of January, 1878, by a two-thirds vote of both houses, over the veto of the governor of said territory.[39]

Frye called attention to the fact that section 1889 of the Revised Statutes of the United States declares that "the Legislative Assemblies of the several territories shall not grant private charters of especial privileges."[40] After further clarification, Frye argued that it was up to the Congress of the United States to disapprove and annul the act of the Legislature of the Territory of New Mexico. The bill passed after the third reading.[41]

Axtell was no longer governor when Congress passed this act, so he could not have savored the result as much as he would have if he had still been in office. He continued his activities in New Mexico and in 1882 he received an appointment to the Chief Justiceship of New Mexico. From this vantage point he presumably continued to keep an eye on the Jesuits.

In the meantime the day-to-day business of teaching had to continue at the college. The new quarters were much more suitable. The building was described by the Eastern scholastic, Mr. Hughes:

. . . a two-story structure whose walls were made of the usual material of the country, *adobes* (bricks of mud and straw), and stuccoed with a mixture of adobe and lime. It comprised the main building about two hundred feet long and thirty feet wide. Although it is the pride of Las Vegas, it is not a very magnificent affair; but it is infinitely superior to the old building.[42]

With the experience of the first year behind them the Jesuits were in a better position to take stock of their position and prepare for the future. The "Prospectus" for 1878-1879 gave more definite information about the organization of the school. It states that there were two distinct departments, a preparatory and higher. The former was purely elementary and might last

---

[39]*Congressional Record,* Vol. VIII, part I, 1879, p. 734. William Pierce Frye was a member of the House of Representatives for Maine, later he became a Senator, cf. DAB vol. VII, pp. 51-52.

[40]*Ibid.*

[41]*Ibid.*

[42]W.L., vol. IX, 1180, p. 1934.

from one to two or more years, during which primary lessons in English, Spanish, writing, spelling and arithmetic would be taught. The latter department was intended to prepare the students for a commercial career. The courses offered were English and Spanish composition, a full course in arithmetic, bookkeeping, and elements of history and geography. Courses in algebra, geometry, and natural philosophy were available for qualified students. The college was true, at least in principle, to the Jesuit classical tradition for a class in Latin was offered, but it was optional.[43] There was a slight increase in the faculty which was now made up entirely of Jesuits.

One of the most significant additions to the faculty was Joseph M. Marra, who was assigned to the position of Prefect of Schools. Marra, thirty-five years old, was a much-traveled man. Exiled with his fellow Jesuits after 1860, he spent time in Ireland, France, Spain and finally the United States. He studied theology at Woodstock in Maryland and as a priest joined the members of his Province in the New Mexico Mission. He was destined to become the most effective man in the Mission after the founder Gasparri. As Prefect of Studies in the college he was to leave his mark on the development of that institution. Mr. Hughes, who worked with him in Las Vegas, wrote, "The organization of the classes was effected by the labors of the Prefect of Studies, Rev. Father Marra, to whom is due in a great measure the success that has thus far been gained."[44]

Life in a boarding school can be dull and monotonous. To alleviate the monotony a number of societies were organized such as the Sodality of the Immaculate Conception, the Las Vegas College Literary Society, the St. Cecilia Society, the Athletic Association and the Las Vegas College Band. The band, directed by the layman P. A. Marcellino, performed at the closing exercises in 1881. Following a time-honored tradition of training a sound mind in a healthy body, the Athletic Association was established "to promote the practice of healthful exercise of the body, and at the same time to conduct with greater regularity the games and sports of the students."[45]

The first four years of the college had been years of hope and some modest accomplishments. The student body had increased and more Jesuits were assigned to the faculty. The fifth year the college reached a milestone that is reflected in the catalogue for that year. For the first time a seven-year course[46] was outlined that led the students through rudiments; third, second

---

[43]L.V.C., Cat., 1878-1879, p. 3.

[44]W.L., vol. XIII, 1884, p. 47.

[45]L.V.C., Cat., 1880-1881, p. 18.

[46]Power states that the seven-year course was conventional for Catholic Colleges, *op. cit.,* p. 240.

and first humanities; poetry and rhetoric; and a culminating course of philosophy. Students completing these courses in the classical department could earn the degree of bachelor of arts. If such a student should spend one more year in the further study of English literature, mental philosophy and the natural sciences, or if he had proof that he had studied or practiced successfully a learned profession for two additional years, he could receive the degree of Master of Arts.[47]

The perennial problem concerning the place of the commercial course in Jesuit education is clearly evident in the catalogue for 1881-1882. The "Prospectus" states that "owing to the special requirements of this Territory, the course of studies is mainly commercial, and comprises two departments." Conscious of the Jesuit tradition and in defense of it the "Prospectus" points out that the study of the classics was now optional and offered at no extra charge. But it was the aim and desire of the Directors gradually to develop the "Classical Department" into one general system of education. Experience proved—claimed the "Prospectus"—that a solid classical training, together with thorough instruction in all the branches of mathematics, was calculated to produce far better results than any exclusive commercial drill. The commercial course offered a five-year program. The students progressed through third, second, and first grammar class to second and first rhetoric class. Having completed these courses successfully, the student would receive a "Certificate of fitness for commercial pursuits, and after spending two additional years at the college in the further study of Physics and Chemistry, and of Geology, Mineralogy, Higher Mathematics, Astronomy, Logic, Metaphysics and Ethics, could receive the degree of Bachelor of Science."[48]

The reference to the degrees of Bachelor of Arts, Bachelor of Science, and Master of Arts is puzzling in the light of the struggle with Governor Axtell over incorporation and the right to award degrees. There is no evidence that any degrees were awarded in the eleven-year history of Las Vegas College in spite of the fact that the catalogue for 1881-1882 has this statement:

Having complied with the provisions of the general law of New Mexico, Twenty-fifth Session, Chapter XL, the College is thereby "empowered to grant diplomas, confer degrees and all other literary honors, usually conferred" by similar institutions of learning in the United States.[49]

---

[47]L.V.C., Cat., 1881-1882, pp. 13-17. Power writes "most colleges in the early United States awarded master's degrees, but they did so without the formalities of course work, examinations, or dissertations." *Op. cit.,* p. 109.

[48]L.V.C., Cat., 1881-1882, p. 3.

[49]*Ibid.*

The college had come a long way in five years. Personè with the assistance of Marra and the faculty had achieved some stature. The President was a kind man who could make the most of the opportunities at hand. An anonymous writer recorded that he undertook the task of running the new institution at a time when the office of president was far from being a sinecure:

Besides providing for his numerous religious family when the means of communication and transportation were meager, to say the least, he had quite frequently to take the place of the teachers who were on occasions prevented by other occupations from attending to their classes. Yet in spite of these difficulties all went well; the college developed and prospered, the boys were numerous, high standards of study were maintained, and the town was proud of its seat of learning.[50]

One additional note for that important year. The catalogue records the interest of the authorities about the books and newspapers that were read by the students, as well as the letters they wrote. This matter, of course, has been a perennial concern of authorities in boarding schools. Censorship has unsavory connotations but it was and would remain in effect for some years to come. Under the heading "General Regulations" prospective students were informed:

To avoid all objectionable communication between the boarders and outsiders unknown to the College Authorities, the latter reserve to themselves the discretionary power of inspecting all letters, books, newspapers, etc., either directed to or sent by the pupils.[51]

The story of Las Vegas College would not be complete without mention of the contribution of the Jesuit brothers. They were not directly involved in the academic life of the institution but their services were invaluable. A College without an endowment and just barely subsisting on tuition payments that were notoriously slow needed all the free help it could get. Lay brothers (Temporal Coadjutors) have been indispensable throughout the history of the Society of Jesus and they certainly were a boon to the men of the Mission of New Mexico. From the very beginning Vigilante and his successor Gasparri could count on the two brothers who came to the United States in 1867. Gradually their number was increased. They took care of menial and not-so-menial tasks around the school. They were tailors, carpenters, sacristans, infirmarians, and custodians of the wine cellar, and, perhaps most importantly, cooks. It is perhaps characteristic of their work that the editors of the catalogues of the Dispersed Province of Naples sometimes noted after a lay brother's name the words *"ad omnia"*; loosely translated, this means

---

[50]W.L., vol. 53, p. 389.
[51]*Op. cit.,* p. 5.

"ready for everything." These men were not dullards nor did they lack imagination. We have the testimony of Mr. Hughes about the versatility of the cook when great demands were put upon his ability to prepare appetizing dishes in the midst of a serious drought that caused, among other things, a serious shortage of meat since the cattle and the flocks had been driven elsewhere for pasture. Hughes reported:

> The poor Brother cook was at his wit's end, but he was an inventive genius, he labored hard to concoct dishes that would please the palates of his customers and as far as the boys were concerned, he succeeded.[52]

In 1882 the death of Donato Gasparri, who had worn himself out working in the Mission, forced Superior Aloysius M. Gentile (1880-1887) to find a man to take over in Albuquerque, and he chose Personè for that position. He then designated Dominic Pantanella, who had just been assigned to the Mission, as President of Las Vegas College. Pantanella who had been teaching Jesuit seminarians at Woodstock in Maryland for some thirteen years was destined to be the second most important builder in the history of the college. His career for the next thirty-nine years would be identified with the institution. He was a gracious and devout man who had an uncanny ability to persuade people to help the Jesuits in their apostolic and educational work. Since Personè had spent himself in keeping the college operating more or less smoothly, he did not have the time or energy to spend to improve the material facilities of the institution. Michael Hughes, the Jesuit scholastic who had been loaned to the Mission by the Maryland-New York Province for a period of four years, described the impact made by Pantanella as follows:

> He went to work at once, to continue the good work that Father Personè had begun, and, in the course of a few months, great improvements were made about the house. Classrooms, chapel, dining rooms and the Fathers' private rooms were all put in excellent condition; new desks and benches were brought all the way from Chicago for the classrooms; excellent teachers' desks, made by a Las Vegas firm, were put in. Nor was he idle outside the house. In less than a month, he had made friends everywhere, and he easily persuaded them to give substantial token of their kind feeling for the college.[53]

A few months after such an auspicious beginning, Pantanella's attention was diverted elsewhere. The Vicar Apostolic of Colorado, Joseph P. Machebeuf, had attended the closing exercises of Las Vegas College in 1883; he asked Gentile, the Superior of the Mission, to send Jesuits to establish a

---

[52]W.L., vol. XIII, 1884, p. 43.
[53]W.L., vol. XIII, 1884, pp. 46-47.

college in Colorado.[54] Pantanella seconded the bishop's request and soon began his travels in support of Machebeuf's proposal. For the better part of his nineteen months as President of Las Vegas College he was away from the institution. Troy writes that because of his many travels to Denver, Pueblo, and even Europe in the interest of the proposed institution in Colorado he was in no way able to attend to the business of the college.[55]

Pantanella personally presented the case for another college in Colorado to the General and his advisors. He must have been very persuasive because he won the General's approval. On August 10, 1884, he was appointed Vice-Rector of the proposed college that was to be opened at Morrison, Colorado. On the same day Personè was asked to resume the presidency of the college in Las Vegas.

Personè had to begin where he had left off. His most pressing problem was the remodeling of the building. This was necessary because the public response to the efforts of the college were such that there was not enough room for the students who applied. In 1884-1885 there were two hundred forty-six students: seventy-eight boarders, eight half-boarders, and one hundred sixty day students. Surprisingly, twenty of the boarders were from the Republic of Mexico. The necessity of expanding the facilities had been recognized and it was becoming obvious that the project could not be postponed. Troy wrote:

> Meanwhile the number of students increased and the college needed to be enlarged. At that time there was in the college a certain Master Edward Barry who had studied architecture in Europe. He was given the task of drawing up plans for the addition. It was to be built on the east side of the college and replace the one-story building that stood there.[56]

Work on the remodeling began on July 25, 1885, and the new foundation was blessed by Personè on August 13th.

In light of subsequent events it is difficult to understand the decision to build at that time. No doubt the Superior and his advisors did not realize what lay ahead of them, that they would move the college from Las Vegas to Denver within three years. Early in 1886 human factors began to complicate the Jesuit operation in Las Vegas. The coming of the railroad in 1879 had changed the character of the town and an increase in the population had given rise to "New Town" or East Las Vegas near the railroad station. To provide for the needs of the increasing population, another parish was established.

[54]Edward R. Vollmar, S.J., *History of the Jesuit Colleges of New Mexico and Colorado, 1867-1919* (Unpublished Master's thesis, St. Louis University, 1938), p. 63.

[55]Troy, *op. cit.*, p. 129.

[56]Troy, *op. cit.*, p. 129.

The existence of this new parish under the direction of the Jesuits was not a welcome development in the eyes of the local diocesan pastor, Father Joseph Coudert, and the good will that he had demonstrated toward the Jesuits was soon eroded. His growing opposition led him to challenge the practice of the Jesuits of preparing younger students for their first communion to be received in the college chapel. Coudert maintained that first communion was the responsibility of the pastor of the parish. The pastor appealed to the Archbishop, John B. Salpointe, who had succeeded Lamy in 1885, and soon the controversy reached such proportions that it was taken up by the authorities in Rome. It is beyond the scope of this history to follow the developments of this dispute. It is referred to here only because it is probably one of the factors that led the Jesuits to decide that there was little future for their educational endeavors in Las Vegas. The fact is that a new building was in progress in Denver during the year 1887-1888. Records of the discussions between the Superior of the Mission and his consultors are sparse but there is no doubt about the final outcome. The catalogue of 1887-1888 had as its frontispiece a photo of the new building in Denver and title page read "Las Vegas College—To Be Known Henceforward as College of the Sacred Heart, Denver, Colorado."[57]

The citizens of Las Vegas were not pleased with these developments. They held a demonstration at the college protesting the decision to move, but it was too late. Some blamed Archbishop Salpointe for allowing the Jesuits to depart. Correspondence about this matter found its way to the Roman archives of the Society of Jesus. A certain F. A. Manzanares wrote to Salpointe on October 17, 1887, and enclosed a donation for the Holy Father; the letter continued, "and the balance to yourself. . . but to be candid, sincere and frank with you I *very much dislike* your course in allowing the Jesuit Fathers to leave this country." The Archbishop answered on the same day:

> The fact is that I pursued no course whatever in the matter but had to remain purely passive listening only to the contradictory sayings of many people on the question until a few days ago that the Rev. J. Marra gave me the official notice to what had been determined about the final location of the college.[58]

One is tempted to wonder how the whole matter would have been handled by Archbishop Lamy, who had resigned from his office in 1885 shortly before the controversy had begun to come to a head.

---

[57]L. V.C., Cat., 1887-1888, p. 1.
[58]S.J.A., Rome.

Chapter 2

The Morrison Experience

The Neapolitan Jesuits had a well-established base of operation in the Territory of New Mexico by the end of the decade, 1867-1877. During that period significant changes took place in the region of the north of New Mexico. That area had been neglected by the Spaniards and the government of the Republic of Mexico because, according to available reports, there was not much there to warrant further extension of their limited manpower. There was little change when the territory acquired a new owner with the purchase of this vast territory from France in 1803. The government of the United States commissioned three expeditions to explore the newly acquired region. The reports of the explorers confirmed the fact of the vastness of the territory but offered little encouragement to those who hoped for fertile lands rich in mineral resources. The leader of the third expedition, Stephen H. Long, described the region as the "Great American Desert", a designation that persisted and proved to be the basis for a controversy among historians well into the twentieth century.[1]

In spite of these discouraging reports there was some activity in the region. Enterprising trappers, searching for beaver pelts, sought their prey in the mountains and along the many streams. Resourceful traders found a ready market for their goods in New Mexico and made regular journeys over the Santa Fe Trail which passed through the southeastern part of the future Territory of Colorado. Since there was seemingly nothing to attract these men to other parts of the region the Indians kept relatively peaceful possession of their lands. This peace was shattered after 1858 when gold was discovered along the creeks that flowed into the South Platte.

The history of the period during which the gold seekers flocked into the region and of the organization of the Territory of Colorado has been recounted by very able historians and need not be repeated here. Our primary concern is to recall how the authorities of the Catholic Church responded to this new challenge.

Since the region was considered an extension of Kansas Territory, the primary responsibility for the Catholics moving into Colorado rested with

---

[1]W. Eugene Hollon, *The Great American Desert Then and Now* (Lincoln, University of Nebraska Press, 1975), p. 65.

the Jesuit bishop of that jurisdiction, John Baptist Miège, who knew enough about the region to realize that he did not have enough priests to enable him to spare even one who could be sent to minister to the needs of the Catholics who were migrating into the region. Miège wrote to Peter Richard Kenrick, Archbishop of St. Louis, requesting him to petition the authorities in Rome to transfer the territory to the jurisdiction of the bishop of Santa Fe. When Lamy learned about this added responsibility he was not pleased but he could not refute the argument that he was closer to Colorado. The hard-pressed bishop discussed the matter with his Vicar General, Joseph P. Machebeuf, who appreciated his superior's quandry and was not too surprised when Lamy suggested that he was just the man to undertake the responsibility. Machebeuf, by this time a seasoned missionary, agreed. All he asked for was one priest to assist him and some money for necessary expenses.[2]

In September, 1860, Machebeuf, with the recently ordained John B. Raverdy, journeyed north to undertake the Herculean task of ministering to the Catholics in an area about half the size of France. It did not take long for the two priests to realize that they were dealing with an entirely different situation than the one they had known in New Mexico. In that territory they had been dealing with people who had a culture that was some two and one-half centuries old. The placidity of many of the Spanish-Americans was in sharp contrast with the drive of the newcomers who were pouring into Colorado. They brought with them a knowledge of democracy gained in Nebraska, Missouri, and Kansas. Professor Lamar caught the spirit of this contrast when he wrote:

> Never had frontier democracy blossomed so vigorously. With popular sovereignty in the saddle the northern part of Bent's old empire was already a far cry from the tradition-bound and caste-conscious territory of New Mexico. A new kind of democratic, middle-class, commercial-minded frontier had arrived on the borders of the Spanish Southwest.[3]

From the perspective of the fourth quarter of the Twentieth Century, it is amazing to see what Machebeuf accomplished in Colorado in the eight years 1860-1868. He visited the villages and mining camps, traveling by horse and buggy or any conveyance he could manage to acquire. Denver was his base of operations and it is amazing that he could find the time and energy to make the presence of the Church felt in that growing town. In 1868 Colorado was

---

[2]Horgan, *op. cit.,* pp. 276-277. The standard biography of Bishop Machebeuf is that by W. J. Howlett, *Life of the Right Reverend Joseph P. Machebeuf, D.D.* (Pueblo, Colo., The Franklin Press, 1908).

[3]Lamar, *op. cit.,* p. 217.

detached from the ecclesiastical jurisdiction of Santa Fe, set up as a Vicariate Apostolic and entrusted to Machebeuf.

One of Machebeuf's major concerns, besides obtaining priests to care for the Catholics in his charge, was to find men and women who would educate the young. As early as 1864 he was fortunate in obtaining the services of a few Sisters of Loretto from Santa Fe who opened St. Mary's Academy. He was not to have such ready success in finding a religious order of men to open a school for boys. He had hopes that the Jesuits who were already working in Southern Colorado would be able to undertake that task but there was greater need of their services in pastoral work. The provincial of Naples had assigned more men to the New Mexico Mission. In eight years the number of men working in the Southwest increased from fourteen in 1872 to fifty in 1879.[4] The first Jesuits to work in Colorado came to Conejos and Pueblo in 1872; 1875 found them in Trinidad. Finally, in 1879, they opened a parish in Denver. Though they had been involved in educational work in Las Vegas since 1877, they were not yet in a position to staff another school.

Machebeuf was not easily deterred from keeping up the pressure on the superior of the New Mexico-Colorado Mission. We have seen that he won the support of Dominic Pantanella, the president of Las Vegas College, 1883-1884.[5] Pantanella went to Rome to persuade the General of the Jesuits to approve the proposed college. While he was in Europe he recruited Jesuits for a faculty. In the meantime the bishop purchased a hotel in the small town of Morrison some sixteen miles southwest of Denver. The hotel was called the "Swiss Cottage" by some; others knew it as the "Evergreen Hotel." Machebeuf deeded the property and building in fee simple to the Jesuits and urged them to open the school as soon as possible. Pantanella returned from Europe in August, 1884. The superior, Aloysius M. Gentile, sent him to Denver to explain to the bishop that it was impossible to open another school that year. The Jesuits realized that they could not start a school without a faculty and students. They also knew that certain adjustments were necessary to convert a hotel into a college. The bishop was persistent, however, and in the end he prevailed. These events were recorded by the diarist who, quite obviously, had not yet mastered the English language. The diarist wrote:

The Bishop prevailed, and on August 6th, Father Pantanella having visited for the first time Morrison with the Bishop accepted to open the College and gave at once orders to have the estimate for the changes needed. On the following Sunday, August 10th, the contract was

---

[4]CDPN. *Passim.*
[5]Cf. *supra,* pp. 20, 21.

signed. He returned to Las Vegas College to inform Rev. Fr. Gentile, S.J., Superior General of the Mission. Many times the consultors of the Mission met in Las Vegas College. Father Pantanella was appointed to be the Vice-Rector of Morrison College. He left Las Vegas and arrived at Morrison on August 21st, where he was the only Jesuit, till September 3rd Mr. Deane, Brother Wallace and Brother Celaya from Las Vegas College, Brother Dominguez from Trinidad arrived at Morrison.[6]

Morrison, a small town at the mouth of Bear Creek Canyon adjacent to the Red Rocks area, was named after a George M. Morrison who came to Colorado in 1859, as so many others did, in search of a fortune. After some experience in mining in the Idaho Springs area he abandoned the search for gold and settled down near the mouth of Bear Creek Canyon. He explored the area and discovered a huge bed of gypsum. Morrison constructed a mill for grinding the gypsum.[7] Soon he realized that the growing town of Denver could use some cut stone and was the first man to deliver such to the city.[8]

Certain resourceful men in Denver became interested in the new town which was named after the resourceful Morrison, and decided to build a railroad that would give better access to it. A group of Denver businessmen headed by the ever-enterprising John Evans incorporated the Denver and South Park Railway on September 30, 1872. In October they established the Morrison Stone, Lime and Townsite Company for the purpose of developing and exploiting the raw materials in the area. The railroad reached Morrison in 1873 but it was destined to be terminated there, contrary to the aspirations of the backers of the project. Two factors accounted for the failure of the railroad builders to continue into the canyon. First, the "panic" of 1873 created financial difficulties for Evans and his associates. Second, there were promoters of a different route to the interior of the mountains through the Platte Canyon; this proposal seemed more practical and attracted more support than the backers of the Denver and South Park Railway would enlist for their project. The decision to stop at Morrison did not end the usefulness of the railroad. For some time the train made regular trips from Denver to Morrison, sometimes as many as four round trips a day.

Sam Arnold described one trip from Morrison to Denver as hauling flatcars loaded with slabs of cut marble; red, white, and even blue sandstone; flatcars stacked high with baked red bricks; freight cars bulging with sacks of

---

[6]*Morrison College Orgin and Diary*, p. 1., RCA.

[7]Sam Arnold, *The View from Mt. Morrison The Story of a Colorado Town* (Denver, The Fur Press, 1974), p. 10.

[8]Wilbur Fish Stone, Editor: *History of Colorado* (Chicago, The S. J. Clarke Publishing Co., 1919), Vol. IV, p. 507.

cement, gypsum, hay and grain; and passengers.[9]

John Evans was so enthralled with Morrison and its surroundings that he decided to build a first-class resort hotel there. The building when finished ''boasted a stone two-story structure with 42 rooms, parlors, a billiard room, a dancing pavillion, and fine grounds.''[10] Evans' dream of a successful resort was not realized; he sold the property and building to Bishop Machebeuf of Denver who deeded it over to the Jesuits in fee simple in 1884.

Father Pantanella, yielding to the persistent pressure of the bishop, expended every effort to prepare the building for the opening of classes. Realizing that the school needed a name, he called it the College of the Sacred Heart.[11]

Morrison was the scene of hectic activity during the last days of August and the first two weeks of September. On the 15th the College of the Sacred Heart opened its doors. It had an impressive faculty thanks to the efforts of the hard-pressed president who had done some recruiting for teachers when he was in Europe during the year before the opening of the college. The superior of the Mission, Aloysius M. Gentile, did not have men to spare, but, somehow, Pantanella managed to assemble a cosmopolitan group of men. The president assumed the added duties of treasurer and buyer. The faculty consisted of Charles Chappuis of the Province of Paris, chaplain, teacher of geometry, higher mathematics, French, piano and vocal music; Joseph Arthuis of the Province of Champagne, assistant chaplain, teacher of evidences of religion, German and physical culture; Inigo Deane of the Maryland-New York Province, prefect of schools and studies, teacher of first class of English, elocution, arithmetic, drawing and painting; Henry Sauve a scholastic from Las Vegas, chief disciplinarian and teacher of second class of English and violin; Francis Kowald of the German Province by way of the Buffalo Mission, teacher of third class of arithmetic, German, bookkeeping, commercial law, penmanship, director of the Acolytical Society and of Liturgical Services, and sacristan; three lay brothers, Patrick Wallace, Prefect of Health, teacher of third class of English; Manuel Celaya, teacher of Spanish, tailor, mender, and wardrobe keeper; and Joseph

---

[9]Arnold, *op. cit.,* p. 15.

[10]Arnold, *op. cit.,* p. 18.

[11]Some individuals would persist in using the name of the town; for example the diarist recorded on the first page of the diary ''Morrison College.'' Father Pantanella was well known for his devotion to the Sacred Heart of Jesus and would insist that this venture as well as the one that he would start in Denver should be known by the name which he had chosen.

Dominguez, chief cook and dispenser.[12] There is something intriguing about such a gathering of Jesuits in a small mountain town at the foot of the Rockies in 1884; it is also amazing when one reflects that this faculty was to expend its efforts for some twenty-four students.

Since there had been so little time to prepare for the opening of the college, it is not surprising that there were so few students. In fact, the students came at intervals during the first days of school. Two students, John and David Walker, sons of J. Brisben Walker who was to play a decisive role in the history of the college, arrived on the 13th of September. Others arrived between the 15th and the 22nd.[13] When school was well under way there was an excellent ratio between faculty and students. The average age of the students ranged from twelve to eighteen; one interesting exception was a youngster who was only seven years old. Kowald commented on the ratio between teachers and students:

> One great advantage for the students, no doubt, resulting from such numerically smaller classes, was the greater personal interest and closer attention afforded and bestowed upon each individual student by his respective teacher, in the line of encouragement and advancement in studies as also in conduct and education in general, so that sure and constant progress was inevitable and failure well might be impossible under such-like guidance and direction.[14]

Kowald wrote from the vantage point of nearly fifty years. He admitted with remarkable candor that the Morrison institution might well be styled a "Select High School, rather than a college as regards the various grades and classes."[15]

One of the few sources of information about the first year at Morrison is the brief brochure which was published late enough in the academic year of 1884-1885 to include the program for the closing exercises. An interesting feature of the introduction is the emphasis that is placed on the use of the

---

[12]Francis X. Kowald, *Sacred Heart College, Morrison, Colorado 1884-1888*, Typescript, R. C. Arch. p. 3. Kowald was a novice in the Society of Jesus when he came to Morrison. A native of Germany, he came to the United States and was accepted as a novice in Buffalo. He had tuberculosis which almost cost him his life. He survived, however, and worked for many years in the United States. His provincial in 1935, Samuel H. Horine, S.J., suggested that he write his reminiscences of his years at Morrison. Kowald complied with the provincial's request and wrote the history with the subtitle "A Brief Historical Sketch and Some Reminiscences." There is a nostalgia in his account and it is obviously a labor of love. The memories of his four years at Morrison were pleasant and Kowald wrote with a freshness and a great awareness of detail that makes his account very interesting and valuable. He was seventy-three years old when he undertook the task. He died on October 8, 1937.

[13]*Morrison College, Origin and Diary*, pp. 1-2.

[14]Kowald, *op. cit.*, p. 34.

[15]*Ibid.*

English language; the statement reads, "The language of the school and the one to which most attention is devoted is the English." However, it is noted that during the week there are certain recreation periods appointed for French, German, or Spanish conversation.[16] The same document records that the charge for board and tuition per session of five months was $120.00 with an added $10.00 for washing and mending. There would be an extra charge for vocal and instrumental music and drawing. However, German, French, Spanish and Italian were free.[17] There was no provision for day students, probably because the authorities realized that there was little possibility of attracting such students from Morrison which was still a very small community.

The faculty endeavored to make the closing exercises on June 26, 1885, as impressive as possible. The program gives an example of the diversity of the programs offered during that first year. There were dramatic presentations in German, Spanish, French, and English. Gold and silver medals were awarded. The donors of these prizes were all ecclesiastics who were willing to encourage the Jesuits in these educational enterprises in Morrison: two archbishops, James Gibbons of Baltimore and John B. Lamy of Santa Fe; two bishops, Joseph P. Machebeuf of Denver and James O'Connor of Omaha; five priests, T. J. Nugent of Cheyenne, Nicholas Matz of Georgetown, Robert F. Byrne of Colorado Springs, M. A. Kennedy of Lincoln, and Charles Personè, S.J., of Ysleta, Texas.[18] The generosity of these supporters was no doubt due to the tireless efforts of Dominic Pantanella.

College life at Morrison was a far cry from what it has become in the Twentieth Century. In a very rustic setting some sixteen miles from the growing city of Denver, the horizons of the students were definitely limited. The then prevailing philosophy of education of Jesuit institutions which assumed that the teachers took the place of parents was certainly followed at Morrison. Pantanella was a kind father who was eager to provide for the needs of all those entrusted to his care, faculty members as well as students. The boys had few diversions beyond those that could be found on a playing field that had its natural hazards; they played whatever games could be improvised at a moment's notice. They could explore the surrounding area and climb mountains, but when they went hiking into the foothills they were always accompanied by a Jesuit or two. Excitement was furnished when the students were reminded that they were living in a frontier town. One such

---

[16]Brochure, *The College of the Sacred Heart,* 1884-1885, p. 1.
[17]*Op. cit.,* p. 3.
[18]*Op. cit., passim.*

occasion was a shooting in town at a local bar when two men shot one another. Pantanella attended both men and baptized one, but the other refused his offer of help. Both were dead by the 19th of April, 1885.[19] Occasional flash floods that caused extensive damage along Bear Creek furnished a topic for conversation for some days. Then there were the frequent visits of Bishop Machebeuf who seems to have demonstrated an intense interest in his investment. He was a well-known missionary and a colorful character who hobbled about with the help of a cane (he had been injured in a buggy accident). The Bishop also had a problem controlling his saliva and when he celebrated Mass there ''was the frequent demand of a cuspidor, to be placed and adjusted within convenient range, or reach, all of which was novel and distracting to say the least, for one (Kowald) who had never assisted at a Bishop's Mass, and was still a novice and inclined to take a comic view of the happenings.''[20]

By the middle of the first year things were moving along quite smoothly. A certain A. A. Salazar visited the school in February 17, 1885, and recorded his impressions in a letter to J. A. J. Valdes of Walsenburg, Colorado. The letter made quite an impression, so much so that it was published in the *Aunciador* of Trinidad, and reprinted in the brochure. After describing how he admired the class of gymnastics, he continued:

Plenty of such systematic exercises, an excellent table (I visited, of course, the dining rooms also) and general cheerfulness and comfort account for the rosiness and bright looks of all the boys without exception, and account, too, for the fact that no doctor has ever been needed in Morrison. Healthy and full of spirits in recreation, the boys show the polish of manner that the Jesuits know so well how to communicate.[21]

Obviously this rosy picture did not include some of the clouds that are present in every boarding school. Because accessibility to the school in Morrison was not as convenient as some might have wished, students were required to remain at the school for both terms, foregoing such welcome breaks as might be afforded by vacations at Christmas and Easter seasons. One student devised a plan, the effect of which would be to give all the students an extended holiday. He planned to burn down the building and might have succeeded if it had not been that the cook and his assistant detected the smoke and extinguished the fire. Word of the near disaster spread quickly among the Jesuits, who prudently kept it from the students who had retired. The prefect of schools, Inigo Deane, was ready when one of

---

[19]*Morrison College Origin and Diary*, p. 6.
[20]Kowald, *op. cit.*, p. 20.
[21]Brochure 1884-1885, p. 5.

the students, fully dressed, urgently requested that he be permitted to get some fresh air. Kowald recorded:

> He was refused and gently told to go to bed and his illness would disappear. A brief quarter of an hour elapsed and the same request came from the same boy now more excited than before, evidently under the impression the fire must be fully ablaze. Then the Dean took him aside into one of the prefect's rooms and put him through a grilling star-chamber cross-examination. Reluctantly the boy was constrained to own the evidence of facts discovered and of his own guilt and was expelled early the next morning.[22]

A somewhat more presentable brochure was published late in 1886. The word "catalogue" is not used on the title page. The introductory remarks reveal that the author was concerned with acknowledging the Jesuit commitment to the classical tradition but was facing up at the same time to the impracticability of following that tradition in the situation in Morrison, Colorado. The statement reads:

> While appreciating the value of the ancient classical languages as a means of education, the Directors of the College believe that their value may easily be exaggerated and that much of the time commonly devoted to the study of them might with more profit be given to the study of the vernacular.
>
> English, in their opinion, should not be subordinated to Latin and Greek, but amongst the languages studied in an English-speaking country, should receive the first and fullest attention.[23]

This is a surprising statement, one which was more applicable in Las Vegas. Another interesting feature of this brochure is the emphasis that is given to the sciences, especially to physics, botany and physiology. It is noted that they are not only recommended but are to be considered "valuable not only for the knowledge they impart but as a mental discipline."[24]

The authorities seemed to be hesitant to even mention the commercial course in the statement in the brochure. But it is evident from another source that commercial subjects were offered; the authority for this is Francis X. Kowald, who taught these classes himself. He is listed among the faculty as the teacher of German, bookkeeping and penmanship. In his history of the school at Morrison, he writes with a great deal of modesty about his efforts to teach bookkeeping, embracing single-entry, double-entry and banking system. He adds that the course "was taught by an expert accountant, who also

---

[22]Kowald, *op. cit.*, pp. 44-45.
[23]Brochure: *College of the Sacred Heart,* Morrison, Colorado, 1885-1886, pp. 3-4.
[24]*Op. cit.*, p. 4.

published an original and valuable set of notes on bookkeeping, of some eight pages, including a complete list of definitions, aids, and manner of keeping accounts, so as to dispense with the textbook itself.'' Later in his history Kowald could not resist mentioning that during the first years of the college the members of the commercial branches were the more numerous and better-paying element.[25] The problem concerning the place of the commercial courses in the curriculum was to plague the college for years to come. It was not a problem for Sacred Heart College alone. Edward J. Power, writing in 1972, concluded that Catholic colleges reluctantly allowed the teaching of commercial courses, and continued:

> Thus, elements of institutional self-preservation dictated the compromises which in the end allowed the commercial course a high degree of security in the Catholic college, despite the fact that its very existence ran counter to the announced educational philosophy of the institution wherein it found a home. This inconsistency proved in time to be troublesome and had a permanent effect on the educational standing of the commercial course, department, or school in the life of American Catholic colleges. Commerce was an educational stepchild, to be put up with and kept, but always to suffer from lack of genuine love.[26]

Any effort to build a stable faculty in a Jesuit college proved to be quite a challenge. The president was not as free as he would have liked to be; he had to accept men who were sent by higher authorities. Of course, he could endeavor to borrow men from other provinces but he needed the consent of an individual's provincial and that of the Superior of the Mission. Moreover, Jesuit superiors assigned young men who were in training for the priesthood to teach in schools as part of the seasoning that was needed to prepare them for their life's work. As a result there was a regular turnover in Jesuit schools. However, Sacred Heart College in Morrison moved into its second year with a loss of but two men while six new men came to supplement the staff. Two of the newcomers were men destined to have an impact on the history of the college; one of them was Armand William Forstall, a scholastic, twenty-six years old, a member of the Province of Champagne, who later joined the New Mexico-Colorado Mission. Since he spent only one year at Morrison, we will consider him more at length later on. Later he rejoined the faculty and became an institution. The second man was Hugh L. Magevney, originally from Memphis, who became one of the greatest assets of the school for a period of ten years. He was an orator with florid style and a great entertainer cast in the mold of those who made life in the rugged frontier

---

[25]Kowald, *op. cit.,* p. 36 and p. 123.
[26]Power, *op. cit.,* p. 233.

somewhat endurable. Magevney, forty-years old in 1885, had a checkered career before he arrived in Morrison to join the faculty. As a Jesuit scholastic he had studied under Pantanella at Woodstock in Maryland, but for reasons known only to himself and his superiors he withdrew from the order and became a diocesan priest. In 1885 he sought readmission into the Society of Jesus and relied on Father Pantanella to help him achieve this end. His friend made this possible on condition that Magevney make a year's novitiate while teaching at Morrison. The catalogue of the Province of Naples lists him as a novice as of June 20, 1887.[27] However, Pantanella's decision was not well received at the headquarters of the Society of Jesus. Someone with an eagle eye detected an irregularity in the readmission process and the Superior of the Mission was informed that it was not possible to accept Father Magevney in the Society.[28] It must have been a sorrowful Pantanella who had to inform Magevney of the decision.

However, there was no reason to prevent the colorful priest from remaining on the faculty and he became an invaluable member of the teaching staff for some ten years. One of his colleagues wrote of him:

Even at that early period (he) had achieved a vast reputation and universal acknowledgement from the public, as a born orator in preaching and lecturing, an efficient, congenial and interesting teacher in the classroom and entertaining companion in conversation and recreation with full command and control of the English language, mingled with the fluid, florid, and vigorous style and vivacity of description of a Southerner, who hails from Memphis, Tennessee.[29]

The composition of the student body did not change significantly when studies were resumed in September, 1885. Word must have been getting around since there were sixty-seven applicants for admission; only thirty-one of these were accepted. With a faculty of twelve, an excellent teacher-study ratio was assured. Each student had an enviable opportunity to benefit from a broadening experience. The members of the faculty came from very diverse backgrounds, and there were representatives among the students from twelve different states besides Colorado: Kentucky, Wyoming, Massachusetts, Nebraska, Maryland, Illinois, Wisconsin, Ohio, Pennsylvania, Michigan, New York and Louisiana. There were twelve students from the state of Colorado. One distinguished student, Henry Casimir Vidal, claimed France as his native land.

---

[27]CDPN, 1887, p. 27.

[28]Correspondence in *Archives of the Society of Jesus, Rome: Mission. Assist. Ital. a die 18 Aug., 1873 ad diem 15 Maii 1906, vol., II, passim.*

[29]Kowald, *op. cit.,* pp. 53-54.

Given the relatively isolated location of the school, there was not much opportunity for outside diversion. Of necessity faculty and students had to devise their own entertainment, and plenty of opportunity to do so was provided. Music provided an outlet, and the students seem to have made the best of the training that was offered. The program for the closing exercises on Wednesday, June 30, 1886, is quite impressive. The musical part of that presentation included the *Overture to Tannhauser* by Wagner, Mozarts' *Symphony in C,* Haydn's *Sonata VII,* and selections from Rossini's *Barber of Seville* and Bellini's *Romeo e Giulietta.* The oratorical part of the program presented some selections from the classics as well as the scene of the battlefield near Shrewsbury from Shakespeare's *Henry IV.* This must have been very heady material for Morrison, Colorado, 1886.

Medals were awarded to students of outstanding achievement during 1885-1886. Ten gold medals were bestowed, one of which was donated by James Cardinal Gibbons, Archbishop of Baltimore. Moreover, nine silver medals were granted. The donors of the medals form an impressive list of churchmen who were willing to give a vote of confidence in the new school. Most of the awards came from the priests working in Colorado, but one came from the Bishop of Leavenworth and another from the Bishop of Omaha. The gold medal for elocution was donated by the Rev. John A. McCullum of Brooklyn. To encourage competition a Legion of Honor was established "for the purpose of exciting emulation amongst the students and of rewarding such as have distinguished themselves in good conduct and studies."[30]

It is evident that the Morrison operation was very much a self-contained one. Some effort was made to establish outside contacts such as those made by the scholastic John N. Cordoba during the academic year 1886-1887 when he endeavored to organize senior and junior athletic clubs. Cordoba developed a baseball team, though it must be admitted that the terrain in Morrison did not make a perfect baseball field possible. Nevertheless, the coach persisted and once he had a team in operation he looked for games with any organization that could field a team. He managed to challenge teams from Golden and Denver. Kowald recalled that when things did not go well for his team Cordoba, "donning baseball cap and shirt, joined the College team ranks 'incognito' and by clever pitching, fine bunting and stealing of bases won the game for their encouragement and prestige."[31]

---

[30]Brochure, *College of the Sacred Heart,* Morrison, Colorado, 1885-1886, p. 24 and *passim.*

[31]Kowald, *op. cit.,* p. 76. This action laid the foundation for a tradition that persisted into the nineteen twenties, namely that if the opposition should prove too competent, Jesuit scholastics would enter the game and turn the tide.

Hiking, as we have mentioned, was one of the major diversions of the students, who explored the surrounding area. One by-product of this activity was the discovery of a natural amphitheater that has since become known as Red Rocks Park, a landmark for visiting tourists to the foothills of the Rockies. Kowald reminisced about this discovery some fifty years later:

> During the first ramblings in the vicinity of Morrison the identical scholastics accidentally discovered a grand nature-made amphitheater. It consisted of an extensive stretch of almost level ground, shut in on three sides by huge Red-Rocks with high abrupt walls, having the sloping foothills to the west as a background and accommodating entrances or exits to the north and south. The magnificent space was well adapted for exercising their lung power in loud speaking, for which they frequently repeated parts of oratorical speeches, sermons and selections of elocutionary contests and declamations they could call to mind.[32]

The lay brothers were an essential factor in the operation of the college. Manuel Celaya and Joseph Dominguez lived up to the expectations, and the day-to-day needs of faculty and students were satisfactorily provided for. Patrick Wallace did double duty; he performed needed services for his fellow Jesuits and the students and taught the preparatory class. Students who wished to study music were able to take violin lessons from him. This small contingent of lay brothers was augmented when Benjamin Tovani joined the community as a novice in 1885. Tovani sailed from Naples with the intention of joining his brother, Sabatino, in Morrison. Unfortunately, he sailed on the wrong ship; instead of reaching an American port he landed at Vera Cruz. A young man of nineteen he might have been expected to be dismayed. He evidently was not. Kowald recorded that "he worked and begged his way with difficulty and delay to the Land of Liberty. . . By odd jobs here and there, and occasional friendly rides offered, he gradually found his way at length to Colorado, after some six months intermittent travel, and finally arrived at Morrison."[33] He made his novitiate at Morrison and pronounced his vows on October 29, 1887. He was destined to remain in the same community, first in Morrison and then in Denver, for the rest of his life.

There were many distractions in Morrison during the last two years of Jesuit activity in the town. It was increasingly evident that Morrison was not intended as the permanent site for the college. There were obvious problems that could not be solved, for example, the difficulty of access and the impossibility of attracting day-students. As early as October 23, 1885,

---

[32]Kowald, *op. cit.,* p. 92.
[33]Kowald, *op. cit.,* pp. 3-4.

Aloysius M. Gentile, Superior of the Mission, together with Salvatore Personè, President of Las Vegas College, and Charles M. Pinto, Pastor of Holy Trinity parish in Trinidad, came to Morrison to discuss the possibility of purchasing property in Denver.[34] Evidently this meeting did not lead to any definite decisions.

In 1886 a new prospect opened up; this one was in Colorado Springs. Robert F. Byrne, Pastor of St. Mary's Church, had been a Jesuit and while attending classes in Woodstock, Maryland, he had become acquainted with Dominic Pantanella. Later he left the order for reasons of health but completed his theological studies and was ordained to the priesthood. He came West and was assigned to the parish in Colorado Springs. When he heard Pantanella's project of starting a college in Morrison he renewed his acquaintance with his former mentor. One of the silver medals awarded at the closing exercises in June, 1885, was donated by Father Byrne. Father Pantanella traveled to Colorado Springs in August, 1886, evidently to visit his former student. Details of their conversation have not survived but subsequent events suggest that the visit was not merely a social one. Within a few months Father Byrne had made preliminary arrangements for the purchase of a piece of property in the Springs and had persuaded the civil authorities to agree to allow ready access to the property under consideration. On March 14, 1887, Pantanella left for Trinidad to discuss with the superior of the Mission and his consultors the possible relocation of the school to Colorado Springs. On the 19th, Gentile, Personè, Marra and Pantanella came to Morrison and on the next day they announced that the college would move to Colorado Springs. On April 2, 1887, Pantanella returned to Morrison after another visit to the Springs with the information that he had purchased twenty acres of land for the College.[35]

In all of these proceedings Pantanella had proceeded without reckoning with his friend and benefactor, Joseph P. Machebeuf. When the bishop became aware of the plans to move to Colorado Springs, he let it be known that such a move would not receive his approval. It would be interesting to read the minutes of the meetings that took place in Denver between the Bishop and Joseph Marra, Superior of the Mission since January 1, 1887. Father Marra was accompanied by his consultors, Salvatore Personè and Charles Pinto; Pantanella joined the conference that was held from June 6th to the 9th, 1887. Finally, it was announced on June 22nd that the college

---

[34]*Morrison College: Origin and Diary,* p. 10.
[35]*Morrison Diary,* pp. 22-23.

would relocate in Denver.[36] Kowald, who was in the midst of the rumor factory at Morrison, reminisced years later:

As soon as the Rt. Rev. Joseph P. Machebeuf, Bishop of Denver, however, became aware of the project, he insisted that any contemplated new College Building must be placed in Denver, the Metropolis of his Diocese, according to plans and stipulations agreed and decided upon from the beginning when he purchased and donated the Morrison College-Building, which was intended only as a temporary location for the future and chief educational institution of his Diocese, to be erected in Denver.[37]

The Jesuits were embarrassed but they could not refute the arguments of the bishop. They had to choose between Machebeuf and Byrne, and there was no doubt about the choice they had to make. Bryne was so upset by this turn of events that he resigned as pastor and left the diocese. He found a welcome in the then diocese of Los Angeles and was stationed at the Church of St. Catherine on Catalina Island.[38]

After the decision had been made, Pantanella took the necessary steps for a relocation of the college in Denver. It was an immense task but he proved equal to the challenge. In anticipation of the move to Denver the catalogue of Sacred Heart College for 1887-1888 suggests a conscious effort to model itself on the catalogues of Las Vegas College. It is by far more detailed than the three previous bulletins published for Morrison. There is a conscious effort to show continuity between Las Vegas College and the College of the Sacred Heart, valuable evidence in itself for any debate over the founding date of Regis College. The opening statement in the ''Prospectus'' reads in part:

The College of the Sacred Heart, . . . , is not a new college in any sense but that of location and building. It is the consolidation of the Jesuit College of Las Vegas, New Mexico, founded, Nov. 7th, 1877, and that of Morrison, Colo., founded, Sept. 15th, 1884.[39]

In this catalogue for the first time, we find two distinct departments, the collegiate and the academic. The text is obviously modeled on the catalogue of Las Vegas College. The collegiate course covers the standard division into four years, philosophy, rhetoric, poetry and humanities, while the academic offers subjects over a three-year period. In reference to the

---

[36]*Morrison Diary,* p. 27.

[37]Kowald, *op. cit.,* p. 110.

[38]Kowald, *op. cit.,* p. 111. The author was greatly indebted to Father Byrne who visited Morrison at a time when Kowald was near death. Byrne had a personal interest in tuberculosis and had learned about a remedy. He recommended the remedy and it proved successful.

[39]*Catalogue of the College of the Sacred Heart,* Denver, Colorado, 1887-1888, p. 9.

academic we find the words "High School" used for the first time when the explanation is given that "this department aims at imparting such an education as is usually given by the High Schools and Academies of our country."[40] A third course is listed, the commercial. An explanation seemed to be in order: ". . .this course offers to those who cannot or will not avail themselves of a regular classical training, the means of acquiring a good English or Commercial Education. . . . It is completed in four years, and prepares students for Commercial pursuits."[41]

A few words about tuition are in order because some changes were made before the move to Denver. It seems that there was a lack of complete communication between Morrison and Las Vegas since both catalogues for 1887-1888 were published late in the year and intended for the up-coming academic period. The Las Vegas statement about tuition and board per session of five months called for a fee of $100.00, whereas the Morrison catalogue has $120.00. It was finally agreed that a standard fee for tuition be charged for day students; it was an astonishing $5.00 a month.[42]

The excitement over and interest in the developments in Denver during the year 1887-1888, while the new building was being constructed in Denver, did not entirely disrupt the even course of events in Morrison. Students had to be fed and taught, and closing exercises worthy of a school which most seemed to have loved had to be prepared. The program, published in the catalogue for 1887-1888, demonstrated a diversity of presentations equal to those which had been given the two previous years. There was a dramatic presentation entitled "King Alfred" and two dialogues which offered the students a chance to display their proficiency in the modern languages, "Die Spartanische Mutter" and "Cada Buhonero Alaba Sus Agujas." A third dialogue, in English, depicted "The Death, Burial, and Resurrection of Morrison College."[43] Upon this bittersweet note the history of Jesuit education in Morrison came to an end.

After the move to Denver the Morrison buildings and property remained in the possession of the Jesuits. For some twenty-one years it was used as a villa, that is, a place of rest and recreation for members of the Jesuit Community in Denver. In September, 1909, the members of the Board of Trustees met and after some consideration voted on a motion made by A. M. Bertram:

Resolved that the action of the President and Treasurer of the Board of

---

[40]*Op. cit.,* p. 27 and *passim.*
[41]*Op. cit.,* p. 32.
[42]*Op. cit.,* p. 8 and p. 15.
[43]*Op. cit.,* pp. 42-43.

Trustees of the Corporation of the College of the Sacred Heart be ratified in making good and sufficient deeds to the property at Morrison, Colorado, formerly occupied as a college and bring Block number fifteen (15) on the plat of the town of Morrison in favor of the Colorado Resort Company upon the payment of the sum of seven thousand five hundred ($7,500) dollars.[44]

The motion passed without a dissenting vote. The deed remained in escrow until March 1, 1915; by that time the final payment had been made and the property was turned over to the Colorado Resort Company.[45] It is an interesting sidelight on history that the man representing the Colorado Resort Company in this transaction was J. Brisben Walker, who was to play such an essential role in making it possible for the Jesuits to move to Denver.

---

[44]*Minutes of the Board of Trustees, College of the Sacred Heart,* Sept. 7, 1909, pp. 66-67.
[45]*Op. cit.,* March 1, 1915.

Chapter 3

Denver- A Self-Contained Operation

1888-1919

During the academic year 1887-1888 Pantanella was involved in many things; not the least of his tasks was that of pouring oil on disturbed waters in Colorado Springs after the aborted attempt to transfer the college to that town. When Bishop Machebeuf made it clear that he would not sanction the move, the distraught president set his sights on Denver and immediately began to plan for the future. That future had to be made more secure by establishing a firm foundation according to the law that would be recognized by the legal authorities. Fortunately, the State of Colorado cooperated in this matter by approving the General Statutes of the State on March 14, 1887. Chapter Nineteen of the Statutes provided for the formation of corporations, and the Jesuits moved as soon as practicable to form such a legal entity.

On April 19, 1887, Pantanella met with Fathers John B. Guida, Carmelus Polino, and Stephen Robert in the residence of Sacred Heart Parish in Denver. Guida moved that Pantanella be elected the chairman and Stephen Robert the secretary. It should be noted that all the Jesuits working in Colorado had been informed of the meeting and had authorized Father Guida as their proxy. The chairman and secretary were approved without a dissenting vote. Pantanella then informed the members:

. . . the present meeting had for object the information of a corporation to be composed, if found expedient, of all members of the Society of Jesus residing, now and from time to time hereafter, in the State of Colorado, for the more convenient conduct of the affairs and management of the properties of said Society of Jesus, as well in Colorado as in any other States and Territories of the United States of America.[1]

Guida then informed the members present that he was authorized to act as proxy for the Jesuit priests and scholastics living and working in Colorado; he testified that he had the signatures of each member. Voting to recognize the votes by proxy, it was moved, seconded, and approved:

that all members of said Society of Jesus residing in the State of Colorado form themselves into a corporation for the purpose of conducting the religious, educational and other benevolent institutions, which the Society of Jesus may now and hereafter have in Colorado or in any

---

[1]*Trustees Meetings, St. Ignatius School and Mission Society,* p. 2.

other States of this country subject always to the rules and constitutions of said Society.[2]

The corporation was to be named "The Saint Ignatius School and Mission Society." The next item on the agenda was the adoption of a constitution. There is no need to examine the whole constitution here but mention should be made of two of the more pertinent articles. Article III provided for the annual election of the members of a Board of Trustees who would be empowered to elect the officers of the association, adopt a corporate seal, and make bylaws to regulate their own meetings and those of the association. Article IV provided that the Constitution could be amended by a two-thirds vote of the members of the association.[3]

After approving the constitution, the four Jesuits who were present proceeded to propose members for the Board of Trustees. There were no surprises among the men recommended, who were Joseph Marra, Superior of the Mission; Aloysius M. Gentile, his predecessor in that office; Dominic Pantanella, president of the College of the Sacred Heart, Morrison; Charles M. Pinto, Superior of the residence in Trinidad, destined to succeed Father Marra as Superior of the Mission; and John B. Guida, Superior of the residence in Denver. Stephen Robert was to continue as secretary of the Board. As such, it was his duty to obtain the confirmation of the proceedings by all the Jesuits residing in the State of Colorado. The decisions of the initial meeting were ratified by all concerned on April 28, 1887, and the document was duly recorded in the office of the Colorado Secretary of State, James Rice, on July 23. Mr. Rice affirmed that he acted in conformity with the provisions of Chapter Nineteen of the general statutes of Colorado.[4]

While the legal technicalities were being attended to, Pantanella and Guida were busy trying to obtain property and money. In the acquisition of land they were fortunate beyond their most sanguine expectations. During Pantanella's four years at Morrison he had become acquainted with John Brisben Walker, who lived in the vicinity and whose two sons attended the college. There was little that was drab in the career of this entrepreneur. Born in 1847 near Pittsburg, he received his early education at Gonzaga and Georgetown Colleges. In 1865 he entered the United States Military Academy at West Point; in 1868 he resigned from the Academy and went to China with the newly appointed minister where he served as a military adviser during the reorganization of the Chinese military service. After two years he returned to the United States, amassed a small fortune in West

---

[2]*Op. cit.*, p. 4.
[3]*Op. cit.*, p. 6.
[4]*Op. cit.*, p. 9 and pp. 11-12.

Virginia, then lost it in the financial panic of the Seventies. He then ventured into the field of journalism. But he was restless and in 1879 he moved to Colorado where he purchased sixteen hundred acres of land near Denver and developed a highly successful alfalfa ranch. Later he purchased over five hundred lots of bottom land in Denver.[5]

Denver at the time was a burgeoning town, and since 1868 it had been the capital of the Territory. The real estate business was thriving and it was fortunate that the Jesuits had a friend in John Brisben Walker, who was Vice-President of the Berkeley Farm and Cattle Company. Eager to increase the value of his holdings, Walker concluded that a college in the area would make it easier for him to develop his property. Accordingly, on July 22, 1887, he donated forty acres of land to Dominic Pantanella and John B. Guida with the stipulation that the Jesuits should:

> . . . erect and maintain a College designed for the education of youths and young men, at some point near the city of Denver; the building thereof to be not less than 297 feet long, nor less than sixty feet in height, and to contain at least four floors, the walls of which shall be built of stone.[6]

Ten more acres were donated by L. K. Perrin and his associates who were "anxious to have said building constructed and said college maintained, that the value of their lands may also be increased."[7]

Walker very generously gave the Jesuits the opportunity to choose any forty acres they wanted from the unoccupied holdings of the company. Pantanella was tempted to choose property near the present West 38th Street, about a mile south of St. Vincent's Orphanage, but Kowald recalled:

> This locality was already allotted for residential purposes, within the City-Limits and enjoying the privileges and benefits or advantages and accommodations accruing therefrom, such as city lights, water, fire and police protection as also sidewalks with trees set on either side of the graded and gravelled streets with the guarantee of having in the very near future two trolley-car lines, running on a time-schedule of fifteen minutes regular service each.[8]

Attractive as this site appeared, it did not satisfy Pantanella. Kowald tells the story that the president of the college in Morrison thought this possible location would be unsatisfactory because of "the close proximity of the orphan asylum, which might be confounded by visitors and sightseers with _

---

[5]Frank Luther Mott, "John Brisben Walker," DAB (New York, Charles Scribner's Sons, 1943), pp. 347-348.

[6]Property Deeds, R.C. Arch., p. 2.

[7]*Op. cit.,* p. 3.

[8]Kowald, *op. cit.,* p. 146.

the college building and thus detract from the latter's prestige and importance as also the possible moral danger for college students flirting with the orphan girls."[9]

Kowald takes a dim view of this reasoning. Nevertheless, it is clear that Pantanella rejected the site in favor of the one on which the college now stands. This area was not developing as much as the alternative one but it too has a magnificent view of the mountains, a view that sweeps from Long's Peak in Rocky Mountain Park to Pike's near Colorado Springs. It was deemed advisable to exchange the ten acres given by L. K. Perrin for ten acres that were contiguous to the chosen site. Once again Kowald, years later, registered a criticism of this decision when he wrote that the exchange was not a wise one since it involved giving improved and valuable land for ten acres of unimproved property even though the new acquisition gave the college-to-be fifty continuous acres. The critic of this decision added:

> . . . the former ten acres, being residentially better located and of much higher value, could have been held over for some years and thus highly increased in value, could have been sold for more than ten times its original estimate and help liquidate a great portion of the College debt.[10]

Pantanella was deeply grateful for these gifts, which surely lifted a great weight from his shoulders, and in the early years of the Denver phase of the college's history due recognition was given to the benefactions of Walker and Perrin.

Following a practice that had been in vogue from the beginning of the college, the catalogue for a given academic year was published toward the end of the second session. The catalogue for 1887-1888 recognized the two benefactors in these words:

> To Messrs. Walker and Perrin is due the praise for the magnificent site, of which the college so proudly boasts. No spot within the State of Colorado was so desirable for the purpose; and the generous donation of forty acres from Mr. Walker, and ten from Mr. Perrin, has enabled the authorities to build the College on the most beautiful tract in the vicinity of Denver.[11]

Mr. Walker objected that he did not deserve such recognition, protesting that he made the gift to help promote his own real estate business. Nevertheless, the college was grateful and displayed a portrait of Walker in the hallway near the entrance of the college. The portrait has since disappeared,

---

[9]Kowald, *op. cit.*, p. 147.
[10]Kowald, *op. cit.*, pp. 145-146.
[11]CSH Cat., 1887-1888, p. 21.

and old timers told the story that it was removed after Walker had divorced his first wife. Walker eventually sold his holdings in Denver at a large profit and returned to the East; in 1889 he bought the expiring *Cosmopolitan Magazine* and in five years increased the circulation from 16,000 to 400,000. In 1905 he sold the magazine to William Randolph Hearst.[12]

The acquisition of sufficient land on which to build did not solve all of Pantanella's problems. Obviously, the most important of these was money to finance the building which had been promised when the gift of the forty acres had been accepted. The Neapolitan authorities were hardly in a position to advance the necessary funds, nor were they forthcoming from the superiors of the New Mexico-Colorado Mission. It is doubtful that any bank in Denver would have been interested in advancing a loan for such a project. As things turned out Pantanella was able to borrow from European sources and he received smaller loans from some Americans. There is evidence that he had been working on this project since 1886. On February 12th of that year Aloysius M. Gentile, Superior of the Mission, received an interesting letter from Anton Anderledy, Vicar General of the Society of Jesus. It read in part:

> For my part I have no recollection that I, according of Father Pantanella's assertion, gave permission for the borrowing of twenty or twenty-five thousand scudi so that funds could be gathered for the projected college. Even if the establishment of a college near the city of Denver had been allowed, such a permission did not carry with it a transfer later into the city. Even this could not have been granted unless the reasons for the transfer had been submitted and each of the consultors of the Mission had written to me separately.[13]

More information about this matter is found in the minutes of the Board of Trustees of the corporation under the date of May 17, 1888. It is recorded that:

> Reverend Fr. Marra and D. Pantanella have until the present day borrowed for the construction of said new College a sum of about seventy-six thousand dollars from different parties in Europe and in America for which sums the Society is responsible. Furthermore the St. Ignatius School and Mission Society authorizes said Reverend J. Marra and D. Pantanella to take all the necessary means to complete said new College, in order to open classes in it in the month of next September.[14]

Unfortunately, the correspondence that Father Pantanella carried on dur-

---

[12]DAB *op. cit.*, p. 348.
[13]S.J. Arch., Rome.
[14]*Trustees Meetings 1887-1893*, p. 29.

ing these years has not survived. There is, however, a document presumably in the handwriting of Pantanella that lists the institutions and persons who loaned money to the Colorado Jesuits in their time of need. The list is a tribute to the solidarity of the Jesuits and their willingness to help a struggling mission. It is true that the loans were made as an investment but the interest charged seems reasonable enough. The first entry records a loan from Mungret College, a Jesuit institution in Limerick, Ireland, and the Rev. Vincent Byrne, S.J., on June 1, 1888, approved a loan of $19,451.60 over a period of ten years at five percent interest (the loan is actually recorded as L4057-15-0). Earlier that same year, January 1, 1888, the Jesuit Province of Belgium made a loan of $10,000 at five percent to be paid annually for a period of ten years. Lesser sums were acquired from a number of people in Holland, and a few Americans showed encouragement; the most significant loan came from Rev. Ignatius Horstman (later Bishop of Cleveland) who advanced $5,000 at six percent to be paid semi-annually over a period of five years.[15]

With property and sufficient money for a beginning, Pantanella next had to find a way to get construction under way. According to the agreement with Walker, the proper authorities undertook to ''begin said construction within fifty days from the date hereof (July 22, 1887) and complete the same within eighteen months from the date hereof.''[16] Jesuits were accustomed to use whatever available talent was at hand. In this case they were fortunate to have a member of the Mission who had pursued for some time the career of a draftsman and architect before he joined the Society of Jesus.

Edward Barry, a native of Ireland, came to the United States with some members of his family and made his home in Boston. His health broke down and he moved West with the hope of regaining his strength. He became interested in the work of the Jesuits and in 1881 he applied for admission into the order. He was received as a novice on November 15th, two days after John J. Brown had been accepted. After a year in the novitiate at Albuquerque he proceeded to Florissant, Missouri, where he completed his two years of probation. This experience was followed by two years of teaching at Las Vegas College, after which he went to Woodstock to pursue his studies. It seems that he was not entirely satisfied with the life of a student and felt that he would prefer to get involved in working for the Indians. He wrote to the Secretary of the Interior applying for the position of superintendent of the governmental Indian school in Albuquerque, New Mexico. This letter somehow found its way to Naples where it is filed in the Archives of the Province.

---

[15]R.C.A.
[16]*Property Deeds*, p. 4.

It reads in part, "I have been a resident of Las Vegas, New Mexico, during the greater portion of the four years, from 1881 to 85. . . . During the past year I have been a student at Woodstock College, Maryland."[17] There is no surviving evidence of the kind of answer he received. It is quite clear, however, from Barry's assignment for the academic year 1887-1888 that his superiors had in mind for him an entirely different destiny.

Pantanella and Barry started planning for the new building; the latter had the task of supervising the whole project. His home base for the period was Sacred Heart Rectory in Denver. The Province Catalogue for Naples for 1888 identifies him as a member of that small community and notes that he would be occupied in building the new college (*"operam dat novo collegio extruendo"*).[18]

Working under pressure, Pantanella was able to sign contracts with architects, excavators, carpenters, bricklayers and a company that could deliver the stone which had been stipulated in the agreement with Walker and Perrin. The architects were Dozier and Cozin, who agreed on July 27, 1887, to furnish complete sets of drawings and specifications "and to superintend the erection of the Jesuit College Building to be erected in north Denver."[19]

Ground was broken on September 13, 1887, and work progressed under the watchful eye of the thirty-year-old Jesuit scholastic, Edward Barry, who compiled a record noting all the contracts and the amount of money due to each firm. It is not necessary to go into detail about the various activities that are indispensable for the building of a school. It seems that Pantanella kept a watchful eye on Mr. Barry because there are a number of pages on which the scholastic recorded every item of expense incurred, such as seventy-five cents for a telegram to Chicago, and twenty cents for college photos.[20]

Under the supervision of Barry the work progressed satisfactorily. In fact, a legend that the greater part of the construction was finished in ninety-eight days was created and persisted for a long time. The foundation of the legend was that Pantanella insisted on time limits in most contracts with provision for a penalty if the conditions were not met. Vollmar concluded that the stone and brick work was finished within one hundred days. There was, however, much work to be done on the interior of the building and it was not finished until more than a year later.[21]

---

[17]P.N. Arch.
[18]CDPN, 1888, p. 29.
[19]R.C.A.
[20]R.C.A.
[21]Vollmar, *op. cit.,* p. 89.

The building was an imposing one for those times. Situated on the crest of a hill and crowned with a cupola, it commanded a panoramic view of the Front Range of the Rocky Mountains, the Clear Creek Valley, and Denver. It is true that the building was quite isolated and was to remain so for some time, but, everything considered, Barry and Pantanella had every reason to be proud of the structure.

Life at Las Vegas and Morrison during the last few months of the scholastic year must have been hectic. It was well known that both schools were to be closed and a new beginning to be made in Denver. Preparations for the change were made during the summer. Among the many decisions that had to be made, one had precedence, namely, the appointment of a president, and that decision had to be made by the General of the Society of Jesus since a president of a Jesuit College was also a religious superior. Obviously, the General had to depend on information provided him by knowledgeable men who were on the local scene. The Society of Jesus relied on regular reports about men who gave promise of having a talent for administration. The procedure has no built-in guarantee of success but it has worked fairly well over the years. Two men were under consideration at the time, namely, Salvatore Personè, president of the college in Las Vegas for some nine years, and Dominic Pantanella, who had spent four years in the office at Morrison and two at Las Vegas. Personè was not a dynamic man in the image of a modern college president, but in the years he occupied the position in Las Vegas he proved that he could measure up to the expectations of his superiors.

Pantanella, however, did not have all the required qualifications. But in any assessment of his performance in office, it should be remembered that he found it necessary to be on the move most of the time in his endeavors to relocate the college. Those who preferred an administrator in residence took a dim view of their traveling president. The diarist, for example, noted on June 22, 1888, that there was a great need for organization in the whole administration.[22]

This opinion must have been reflected in the reports that filtered back to the Society's headquarters. The decision was made on July 13, 1888. On that date Anton Anderledy, General of the Society of Jesus, wrote to Joseph Marra, Superior of the Mission:

After your reverence, in accord with your own judgment and that of your Consultors, indicated that in the case of Father Pantanella you had in mind the need of a man for an onerous duty, I was persuaded that that Father is not suitable for undertaking the office of Rector in the College

[22]Morrison College Origin and Diary, p. 59.

at Denver. Consequently I delegate your Reverence to put Father Salvatore Personè in charge of the college for the time being, with the title though of Vice-Rector.[23]

The decision was not popular in the growing community of Denver. Some thought that since Pantanella had raised the money and built the new school he should be the president. A reporter from the *Denver Republican* approached Hugh L. Magevney, a member of the faculty of the college in Morrison. Magevney was well known in Denver because of his many successful appearances in the pulpits of Denver. When asked why Pantanella was passed over, he responded:

It is not right to impose too much labor on the man. Dignity is nothing but responsibility, and honor for a Jesuit is only trouble and annoyance. Father Pantanella himself asked to be removed in order to perfect his work on the building and beautifying the grounds. It will take several years for him to fix up the grounds according to his present plans, and he would have no time for the duties of President.[24]

The reporter sought another interview, one with the man who had been appointed to head the college in its new location, Salvatore Personè. There is no record to show how Personè felt about what might be called the game of "musical chairs." As a Jesuit he felt that it was his duty to accept whatever position he was assigned. He responded to the question of the reporter in a manner typically Jesuit. His answer was that he built Las Vegas College "and Father Pantanella was sent to be President there. It was time to pay him back. He built the Denver College, and I am now sent to be its President."[25]

Pantanella was too good a Jesuit to resent the action of his superiors. He did, however, have the satisfaction of seeing the name he had chosen for the college accepted: The College of the Sacred Heart, the same name he had given to the school in Morrison. Pantanella was a very devout man and since his days as a novice he had practiced a lively devotion to the Sacred Heart of Jesus, a devotion that would remain an important part of his religious life.

The selection of a president was not the only important decision that had to be made during the summer of 1888. Someone had to preside over the transportation of all usable equipment of two boarding colleges from Las Vegas and Morrison to Denver. Adjustments were needed to determine who would teach at the new location. It should be remembered that some of the men in Las Vegas were needed to continue the work of publishing the *Revista Catolica*. Somehow arrangements were made and although it had

---

[23]S.J.A., Rome.
[24]The *Denver Republican,* Sept. 5, 1888.
[25]*Ibid.*

been announced that school was to begin on September 5th, it took five more days before some order began to be evident in the midst of near chaos. The first entry in the diary for the College of the Sacred Heart noted, ''a common daily order is being established and every effort is being made to arrange and put in order the things in the house; rooms are being prepared for the community; study halls, classrooms, and dormitories are being readied for the students.''[26]

In time Personè and his colleagues gained control of matters and orderly procedures were established. In spite of uncertainties and the problems related to relocation, the school accepted 152 students. Twenty-nine of that total transferred from Las Vegas, some of them Mexican nationals, and twenty-seven of the Morrison boys moved to the new site in Denver. The presence of fifty-six of their old students made things easier for the Jesuits. During the first year of the Denver experience ninety-three students enrolled in the classical department, twenty-eight in the commercial and thirty-one in the preparatory.[27]

Twenty Jesuits and one layman made up the faculty; the layman, Mr. D. Boffa, taught violin. Four Jesuits came from Las Vegas to replace the four of the Morrison faculty who had been transferred. There was a significant shift from predominantly Italian personnel to a more cosmopolitan one. Since the foundation of the New Mexico-Colorado Mission, Americans were attracted to its apostolate. True, some came West for their health, but others were simply interested in a mission field which offered various opportunities for the service of the Church. Some of these men entered the Society of Jesus and became members of the Province of Naples. Other Jesuits were loaned to the Mission or were sent to Colorado or New Mexico from other provinces for the sake of their health. For example, Father J. F. Holland came to Denver from the Maryland-New York Province, and Augustus Girard came from the Canadian Mission. Kowald joined the Mission after he became a novice of the Buffalo Mission which had been established by members of the German Province. While at Morrison he became a very sick man but eventually recovered and served the Society well for many years. Armand W. Forstall came to the United States as a Jesuit from the Province of Champagne, but joined the Mission and became an institution at the college. It is not surprising that five members of the faculty were of Irish extraction, William O'Connor, William Lonergan, Joseph Phelan, Patrick Wallace and Hugh Magevney.

---

[26]Diary, 1894, p. 2.
[27]C.S.H. Cat., 1888-1889, pp. 28-32.

We have already mentioned Magevney's contribution to the college at Morrison and noted that he had been dismissed from the Society. Incidentally, when the superiors decided to keep him on the faculty for a few more years, they judged that it would be prudent to cover up the fact that Magevney was not a member of the order. They achieved that by not placing the "S.J." after any of the names of the faculty listed in the catalogues from 1888 through the academic year 1893-1894. Magevney's name disappears from the roster for 1894-1895.[28]

Far from being embittered by the decision to dismiss him from the Society, he was as dynamic and dedicated in Denver as he had been when he began to teach at Morrison. One of his greater achievements was that of founding an association the objective of which was the publication of "a College paper devoted to the improvement of the students in literary work, and intended to serve as a medium of communication between the undergraduates and their friends outside."[29] They decided to name the publication *The Highlander* in recognition of the fact that the college was in the section of Denver known as the Highlands. Magevney enlisted some students whom he had known at Morrison and added willing candidates from newcomers to make up the staff. The first edition appeared in December, 1888, no mean achievement in days when so many adjustments were necessary because of the move from Morrison to Denver. This literary venture was a gamble and the first issue was limited to six-hundred copies. A subscription cost one dollar a year; the price for a single copy was ten cents.

The Highlander aspired to be a combination literary magazine and college paper. The major portion of the publication was given over to essays written by the students. These essays show an amazing breadth of interests. A few titles chosen at random demonstrate how varied the topics were that were the subjects of those literary endeavors. For example, the editors prepared for publication articles titled "Chapultepec," "Thoughts on Pantheism," "Jacques Cathelneau (the peasant leader of the Vendean war during the French Revolution)," "On Music," "Modern English Literature," and "Joseph Addison."[30] The articles may not have been literary gems but they indicate the subjects in which the students were interested. Besides the essays there were columns given to local topics, college notes, and happenings in the daily life of the college. These notes are valuable because they

---

[28]Kowald's memory failed him in this matter concerning Magevney. He writes that he spent three years in Morrison and two in Denver. Actually, his name appears as a member of the faculty in Denver through the scholastic year 1893-1894. The catalogue for 1894-1895 resumes placing the "S.J." after the names of the Jesuits.

[29]CSH Cat., *1888-89*, p. 37.

[30]*The Highlander, passim.*

furnish a supplement to the rather laconic notations in the college diaries. The students were proud of their publication and established a quite impressive list of exchanges. For example, *The Highlander* had an exchange with the *Notre Dame Scholastic,* the *Georgetown Journal, Stonyhurst Magazine* of Lancaster, *The Raven* of Downside, England. *The American Art Journal, The Owl* of Ottawa, and *El Eco de la Juventud* of Orizeba, Mexico.[31]

The Highlanders Association was not the only organization that had been established. Following the venerable tradition of the Society of Jesus, the Sodality of the Immaculate Conception flourished under the direction of Father J. F. Holland. Students had the opportunity to join the St. John Berchmans Society, which provided servers for the many Masses that were offered every day. Other societies afforded opportunities for students to develop their natural talents; for example, the St. Cecilia's Society provided music both for the frequent assemblies and for such special occasions as the closing exercises at the end of the scholastic year.

Since it had long been a tradition in Jesuit schools to train students in *eloquentia,* elocution was a major concern of the faculty. There was an elocution contest every year. Lively competition determined which students would qualify for participation in the final competition which was one of the highlights of the year. Judges were recruited from the Denver Community and it was their duty to pass judgment on the best renditions; the winners were awarded prizes at the end of the year. Elocution proved to be far more successful than debating, even though the Loyola Debating Society was formed with the Rev. Joseph A. Phelan as moderator. For some unexplainable reason debating never met with much success in the history of the college even though honest efforts were made over the years to promote that activity.

The development of the dramatic arts met with a better fate. The stage had its devotees and drama had been an important part of the college life in Las Vegas and Morrison and the tradition continued when the college moved to Denver. On February 22, 1890, the students presented ''Elma'' at the college and the performance was so well received that the moderator of the dramatic society, Rev. William Lonergan, decided with the approval of the president to make a public presentation in the city in the Tabor Grand Opera House on April 10, 1890. The students were enthusiastic and promoted the undertaking as a fund-raising project for the benefit of the library. They were modest in their request for the cost of the tickets, asking fifty cents admission. The play was performed before a full house and received good reviews. A critic wrote in *The Denver Republican:*

----

[31]*The Highlander,* June, 1892, vol. IV, No. 10, p. 159.

The drama was watched with intense interest from beginning to end. The youthful actors performed their parts with great spirit and were frequently applauded. Nothing was omitted in costume or scenery towards contributing to the success of the play. The college chorus received a very warm greeting. All the young actors and participants did themselves much credit and contributed to a very pleasing and instructive entertainment.[32]

The elocution contests, the dramatic presentations, and the preparation they involved must have been welcome to the young men who lived in a very controlled environment. The College of the Sacred Heart in Denver was very much a self-contained institution, one that was isolated from the mainstream of a growing city. The regulations limited the number of visits that parents and friends could make; visiting days were specified, and exceptions were frowned upon. Students were forbidden to leave the college grounds without permission, and as late as 1925 prefects still issued "walking permits" that allowed students to take walks away from the campus. Day students were just barely tolerated and were considered a possible threat to the well-being of the boarders; the regulations regarding day students read, "They are not allowed to associate with boarders more than is absolutely necessary in class and college exercises. It is strictly forbidden to take out letters or go on errands for boarders."[33] Moreover, the authorities continued to reserve to themselves the right to censorship with the discretionary power to inspect all letters, books, etc., either directed to the students or sent by them.[34]

A cursory inspection of the daily order gives the impression of a tightly organized community in which the watchword was discipline. One is reminded of a monastic institution, and it is not surprising that some people in the Denver community concluded that the Jesuits were conducting a seminary, an opinion that survives in some quarters of the city to this day.

There is little wonder then that celebrations and/or festivals were welcomed by faculty and students. Such events provided opportunities to get a change from the ordinary routine. Fortunately, Bishop Machebeuf, during the year of life that was allotted to him, was a frequent visitor. His coadjutor and successor, Nicholas C. Matz, showed a lively interest in the college and continued to visit it on special occasions. These visits provided an opportunity for celebration and the students usually were granted a full or half holiday.

---

[32]*The Denver Republican.*
[33]CSH Cat., 1888-1889, p. 6.
[34]CSH Cat., p. 5.

A number of special occasions occurred in 1888 and in 1890. In October 1888 the two bishops participated in the ceremonies honoring three Jesuit saints who had been canonized, Peter Claver, John Berchmans, and Alphonsus Rodriguez. The festivities lasted for three days. One of the highlights was the blessing of the building, described in *The Highlander* in these words: "The ceremony of blessing the house was most imposing. The clergy in chasuble and dalmatic, the choir in surplice, and the column of nearly one hundred fifty students chanting the hymns through the long corridors, was something very beautiful."[35] On these occasions there were entertainments that gave the students an opportunity to demonstrate their progress in the thespian arts and in the rendition of musical selections. Of course, a banquet was prepared and served and speeches were made by the leading notables.

A second highlight in the early years in Denver was the recognition given to Salvatore Personè, Dominic Pantanella and Pascal Tomassini (Pastor of the Church of Conejos) on the occasion of the twenty-fifth anniversary of their ordination to the priesthood. Bishop Matz and a goodly number of pastors of churches in Denver came to the college on June 10, 1890, to pay tribute to the three Jesuits, and of course the students joined in the jubilation. The bishop preached at the Mass which was followed by a banquet.[36]

A third notable event was the blessing of the statue of the Sacred Heart of Jesus, the gift of the Walkers, parents of J. Brisben Walker. The benefactors paid $1,500 for the statue that has been a landmark on the grounds and is still standing. It was erected on a mound in front of the main entrance, where it dominated the surrounding grounds. The blessing took place on October 9, 1890; the occasion marked the formal opening of the college. The statue, a standing tribute to Pantanella's devotion to the Sacred Heart, has four inscriptions on the pedestal in Latin. Down through the years many translations of the Latin have been attempted, but there has been no concensus regarding the most accurate version. During the early years when Latin was an integral part of the curriculum, it was a favorite punishment (more familiarly known as "Jug") to assign culprits the task of rendering the Latin inscriptions into English. Fortunately for the more modern student, for whom Latin is truly a dead language, a translation was printed in *The Highlander*. The inscription on the north side reads, "This house to the training of boys in piety and arts devoted Thou has prepared for Thyself it is Thine. Do Thou increase and preserve it." On the south, "This field by Thy bounteous hand enriched is redolent for Thee. Grant Thou that our youthful

---

[35]*The Highlander*, Vol. I, No. 1, December, 1888, p. 13.
[36]*The Highlander*, Vol. II, No. 10, June 1890, p. 170.

charge may by steadfast piety sweetest fragrance yield.'' On the east, ''May those who by Thee inspired gave their aid to the raising of this College to Thy Sacred Heart devoted be forever near Thee in the world to come.'' On the west, ''Do Thou rulest the Hearts of men grant us to enjoy in heaven the company of the patrons and pupils whom Thou givest us on earth.''[37]

June 23, 1890, marked a fitting climax to the academic year. On that day the degree of Bachelor of Arts was conferred on four students and that of Bachelor of Science on six, and three students were awarded certificates for the successful completion of the English and Commercial Courses. These were perhaps the first college degrees granted by the Jesuits in either New Mexico or Colorado. The catalogues of Las Vegas since 1881-1882 stated that ''Having complied with the provisions of the general law of New Mexico, Twenty-fifth Session, Chapter XL, the College is thereby 'empowered to grant diplomas, confer degrees and all other literary honors, usually conferred' by similar institutions of learning in the United States.''[38] There is, however, no available evidence that any degrees were conferred in Las Vegas. The previous quote from the catalogue raised a question in this matter. It has been noted that the Congress of the United States had decided that territorial institutions could not award degrees. The catalogues of Las Vegas College for the years 1881 to 1888 do not list the names of students who might have merited any academic degrees.

The prospectus for the year 1888-1889 states that ''The College of the Sacred Heart, incorporated July 23, 1887, by the State of Colorado, and by an Act of the State Legislature, April 1, 1889, [is] empowered to confer University and Collegiate Honors and Diplomas.''[39] The catalogues of the College of the Sacred Heart, however, list them from 1890.

Two of the ten degreed graduates had studied at Las Vegas College and six at the College of the Sacred Heart, Morrison; two were transfers from other schools. Of the four who received the A.B., one was from Zacatecas, Mexico, one from Leadville, and two from Denver. Of the six Bachelors of Science, two were from Milwaukee, one each from Denver, Laramie, Lincoln, and Guanajuato, Mexico. Some of the men who received degrees went east to continue their studies. For example, Henry C. Vidal, P. F. Gildea and James A. Johnston entered Georgetown; John T. Donnellan went to Harvard Law; Michael Estrada to Georgetown Medical; James H. Nichols to Andover, Massachusetts.[40] This was an excellent record for such a small graduating class.

[37]*The Highlander,* vol. III, No. 2, Oct. 1890, p. 28.
[38]LVC Cat., 1881-1882, p. 3.
[39]CSH Cat., *1888-1889,* p. 1.
[40]*The Highlander,* vol. III, No. 1, September, 1890, p. 10.

The year 1892 was noteworthy also for the decision to choose school colors. This may have been just another vestige of a medieval tradition but, for whatever reason, it seemed necessary to make a choice. There is no available record to indicate that this matter concerned students or faculty members in Las Vegas or Morrison. Not unexpectedly, the matter came under consideration because the players on the baseball team felt that they needed colors to identify themselves. As usual in such matters there were as many suggestions as there were persons interested enough to make a choice. Father Alphonsus Mandalari, Prefect of Studies, intervened and recommended that an outsider be chosen as arbiter. Father Mandalari submitted the proposals to the mother of the captain of the baseball team, J. Grattan O'Bryan. Mrs. J. D. O'Bryan recommended the colors of old gold and brown. The editors of *The Highlander* expressed their appreciation:

It is to her excellent taste that the trying problem has been solved. Considering the limited number of colors from which she had to choose, the selection of old-gold and brown is most satisfactory to all concerned. [41]

Another noteworthy development took place in 1893 but since it pertained to the internal affairs of Jesuit government, it will be mentioned here very briefly, principally because the action taken dissolved the St. Ignatius School and Mission Society and established a new corporation to be known under the title "College of the Sacred Heart, Denver, Colorado." [42]

The occasional celebrations were a welcome interlude in a very orderly and generally monotonous life. On the average there were some one hundred fifty students fairly evenly divided between boarders and day students. Much emphasis was placed on performance in the academic life as well as in the manner in which students behaved themselves. Weekly marks of the students' conduct, application and recitations were registered in books kept for that purpose and read publicly in every class and in the study halls. Each month there was an assembly in the college hall with a public reading showing the student's standing in the teachers' and prefects' departments. These records were sent to the parents who were requested to examine them carefully. From the beginning there was great emphasis placed on encouraging the students to be polite. The statement in the catalogue read:

The College expects from all its students the manners and deportment of perfect gentlemen. Politeness is deemed a very important element of education. On the premises, smoking, tobacco chewing, low or profane language, rough, uncouth games of any sort, are not tolerated. [43]

---

[41]*Op. cit.,* vol. IV, No. 10, June 1892, p. 158.
[42]*Trustees' Meetings,* 1887-1893, p. 69-70.
[43]CSH Cat., *1889-1890,* p. 6 and passim.

Some relief was found in training for the presentations of plays and preparing musical programs for the special occasions, such as St. Patrick's Day (one suspects the influence of Hugh Magevney). One special occasion took place on December 17, 1893, when a banquet was served to the teachers and prefects; there is no doubt about the role of Magevney in preparing the menu. The author of the diary was so impressed that he recorded the menu in detail. The banquet started with raw oysters followed by beef broth and Albuquerque catawba. The next course was barbecued pig followed by stuffed ham served with California claret, then roast beef and mashed potatoes. Presuming that appetites were not sated, baked pigeons were offered. Finally, fruit was served with cheese and crackers and, of course, coffee. The diarist adds an interesting note: "It would be advisable to serve the same meal to the Brothers."[44]

Naturally, athletics were an important fact in college life, especially in a school as isolated as the College of the Sacred Heart. In 1895 the students decided to give more formal recognition to this facet of college life. They established an athletic association the objective of which was "not only to afford harmless amusement, but also to promote the physical development of the students by manly games and healthful exercise." The statement of the objective identifies lawn tennis, baseball, handball, and billiards. In the light of future interests of the college it is strange that football is specifically excluded because it was considered "rough and uncouth."[45]

The faculty should not be compared to those of modern Jesuit schools. There is an adage adopted by some more sophisticated American Jesuits that states, "Those who can, do, those who can't, teach." It is not easy to give a satisfactory answer to persons who always think in secular and perhaps selfish terms to the question: "Why does a reasonably intelligent, healthy young man become a Jesuit?" But young men did, and still do, join the Society of Jesus. After receiving a solid training in the basics of the religious life, the seminarian proceeded to an intensive study of Greek and Latin classics. Philosophy followed, after which the young man was assigned to a school to teach. At this stage of his training he knew that he had to do what he was told to do, and he may have found himself teaching a subject about which he knew very little. The system was not perfect, nor did it stress specialization, but on the whole its record for performance was not all bad.

To take one year as an example, one can see what kind of faculty the College of the Sacred Heart had in 1894-1895. Edward Barry, the right arm of Pantanella during the period of construction of the building, had returned

---

[44]Diary, 1888-1894, p. 148.
[45]CSH Cat., 1894-1895, p. 46.

after theological studies and ordination to be Prefect of Studies and Discipline; Dominic Pantanella was professor of evidences of religion, mental and moral philosophy; Raphael D'Orsi was professor of natural philosophy and analytical geometry. These three were priests. All the others were scholastics, that is, Jesuits still in training. William A. Lonergan was professor of poetry, English literature and mathematics; Augustine J. Bertram, professor of special classes; Anthony J. Schuler, professor of humanities. These six constituted the faculty for the more advanced studies. In the Academic Department, one man taught all the subjects to a given year; for example, John B. Schimpf was in charge of First Academic. Laymen taught music. One other layman, Eldridge A. Hyde, taught bookkeeping, commercial law, and elocution. Since there were only some one hundred sixteen students, the teacher-student ratio was ideal, especially in the more advanced years.[46] Given the ambivalent attitude of the Jesuits to the commercial subjects, it is not surprising that during the early nineties the commercial course suffered. The 1892-1893 catalogue, perhaps by oversight, does not mention the commercial course under the section "Course of Instruction." One student, however, John Thomas Watters, received a commercial certificate. In the following year, nine lines have reference to commercial studies compared to four and one-half pages in the catalogue of 1891-1892.[47]

The administration was far from being complex. Salvatore Personè, the President, for three and one-half years, came to Denver after nine years of experience as administrator of Las Vegas College. A kind man, he had sufficient competence in conducting the business of the institution. His ultimate responsibility was to make sure that all the necessities were provided for a faculty of about twenty and a student body that averaged about one hundred fifty. He worked with the Treasurer of the College, Dominic Pantanella, to provide for the daily needs of all as well as to find money to pay the interest due to those who had loaned so much to the institution. It is difficult to formulate an adequate assessment of Personè's administration. A summation written after his death is not very helpful, noting that when he came to Denver he "had once more to face the difficulties inherent in every new undertaking; and again God crowned his labors with success."[48] There is no doubt that the students loved and respected him. *The Highlander* printed an appreciation of his place in the lives of the young men attending the college. In presenting some pictures representing science, piety and art to

---

[46]CSH Cat., *1894-1895, passim.*
[47]CSH Cat., *1891-1894, passim.*
[48]W.L., vol. 53, p. 389.

the president, the delegate of the student body said, ''and as you are the leader of us all, in our efforts to attain them (the ends after which we are struggling), it is only proper that we should let you have some mark of our appreciation.''[49] Personè received a new appointment in January, 1892, leaving Denver to assume pastoral duties in Trinidad.

Joseph M. Marra, Personè's successor, was also superior of the Mission; he took on this added burden seemingly because he could find no one whom he deemed qualified for the position. Marra was a veteran of the Mission, having come to the United States in 1870. After he finished his course of studies he was assigned to Las Vegas where he became a valuable asset for the publication of the *Revista Catolica*. He still found time to perform the duties of the prefect of schools and discipline in Las Vegas College; he filled this latter post for a period of eight years. He became superior of the Mission in 1887. At the time he assumed the office of president of the College of the Sacred Heart in January, 1892, he was responsible for eight Jesuit communities resident in cities as far apart as Denver and El Paso. There were eighty men distributed over this territory, each of whom was under the jurisdiction of Joseph M. Marra.

Marra was a classic example of the dedicated Jesuit. Totally reliable, kind but firm, he performed the duties to which he was assigned with a selflessness that elicited the approbation of his superiors. One who knew him wrote at the time of his death, ''His rich talents, remarkable prudence and genuine piety, his fatherly tenderness, hidden beneath a seemingly austere exterior, all combined to make him a wonderfully efficient instrument in the hands of the Almighty.''[50]

Although the duties of Superior of the Mission called for frequent absences from the college, he still found time to preside over the assemblies when the monthly grades were read. His technique on such occasions was described by the recorder in the College Diary in April 1894, who remarked that the president made some remarks showing his pleasure with those who had performed well but indicating his displeasure with those who had failed to live up to the established standards. The diarist continued, ''three things had caused him displeasure, namely, first, the low marks of the Preparatory class; second, the low marks in the Prefect's Department; and third, the low marks of some boys whom he did mention.''[51] One gets the impression that the president made his point. It should not, however, be concluded that

[49]*The Highlander*, vol. II, No. 5, January, 1890, p. 81.
[50]W.L., vol. 44, 1915, p. 392.
[51]Diary 1892-1895, p. 90.

Marra was a pessimist or that he was unable to give due credit. A year later, June, 1895, the diarist recorded that the president was pleased with the performance of the students. Marra recognized that the general tone of the marks was excellent and he congratulated the new leaders. He concluded by saying that "this was one of the best and happiest school years he had ever experienced."[52]

Marra presided over the affairs of the college for three and one-half years, during which time he endeavored to find a man capable of replacing him. It was not an easy task and it is easy to detect a note of frustration in a letter written to Luis Martin, General of the Society of Jesus. He wrote on January 10, 1896, and reminded the General, "For the last four years now a rector for this college has been asked for in vain. The matter has been often discussed at length in the meetings of the consultors, and more than once I have brought the matter to your Paternity's attention and to that of the provincial, but always to no avail."[53] In the event, it became clear why there was so much anxiety to find a successor. The authorities of the Province of Naples had such a high regard for Marra's ability that they wished to recall him to Naples and appoint him Provincial; they did so in October, 1896. In the meantime, superiors decided to appoint John B. Guida, the founding pastor of Sacred Heart Church in Denver, as president of the college. Jesuits were supposed to be ready for any appointment, but it is doubtful that seven years' experience in building a parish prepared a man for the task of governing a college.

Whether he was qualified or not, Father Guida governed the college for three years, July 1896 to September 1899. His tenure of office seems to have been a holding action for there is not much in the records to indicate that his administration changed anything in the operation of the school. One of the few things he was remembered for was the picture he presented when he went among the students when they were occupied in their activities on the grounds during recreation periods. He moved about dressed in a swallowtail coat and wearing a stovepipe hat.

Every president during these years was deeply concerned over the problem of finances. The income from tuition and board remained at $120.00 for the five-month term, $8.00 per month for half-boarders, and $5.00 a month for day students. This was hardly sufficient to pay the current expenses let alone meet the regular payments due on the interest on the loans that Father Pantanella had obtained. Even if the tuition of each student had been paid it would not have been enough. Unfortunately, some of the students did not

---

[52]Diary 1892-1895, pp. 147-148.
[53]S.J.A., Rome.

pay even though the charges seemed minimal. In the annual report of April 18, 1898, the president of the Board of Trustees, Charles M. Pinto, noted that "of the day scholars, who constitute one-half the number of students, one-third receive their tuition gratis."[54]

In 1892 the Board of Trustees endeavored to promote interest in the college by offering a free scholarship for day students in the classical course to one successful competitor from each parochial school within the city limits. In the same year the authorities were successful in enlisting outside help. They found two benefactors, Count M. Henry Cassell and Edward L. Johnson, LL.D., both of Denver. The former offered two scholarships for day students; the latter gave ten.[55]

The years 1892 to 1896 were critical years. The panic of 1893 took its toll on the college. Enrollment figures for the years 1892 through 1895 reflect the economic condition of the times. Enrollment dropped from 103 in 1891 to 64 in 1892. A slight improvement is noticeable during the next three years. After 1896 there is a return to previous averages. *The Highlander* must have been a casualty of the depression; it is not mentioned in the college catalogue after 1894. Perhaps it is significant that at about the same time the name of Hugh Magevney disappears from the roster of the faculty. Father Magevney's health was not robust and there are references in the diary to many periods of illness. It was a sad day at the college when the colorful Hugh Magevney departed; he was certainly missed in the succeeding years.

At the turn of the century the college was on a fairly stable foundation. Having survived the economic crisis of 1893 the college restored its students to a normal course. No one could predict what the new century would portend. The financial status of the college was just barely solvent. Everyday needs were taken care of largely because the authorities were able to rely on a number of the necessities being provided for by the industrious lay brothers and the laborers who took care of the limited amount of farming that was done. The college had its own laundry and bakery. But at best the authorities were able to meet the barest daily requirements of the faculty and students. The financial report[56] made to the members of the Board of Trustees at the end of the year 1899 revealed how precarious the situation was for a debt-ridden institution:

Cash on hand and in banks
    from last year, January 1, 1899 $ 1,249.34
Cash receipts for 1899   30,080.15

---

[54]*Minutes of the Board of Trustees,* p. 36.
[55]C.S.H., Cat., 1892-1893, p. 32.
[56]*Minutes of the Board of Trustees,* 1893-1923, p. 43.

Total	31,329.49
Cash expenses of 1899	29,682.22
Balance cash on hand and in banks, January 1, 1900	1,647.27
Surplus, January 1, 1900	1,249.34
Receipts over expenses, 1899	397.93

On September 1, 1899, Guida was replaced by John J. Brown. Brown assumed the duties of president of the college at the age of thirty-two, the first American-born man to hold that office. He had not yet completed his training as a Jesuit but such was the dearth of qualified men that superiors decided to appoint him. John Brown had been sent to Las Vegas College in 1880 by his parents who had come to Colorado in 1876 to seek their fortune. They thought that their son should receive a Catholic education. During his first year at Las Vegas young John, age fourteen years, applied for admission into the Society of Jesus. He was accepted and began his novitiate in Albuquerque.

During the subsequent years he was a much-traveled young man. He went through the various stages of Jesuit training in such places as St. Louis, San Francisco, and Woodstock, Maryland, with an incidental return to Las Vegas for experience in teaching at the college in 1887. He was ordained a priest by James Gibbons, Archbishop of Baltimore, on June 28, 1896. After completing his theological studies he was assigned to the college in Denver.

Brown was cast in the mold of a Joseph Marra. He gave the impression of being very austere but underneath was a kind and gentle man. He was, however, quite unyielding where principles were involved. As a religious priest he was strict and took a dim view of those who were somewhat lax in matters of religious discipline. A dedicated son of St. Ignatius, he had a lasting loyalty to the Society of Jesus and the Neapolitan Jesuits who had established the New Mexico-Colorado Mission. Conservative by nature, he governed with caution.

High on his list of priorities was the determination to do anything and everything possible to wipe out the debt that had been incurred by Pantanella when he borrowed the money to pay for building the college. One of his first actions was to have the funds of the college transferred from the personal account of Pantanella to the account of the College of the Sacred Heart. The fact that Pantanella as treasurer of the institution had the money in a personal account is puzzling indeed. The documents are not a bit helpful in shedding any light on the matter. The minutes of the Board of Trustees on May 13, 1901, note that at the annual meeting of the Board it was moved by J. J. Brown, seconded by H. J. Swift and unanimously resolved "that the funds of the college be hereafter deposited in the bank to the credit of the 'College of the Sacred Heart, Denver, Colorado,' and that the funds now in the bank to the personal credit of Rev. D. Pantanella, as Treasurer of the College, be transferred to the said College Account.''[57]

One can only surmise what Brown did that was different from anything that had been attempted by his predecessors. He did, however, succeed in making payments on the debt. He wrote to the authorities in Naples in 1903,

This year we paid off to Mungret on debt $5,000.00. We secured 1/2% reduction of interest from Belgium on $27,000.00 and from Limerick on the remaining $12,817.00 and from all the Hollanders minus one, amounting in all to $309.00 less interest. Since January 24, 1900, the debt has been reduced to $13,182.00, add to this the saving of interest plus the reduction of interest and we have $14,000.00 less to pay and $1,000.00 interest saved every year.[58]

Brown had other problems that needed attention. Not the least of these was the need to keep pace with the times by providing proper lighting for students and faculty. Previous experience in this matter had been exciting but the results had been disappointing, almost disastrous. Pantanella, looking for ways to cut down costs, had awarded the contract for lighting in his new building to the ''Denver Economic Light Company.'' In the event, this move did not prove to be economical. Kowald described the installation of the system and noted that there was an inherent danger due to the fact that the company depended on the use of gasoline to provide light. He continued:

The fuel they used for producing the cheap light was gasoline and only a small tank was allowed by Insurance Companies to rest on the roof to receive the necessary feed-supply of oil, which had to be pumped from a larger tank buried underground at some distance from the College for safety's sake. Small-sized lead-piping, to all appearances securely placed through the joists beneath the flooring, were used to feed the numerous jets of fixtures in every room and corridor.[59]

The system proved to be defective and dangerous. The flow of gasoline was not properly controlled thus creating a constant danger of fire. In fact there were fires in the chapel and in several private rooms. The contract with the company was voided and the college had to turn to petroleum-fed lamps. This method was less dangerous but not very effective. It proved to be cumbersome. Kowald was less than enthusiastic about the requirements of the system when he described it in these words:

. . . the daily rolling about of a specially constructed cart or small wagon truck from door to door, and from floor to floor, in order to

---

[57]*Minutes of the Board of Trustees 1893-1923,* p. 45.
[58]P.N.Arch.
[59]Kowald, *op. cit.,* p. 154.

clean, trim and refill with oil most of the numerous lamps everyday, was no doubt, an unsightly nuisance, besides extra expenditure of time and labor and consequent greater outlay for wages.[60]

In the year 1900 the students and faculty could forget these experiences because electricity was installed. There is a refreshing simplicity in the account recorded in the diary.

Denver Gas and Electric Co. had a force of 15 men working to place their wire in connection with College wires and at 2:55 P.M. the current was turned on. It was found that the wiring of Doss Bros. was faultless. As there was no meter in place we took advantage of this fact to have an all around illumination which was thoroughly enjoyed by everyone. We owe this great blessing of electric light to the generosity of Mr. August Forster's father to whom it will remain a lasting monument. To God and him be the thanks.[61]

Some six months later a telephone was installed. This instrument was not considered an unmixed blessing; such a contact with the outside world had to be jealously guarded. The phone was placed in the president's room on May 27, 1901, and was connected with the city at 5:00 P.M. The diarist was so impressed that he recorded the exact time when the first call was received: 8:15 A.M. on the first day of June.[62] It was to take many years, some seventy-four, before each member of the Jesuit Community had a telephone in his room. Stories persisted for years about the limited access that was permitted to the telephone that remained in the president's room. For example, there was the tale that Brown told at least one member of the Community, Father William J. Fitzgerald, that he should use a penny post card rather than incur the expense of making a phone call.

Brown presided over the college for four years, 1899-1903. Since he had not made his tertianship, a final year in the preparation of a Jesuit for his life's work, it was necessary to relieve him of his office and appoint a successor. In this case, Anthony J. Schuler was designated as the eighth president of the school. Schuler, like Brown, was the son of parents who had come to the West in the hope of making a fortune. The young man became a protege of the pastor of the church in Georgetown, Nicholas C. Matz, who later became the second bishop of the diocese of Denver. Father Matz helped to educate the young man. Schuler attended a mission preached by the Rev. Arnold Damen, S.J., and was so impressed that he decided to become a Jesuit. Marra, superior of the Mission, accepted him. He followed the

---

[60]Kowald, *op. cit.,* p. 155.
[61]Diary, 1897-1900, p. 153.
[62]Diary, 1901-1906, p. 18.

standard course of education in the classics, philosophy and theology. After his ordination in June 1903 he returned to Denver. In September he assumed the burden of governing the college and its Jesuit Community.

Schuler's administration was neither innovative nor imaginative. He did, however, face the current problems and tried to resolve them. In March 1905, the president requested the members of the Board of Trustees to allocate some money for building an addition to the students' recreation room. He pointed out that an added facility would provide more suitable and roomy quarters for the day students. Moreover, more room would be acquired for the student library. The Board approved the proposal but limited the amount of money to be spent to $8,000.00.[63] Schuler was also aware of two of the perennial problems of administrators of private colleges, the regular collection of money for board and tuition and the maintenance of reasonably high requirements for entrance into the school. Regarding the first problem, Schuler discouraged the large number of students paying reduced rates and, of course, recommended greater diligence in the collection of bills. Any administrator who wished to raise standards according to which students were admitted had to be satisfied with exhorting the prefect of studies to be more strict in his judgment of applications.[64]

Another problem had to be considered which had nothing to do directly with the academic but was concerned rather with the role of the Neapolitan Mission on the American scene. The question surfaced in 1906 but was not resolved until 1919. The authorities of the Society of Jesus had decided that some kind of reorganization of the Order's fields of operations in the United States was overdue. Schuler was consulted about the possibility of separating the Mission from the Province of Naples. His answer is interesting, especially in the light of the recent movement in favor of developing bilingual programs. He answered the authorities that the Italian and Spanish languages were necessary (*omnino necessariae*) in the Mission.[65]

In 1906 Schuler was relieved of his office; he had to complete his training as a Jesuit. He went to Florissant to make his tertianship. Sister M. Lilliana Owens, an indefatigable student of Jesuit activities in the Southwest, wrote a biography of Schuler in which she disposed of his three years as President of the College of the Sacred Heart in these words: "Both spiritual and temporal fruits resulted from his labors. The enrollment increased and both the alumni

---

[63]*Minutes of the Board of Trustees, 1893-1923*, pp. 55-56.

[64]*Op. cit.*, pp. 57-58.

[65]P.N.Arch.

and friends of the college loved him dearly. A number of young men entered the novitiate of the Society of Jesus during his administration there.''[66]

Schuler's successor was John J. Brown, the man whom he had relieved of the office in 1903. This time Brown was destined to direct the affairs of the college for fourteen years (1906-1920). After his tertianship Brown had spent two years as pastor of the Jesuit Church in Pueblo; on August 15, 1906, he resumed the presidency of the college in Denver. The catalogue published at the end of his first year reflects a major change in the entrance requirements for the college department. Seen in the perspective of modern times, the requisite preparation seems to be unrealistic; to choose but one example, that concerning Greek, the college demanded:

(a) Grammar-Etymology complete. The more ordinary Syntax.

(b) The translation into correct English of portions of Xenophon's *Anabasis,* Bks. I and II.

(c) Translation into Greek of simple English sentences based upon Xenophon's *Anabasis*. N.B.—In the case of students who have had little or no Greek but fulfill the other requirements, special arrangements may be made by which they may enter the Freshman Class and take Greek in Special Greek Class.[67]

The note does demonstrate that those who formulated these requirements did have a saving sense of the possible. The history teacher might envy an institution that would require entering freshmen to have a knowledge of the essentials of American history as well as the main epochs of modern and medieval history. It is conceivable that applicants who read the catalogue were discouraged, a possibility that might be reflected in a drop in enrollment from 196 in 1907 to 167 the next year. If a student wished to enter the academic department, he was required to take a four-day entrance examination that would be administered during the end of August and the beginning of September, 1907.

During the first years of his second tenure of the office of president, Brown found the college involved in a lawsuit. A student from McCook, Nebraska, Claude E. Bailey, had been enrolled in the class of third academic for the scholastic year 1906-1907. Bailey died at home in January, 1907. His mother hired a lawyer who informed the college authorities on September 13, 1907, that Mrs. Charles M. Bailey intended to bring suit against the college charging negligence on the part of the institution's personnel in caring for her son when he was ill. The case, which took some time to

---

[66]Sister M. Lilliana Owens, *Most Reverend Anthony J. Schuler, S.J., D.D., First Bishop of El Paso* (El Paso, Texas, Revista Catolica Press, 1953), p. 55.

[67]C.S.H., Cat., 1906-1907, pp. 21-22.

prepare, was scheduled for hearing on February 28, 1912, but the lawyer for the college, T. J. O'Donnell, could not attend and the judge granted a postponement. The trial finally began on January 22, 1913, and lasted for a week. Fathers Brown and William A. Lonergan testified and were cross-examined; Dominic Pantanella explained to the court that the college was an eleemosynary institution. On January 28th, the court heard the testimony of Brother Benjamin Tovani, the infirmarian, supported by two doctors. On the next day, January 29, 1913, the judge instructed the jury to bring in a verdict for the defendants.[68]

The president made a report on the whole matter at the annual meeting of the Board of Trustees on January 26, 1914. Brown reported that the judge decided that the college could not be made to pay the damages that were being sought. He did not, however, hand down a decision on the question of negligence. Concerning this matter the report to the Trustees stated:

When the plaintiffs had rested their case, Mr. T. J. O'Donnell, one of the attorneys for the defendant, argued that said plaintiff had not proven their charges and therefore no further proceedings were necessary; Judge Teller, however, refused to so decide, but in giving his opinion he left all under the impression that he agreed with Mr. O'Donnell, and gave as his reason for not allowing the case to drop before the defense had presented its evidence that such a decision might lead to further litigation.[69]

Before the year 1913 had run its course, Brown was faced with another court case. This was a bizarre suit involving the accusation that Dominic Pantanella had alienated the affections of the wife of Robert J. Lowery. On November 24, 1913, an article appeared on the first page of *The Denver Times* reporting that Lowery had brought suit against the college asking for $50,000.00 in damages. The charge caused a sensation since it involved a very religious man who was eighty-three years old. The Catholics of the Denver Community rushed to the defense of the old Jesuit; J. K. Mullen made a public declaration of belief in the innocence of Father Pantanella. The *Rocky Mountain News* quoted Mullen:

How could a life filled as his is throughout with nothing but godliness be misdirected and wrecked at the ebb of its tide by such a terrible thing as this? It is unfortunate—terribly unfortunate that a man whose standing nobody seems to know can come forward and make such charges on nothing plausible.[70]

---

[68]*College Diary, 1907-1914, passim.*
[69]*Minutes of the Board of Trustees, 1893-1923,* p. 77.
[70]*The Rocky Mountain News,* Nov. 25, 1913.

Lowery had made an attempt to have the case prosecuted criminally, but District Attorney John A. Rush informed him that he could not get a conviction on a criminal charge. It took some time to get the case presented in court. On January 15, 1915, the trial began in the court of Judge Wright. After Lowery gave his testimony the Judge dismissed the case. The diarist for the college laconically wrote, "as soon as testimony of Lowery & Co. was finished Judge Wright dismissed suit announcing no case was made by the complainants."[71]

For a man like Brown who would have preferred to preside over a close-knit familial community the members of which were dedicated to educating and being educated, these court cases were disturbing, to say the least. But they were not the only disturbing developments. For example, attacks against the administration appeared in *The Denver Post.* In September and October, 1908, a number of cases of typhoid fever were detected at the college. In one instance the press reported that one of the students who was sent home died as a result of the fever. People in Denver became concerned and the health department intervened. After an investigation it was discovered that the milk that had been delivered to the college was contaminated. It was also learned that the announcement of the death of a student turned out to be premature; the young man recovered. The reporter responsible for the story came to the school and apologized to the president.[72]

Brown's personal status as a Jesuit underwent some changes during the years 1911 to 1915. In February, 1911, he became a full-fledged rector of the community, an appointment that made him somewhat more independent in his administrative office. A year and one-half later he became Superior of the Mission (August 19, 1912), succeeding the tired and worn-out Joseph Marra. In 1915 Brown escaped an even greater responsibility. He had been preconized as the first bishop of the newly created diocese of El Paso, Texas, at the papal consistory on January 22, 1915. He protested his lack of ability for such an office; the Roman authorities heeded his protests and accepted his resignation in June, 1915.

In spite of the problems that took up most of his time and energy, Brown somehow found time to do some building. In 1911 he managed to get approval for the construction of a gymnasium, a facility that was badly needed. By 1912 the gym was ready for use. It is not an imposing structure by modern standards but it served a very useful purpose until 1960. Over the years it provided suitable space for basketball, student assemblies, and

---

[71]*College Diary, 1914-1922,* p. 14.
[72]*College Diary, 1907-1914,* pp. 59 and 62.

elocution contests. An entry in the diary for April 10, 1914, recorded that about a thousand people attended the elocution contest that was held in the gym.[73]

The impact of the war on college life was hardly noticeable. In fact the enrollment for 1917 and 1918 was higher than it had been in the previous years. There is no evidence that the few Italians on the faculty or in the Jesuit Community caused any problems after Italy entered the war. Some evidence of the effect of the war on college life could not be avoided. For example, all but three of the scholastics and lay brothers registered for military service but claimed exemption on the grounds that they were clergymen. Since the seniors left in May to enter military service, there was no public commencement in 1917. In October, 1917, the officials of the college invested $1,000 in Liberty Bonds. By February, 1918, seventy-five students had enlisted. Brown and his colleagues hoped to take part in the war effort. They applied for a government contract that would make it possible for the college to participate in the preparation of young men for military service. Government officials checked the facilities of the school and found them inadequate for their purposes, and consequently awarded the college no contract.[74]

Because of the war years it is surprising, to say the least, to find significant changes in the catalogue of 1917-1918. The Denver Jesuits were some twenty to thirty years behind their sister institutions in the Midwest. This may be partially explained by the fact that the supervision of the college ultimately lay within the jurisdiction of the Province of Naples. Most of the young Jesuits, however, who joined the Mission received their religious training and their college education at St. Louis University. In time, the policies that prevailed in St. Louis had an effect on the Denver institution.

The situation in Denver was not unique. Catholic colleges generally were becoming aware that they were behind the times in matters educational. The seven-year course was falling, or had fallen, out of favor and a four-year high school course was more sharply delineated. Edward Power saw that development quite clearly when he noted that there was a ferment in Catholic colleges since regional accrediting associations began in the 1890's to be formed in the United States, associations that took a dim view of the seven-year course. Power continued:

> Outside pressures, then, rather than internal, self-generating reforms recommended a four-year college course, and Catholic Colleges while seeking the blessing of an accrediting association, were disposed to keep their hands on preparatory instruction, and they did so by organiz-

---

[73]*Op. cit.*, p. 159.
[74]*Diary, 1914-1922, passim.*

ing the first three or four years of their regular curriculum into a separate preparatory, or high, school which they maintained on their own campus.[75]

The officials of the College of the Sacred Heart were very reluctant to move along with the mainstream of American education. However, they began to realize that they must at least recognize the trend. In 1904 the words "High School" appear in parenthesis after the heading "Academic Department." In 1909 entering students are placed in Fourth Academic and the catalogue specifies that the applicant for admission must have completed the seventh grade. Such students had been previously identified under the heading "Preparatory."[76] By 1916 the distinction between high school and college is even more noticeable because the former has a separate section in the catalogue. Finally, the author of the history of the house for the years 1913 to 1920 wrote that "it now takes 4 years high school and 4 years college course to obtain an A.B. Degree."[77]

The preceding provides a background for the breakthrough in the catalogue for the year 1917-1918. The change is all the more understandable in the light of a note added to the minutes of the meeting of the Board of Trustees on January 3, 1917. The note stated, "Then the meeting adjourned after informal discussion of some special needs of the hour in regard to the present day movement toward College Standardization."[78]

The catalogue for 1917-1918, after a brief statement about the kind of education the college offers, makes it clear that there were two divisions, a college and a "standard" high school. The former offered four different programs of strictly collegiate instruction: a school of arts, conferring the degree of A.B.; one of science, conferring the degree of B.S.; another of philosophy and literature, offering the degree of Ph.B. and Litt.B.; and finally the school of premedical studies. It is worth a passing note that the word "Standard" appears in boldface print five times on the same page. The high school division is not to be outdone; it, too, has four different programs of instruction: classical, scientific, literary, and commercial.

The presentation continues with a disquisition on "Educational Principles and System" which emphasizes intellectual and moral training, though physical well-being and training are also mentioned. There follows a statement quoting the department of colleges and secondary schools of the Catholic Educational Association regarding the standards that a college

---

[75]Power, *op. cit.,* p. 242.

[76]*Catalogues, 1903-1912, passim.*

[77]R.C.A..

[78]*Minutes of the Board of Trustees, 1893-1923,* p. 82.

should meet. Departments and courses of collegiate instruction are listed, biology, chemistry, English, and so forth. The departments of Greek and Latin offered a rather impressive list of courses. It is worth passing notice that under the heading ''General Requirements'' there is a statement that a minimum of 144 semester hours were needed to earn a degree.

This same catalogue has a separate section for the High School. Rev. William J. Fitzgerald is listed as the principal (he is entered on the college roster as dean). The statement on the objectives of the high school stresses the importance of a classical training but bows to the inevitable in acknowledging that practical and commercial courses merit consideration. The program for the annual commencement on June 16, 1918, states there were only two graduates from the college; at the same time, there were eighteen who received diplomas of graduation from the high school.[79]

The catalogue sets board, lodging, and tuition at $350.00 a year and tuition at $60. For the first time, the faculty members have their degrees noted; five were Masters of Arts, and six were Bachelors of Arts. No doubt this was done to conform to the standards of the Catholic Educational Association which required that ''The Professors of the Standard College should have a College degree or its equivalent. . . .''[80]

The year 1919 was an interesting one, one that must have weighed heavily on John Brown. Since finances constituted one of his major concerns, it is surprising that he permitted the students to start a school paper bearing the name *The Brown and Gold*. It is true that the cost for the first numbers was minimal since they were mimeographed and not printed. It was not an easy undertaking. An early introductory editorial, October 1919, noted:

In spite of the good wishes and good start the ''Class of 1919'' gave us, we have no little difficulty in surmounting the obstacles we found ahead of us. . . . Hoping that our efforts will meet with the approval of our friends, ''The Brown and Gold'' is for the second time given to the favorable consideration of the Faculty and Student-body of the College of the Sacred Heart.[81]

The editors planned to resume the policies of *The Highlander* and print selected essays along with short notices about campus events. The response was sufficient to permit printed copies by December, 1919. The paper sold for ten cents a copy or seventy-five cents a year. The December 4th, 1919, issue carried a picture of the president of the newly founded Republic of Ireland, who visited the college on November 31, 1919. DeValera shook

[79]*Catalogue 1917-1918, passim.*
[80]*Ibid.*
[81]*The Brown and Gold,* vol. II, No. 1, October, 1919, p. 1.

hands with each member of the faculty and student body, and asked the president of the college to grant a holiday in honor of the Irish Republic. The account concluded, "but the farewell given him assured Mr. De Valera that he was going away with the sympathy and loyalty of 250 young Americans."[82]

In May, 1919, an event took place that put considerable pressure on the troubled president. The outcome showed that Brown was capable of taking a stand, an extremely unpopular one in some quarters, and proved him to be a man of courage. Forty-two students, reacting somewhat exuberantly to the spirit of spring and because the scholastic year was drawing to a close, sought permission to go to town and do some celebrating. The request was denied but the students went anyway and did not return until early the next morning. The dean, William J. Fitzgerald, who was also in charge of discipline, met the students and checked them in. Next morning forty were expelled; two were spared because they had been coerced to join the group. There was an immediate reaction on the part of the parents of the expelled students but Brown stood his ground. The parents received a letter informing them that:

> The Board of Trustees met at once to consider what action should be taken in the matter. It was seen that there was nothing for us to do but to send all of the delinquents home, and this was therefore decided upon.
> You see for yourselves at once, as we saw, that such an open, flagrant defiance of authority, if overlooked or minimized in any way, would establish a very dangerous precedent, one that would be utterly subversive of discipline, order and authority, not only for the rest of this year, but for several years to come.
> Hence the above measure had to be adopted, painful as it is and much as it may cost the College in every way, as the only logical one under the circumstances.[83]

The action brought the college to the attention of people far and wide in the United States. There was notice of this event in the *Ave Maria,* published at Notre Dame University, for May 31, 1919, and in the New Jersey *Monitor* for June 14, 1919. Dire predictions about what this whole matter would mean to the college, especially with regard to enrollment, were not fulfilled. In fact the number enrolled for the scholastic year 1918-1919 was 261, for the next year, 289, and the year after that, 310.

A major problem confronting Brown during his final years as superior was the necessity of taking care of the details connected with the dissolution of

---

[82]*The Brown and Gold,* vol. 2, No. 11, Dec. 4, 1919, p. 1.
[83]A copy of the letter found in the *Diary,* 1914-1922.

the New Mexico-Colorado Mission. In June, 1908, the Holy See had declared that America was no longer regarded as missionary territory. A logical conclusion of this decision was that the responsibility of the Province of Naples for the Mission should be terminated. This matter had been under consideration since 1906. In that year Schuler had been asked for his recommendations concerning the possible dissolution of the Mission. Two years later the question was presented to Brown who argued against the separation. Brown, one of the first Americans to join the Mission, had developed a deep loyalty to it. One of the more cogent arguments in his answer to the Provincial was that if the Mission became completely Americanized, there would be no priests to take care of the Spanish-speaking people and the Italians in the region. Evidently, the prevailing opinion in Naples and Rome was that the Mission should be separated from Naples and the territory be divided between the American provinces of Missouri and New Orleans. The logical division would be to assign Colorado to the former and western Texas and New Mexico to the latter province.

Brown's response to his superiors revealed his deep concern about the future of Jesuit activity in the Southwest. He argued that the American provincials would be tempted to send their sickly men to live in the healthy climate of the West and added that the superiors of the Missouri Province "would surely try to make conditions suit them instead of suiting themselves to the conditions. This would thwart God's work here for years to come."[84] Brown's clinching argument was that the bishop of Denver would not approve of the change and might ask the Jesuits to leave the diocese.

Roman authorities proceeded with their proverbial slowness and it was not until the fall of 1917 that the Jesuit General, Wlodmir Ledochowski, appointed J. Burrowes, Provincial of the Missouri Province, as Visitor to the Mission with charge of finding a satisfactory solution for the separation of the Mission from the Province of Naples. Burrowes submitted his report on April 22, 1918. He suggested that it might be possible to allow the Mission to continue under a superior who would be dependent upon the provincial of Missouri but added that he doubted that it could survive under such an arrangement. His second recommendation, the one that had been under consideration ever since the matter was broached, was that the Missouri

---

[84]S.J.A., Rome. The notion of using the college as a health resort persisted down to the 1940's. An ambulance had been called to transport an ailing Jesuit to the hospital. Mr. Ed. Williams, who was in charge of publicity, inquired after a few days about the priest since he missed seeing him around the college. Someone told Williams that the Jesuit had been taken to the hospital, and inquired whether or not Williams had seen the ambulance. He responded that he had but thought that the drivers were delivering a new faculty member from St. Louis University.

Province should incorporate Colorado and that New Mexico and El Paso should be attached to the Province of New Orleans.[85]

The final decree, promulgated on August 15, 1919, terminated the responsibility of the Province of Naples for the Mission and incorporated Burrowes' recommendation concerning the division of the territory. It was Brown's duty as superior of the Mission to make the official announcement to the Jesuits under his jurisdiction. A letter dated August 10, 1919, was sent to the parishes in Texas, New Mexico, and Colorado, and, of course, to the college. It was a sad day for the superior when he wrote to his fellow Jesuits:

> Beyond all doubt every one of us will feel this division and separation, this loss of our identity, most acutely, even though we may accept it in a spirit of perfect resignation and as coming directly from the hands of God. This, we know, will render the sacrifice all the more meritorious to us.[86]

Brown and his consultors undertook to do what was necessary to carry out the prescriptions of the official decree. For the most part the men were to be assigned to the Province that took over the houses in which they resided at the time the Mission was separated from the Province of Naples. The Missouri Province gained seventy-six men; forty-three others became members of the Province of New Orleans. Those men who had come from Italy were granted the option of remaining in the United States or returning to Italy.[87]

Brown, moreover, had to find a way to raise one hundred thousand dollars ($100,000) to be given to the Province of Naples as a token of appreciation for the efforts that had been made during the years 1867-1919 to supply men and resources for the Mission. This was possible because, according to Burrowes' report, the Mission was in good financial shape at the time of his visitation. The one liability was the college. The Missouri Province inherited an institution that was carrying a debt of $46,000 with $15,000 of this owed to the Belgian Province, $19,000 to the parish in Albuquerque, and $12,000 to the Arca Seminarii of the Mission.[88]

The Province of Naples relinquished responsibility for the New Mexico-Colorado Mission after fifty-two years. During that time the number of men working in the region had increased from five to one hundred fifty-eight.

---

[85]M.P.A.

[86]R.C.A.

[87]*Lettere Edificante Prov. Neap.*, 1919, pp. 160-161. Some of the Italians returned to Italy. One, Januarius Casolaro, who was a member of the Jesuit Community of Gesu Nuovo in May, 1975, informed the author that he sought the advice of his spiritual director, Dominic Pantanella. The latter advised him to return to his native land.

[88]M.P.A.

A good percentage of the personnel was American, though there were some from other European countries who had joined the Mission. During those years the Italians had served the Church well. They had established a printing press and through the *Revista Catolica* exerted an influence among a wide Spanish readership throughout the Southwest. There was a college that was gaining some stature in a region that badly needed Catholic institutions of higher learning. It is difficult to assess the accomplishments of the parish priests who worked in such places as El Paso, Albuquerque, Las Vegas, Trinidad, Pueblo, and Denver. The Catholic Church was better off in the Southwest because of the dedication of men who had left their homeland to spread the good news in what was to them an alien land.

The lay brothers served the Mission well. As carpenters, bakers, cooks, infirmarians, they made projects viable because of their unselfish devotion to duty. The college was helped immensely by their labors. In its earlier years it was able to make the most of the abilities of a man like Brother Patrick Wallace, a capable teacher. Two Italians became institutions at the college, Benjamin Tovani and Anthony Uliano (more familiarly known as Brother Julian). They both served the college well, one for sixty-five years and the other for sixty. They served in many capacities, but the former was more generally identified with the work of infirmarian and the latter with that of porter and tailor. Brother Ben had a hobby that reflected his great devotion to the Blessed Virgin. Over the years he built a grotto that was the marvel of North Denver until a decision was made in favor of greater simplicity and his dedicated work of many years was destroyed and replaced by a more simple shrine. Besides the lay brothers there were others who served the college well. Pantanella had persuaded some of his countrymen to come to Colorado and these men found employment at the college in Morrison and later in Denver. Their contributions have been taken for granted over the years but they were indispensable for the operation of the school. Some were handymen, most took care of the menial tasks. All of them helped a struggling school that was burdened with a debt that threatened its continued existence. The maintenance of the building in Denver and the problem of caring for fifty acres of land were a constant challenge. Water was in short supply. An artesian well supplied water for the essential needs of the faculty and students but until the irrigation ditch which flowed through the property of St. Vincent's Orphanage, six blocks south of the college, was tapped, not much could be done about improving the appearance of the grounds. In time trees made the campus more presentable. Water from the irrigation ditch made possible a small lake east of the main building. This lake served a very practical need for, as Kowald recalled, there were no bathtubs or showers in the building either for the community or for the students, save a makeshift or afterthought, erected within the boiler room in the rear of the building.[89] The lake was used for bathing and swimming and, Kowald added somewhat optimistically, boating.

The availability of water made it possible for the authorities of the school to dabble in farming. Interestingly enough, alfalfa became a special commodity. The diarist recorded that the alfalfa had been cut in the orchard on August 25, 1908; three days later he noted that three tons of the plant had been reaped from the west orchard.[90]

Brown governed the college for one year after its transfer to the Missouri Province. He had governed well, if conservatively, for eighteen years, 1899-1903 and 1906-1920. He had kept the institution alive and turned over a reasonably healthy college and high school to his successor. The students acknowledged their respect for him when they dedicated the annual of 1920 to him with the words, "With cherished affection. . . to our honored President and sincerest adviser in token of our gratitude and esteem."[91]

Brown was relieved of the office of president on August 15, 1920. His career of service was far from being completed. The Provincial of the Missouri Province appointed him superior of St. Stanislaus Tertianship in Cleveland where young Jesuit priests finished their long period of training; Brown held the post for nine years. He left Cleveland in 1931, the year of his Golden Jubilee as a Jesuit, and joined the Community in St. Mary's, Kansas, where he counselled Jesuits who were studying theology in preparation for ordination to the priesthood, filling this position until his death in 1947.

---

[89]Kowald, *op. cit.,* p. 157.
[90]Diary 1907-1914, pp. 54-55.
[91]*The Brown and Gold,* June 1920, p. 4.

Chapter 4

Unfulfilled Dreams

1920-1942

On August 15, 1920, Robert M. Kelley became the tenth president of the college. Kelley, a native of Iowa, entered the Society of Jesus in 1897. He received all of his Jesuit training in the Missouri Province, which at that time carried on educational and parochial work in ten states and in British Honduras. He had studied and taught in St. Louis, Detroit and Omaha. Before his appointment to Denver, he was dean of the College of Arts and Sciences in Creighton University, Omaha. At the age of forty-three he assumed the responsibility of administering a small college and high school that had been established in the year of his birth.

Kelley found a self-contained, almost stagnant institution with little involvement in the affairs of the city of Denver. He had a faculty of nineteen and a student body of two hundred eighty-nine. Of that number there were only eighteen enrolled in the college with two hundred seventy-one in the high school. The boarders were expected to pay $450.00 a year for board, tuition and lodging; tuition for day-students had been gradually increased and in 1920 it was $80.00 for the year. There were, of course, other incidental charges.

These students were taught by Jesuits who had been trained in a strictly classical tradition. For the most part they were competent teachers but would hardly meet the standards that have since been established, at least as far as degrees and capability to do research are concerned. Nine members of the faculty taught the eighteen students that made up the college student body. Five priests and thirteen scholastics taught in the high school; the latter were young members of the Society of Jesus who, after some initial training in the spiritual life, a solid course in the classics, and three years of philosophy, were expected to spend three to five years teaching before resuming their studies in preparation for ordination to the priesthood. The school had, in effect, a competent if not outstanding faculty.

Although the college was, for the most part, isolated on the northern boundary of a growing city it was not unknown in academic circles in the United States and beyond its borders. The *Highlander* had an impressive list of exchanges and some notoriety was gained for the school after the expulsion of forty students. As a Jesuit school the college shared in the reputation of an organization that was world wide. Shortly after the turn of the century certain Jesuits became interested in seismology. In 1909 Rev. Frederick L.

Odenbach, S.J., of Saint Ignatius College in Cleveland (John Carroll University), sent a letter to all the Jesuit colleges and universities of the United States and Canada inviting them to participate in a program designed to establish seismographs at each school that would register the shocks and motions of earthquakes. He wrote that the Jesuits could serve a worthwhile purpose and continued:

> Our Society can make a move which cannot be duplicated unless the Government should organize a bureau of seismology. It is this—to organize a system of observatories with the *same kind of instrument* handled in the same way and these stations to be fairly well scattered N-S-E-W over the continent. Seismograms produced by instruments of different makers are hard to compare and therefore a set of uniform grams such as we could furnish would be a Godsend to seismologists. . . And if, following our example, others of the Society in different countries were to join the movement the result would be unique.[1]

The response of the Jesuits in Denver was prompt. Following the recommendation of Father Odenbach they obtained a Wiechert 80 kilogram inverted pendulum, horizontal component seismograph and contact clock from the firm of Spindler and Hoyer of Gottingen. The seismograph was set up by Father Armand W. Forstall in a basement room under the front steps near the middle of the college building. Forstall was meticulous and conscientious in watching the operation of the machine. He carefully followed every tremor and displayed the records of the more notable earthquakes so that faculty and students could study them. By 1922 the instrument had recorded 253 conspicuous earthquakes. Forstall exchanged reports and publications with stations in Mexico, Japan, Canada, England, New Zealand, China, the Philippine Islands, Italy, and throughout the United States.[2] In time the machine became outdated. Since the college could not afford to purchase a new model, Forstall had to repair the old one. Gradually his name became identified in the city of Denver with the study of earthquakes. Years later, when Gene Lindeberg, a writer for the *Post,* wrote an assessment of Forstall's career, he praised his work with the seismograph:

> He made up in skill what he lacked in research funds, and rebuilt his seismograph, time after time. Yet he knew its limitations. It was mechanical. The sheer weight of even its tinest moving parts was too great for ultra-faint earth tremors to budge. Nevertheless, he got out of it the utmost performance of which it was capable. His work with it gained

---

[1]James Bernard Macelwane, S.J., ed. *Jesuit Seismological Association 1925-1950* (Saint Louis, Central Station Saint Louis University, 1950), pp. 6-7.

[2]CSH Cat., 1922-1923, pp. 15-16.

him international reputation among seismologists.[3]

The work of Forstall was a definite asset, but as Kelley assessed the position of the school as a whole he concluded that he had inherited some liabilities. Not the least of these was the public image of the college in the Denver community. Brown and his predecessors had been so preoccupied with the problem of survival that they had neglected to take their case to the citizens of Denver. The new president decided to remedy the situation. The first step was an attempt to revitalize the Alumni Association that had been organized in 1899. Its record during its first years was less than spectacular due to a lack of leadership. The association was reactivated in 1908 and by 1921 it claimed an active membership of 1,000 members.[4] Kelley challenged the organization by asking them to have a public reception for him. The challenge was accepted. The officers, Martin D. Currigan, president, Earl Frazier, vice president, and Daniel J. Floyd, secretary-treasurer, appointed a committee of interested members to put on the reception. Promising Catholic men of various professions, such as John P. Akolt, Joseph J. Walsh, Leo F. Floyd, Harry L. Luckenbach, M. J. McEnery, and John J. Sullivan, joined the officers in making the necessary preparations. The event took place on October 23, 1920, at a banquet held in the Knights of Columbus Hall. It was attended by Bishop J. Henry Tihen and most of the presidents of the universities and colleges of Colorado. The Governor of the State was represented by Mr. Frank McMahon. The Mayor of Denver sent his regrets; a pressing business engagement prevented him from attending. This affair certainly was a great public exposure of the college before the Denver community.[5]

After his public introduction to the Denver community Kelley tackled the problems of the college with imagination and determination. Within months he initiated three major changes that drastically changed the image of the college and high school. He proposed that the name of the institution be changed, he took steps to gain accreditation from the North Central Association of Colleges and Secondary Schools, and he launched a fund-raising campaign to finance a building program.

Prior to his installation as president there had been concern about the propriety of the use of the name "Sacred Heart" at such events as athletic

---

[3]Gene Lindberg, *Rocky Mountain Magazine, The Denver Post,* Sept. 22, 1946, p. 3. In 1946 Rev. Joseph V. Downey, S.J., became director of the seismological observatory. He continued in the best tradition of Father Forstall, carefully keeping the record of every earthquake. He has been in great demand around the city and gives frequent talks in which he explains the mysteries of these phenomena. The author is indebted to Father Downey for his assistance.

[4]*The Denver Catholic Register,* Oct. 28, 1920, pp. 1-2.

[5]*Ibid.*

contests. A number of the catalogues before 1920 had printed a warning to the students against the use of the name of the school in connection with social and athletic events without express permission. Another possible explanation of the desire for a change in the name was the fact that many people referred to the institution as "The Shack," a nickname suggested by the featured letters on the seal of the college, S.H.C. Kelley took the matter up with his consultors on January 11, 1921. They agreed that a new name should be selected and the Jesuit Community was asked to give some suggestions. The diarist made this succinct entry on May 8, 1921: "Teachers' meeting to select a new name for the college. Many names were proposed but none selected; favorite names seemed to be Regis and New-man."[6] When it was learned that the Provincial and his consultors in St. Louis favored the choice of the name "Regis," that name was adopted. At a special meeting of the Board of Trustees on April 19, 1921, it was resolved "that Article I of the Article of Incorporation of said 'College of the Sacred Heart,' Denver, Colorado, be amended so as to change the name of said corporation from 'College of the Sacred Heart, Denver, Colorado' to 'Regis College.' "[7] Some months later, December 5, 1921, the Board adopted as its seal "Regis College, Denver, Colo., 1888" arranged in circular form, with the monogram "R.C." in the center of the circle.[8]

The change in the name and the seal offered an opportunity to adopt a new coat of arms. The college was fortunate in finding a Jesuit knowledgeable in the art of heraldry. Aloysius Brucker, a priest who was engaged in pastoral work in Sacred Heart Parish in Denver, was engaged to devise a coat-of-arms for the college. Brucker created a heraldic design, the outside circle of which had the Latin words "Collegium Reginum, S.J., Denveriense" with the year 1888 noted in Roman numerals. The center of the shield displays an eagle to denote the association of the school with the Jesuit saint, John Francis Regis, whose name had recently been adopted for the institution. The Jesuit mono-gram "I.H.S.," signifying the name of Jesus, was imposed on the breast of the eagle, and over the head of the eagle the letters of the Jesuit motto, "A.M.D.G." ("For the Greater Glory of God"), were inscribed. The talons of the eagle grasp the motto of the State of Colorado, *Nil Sine Numine* ("Nothing without the Divinity"). This description was printed in *The Brown and Gold* and is summarized in these words, "Thus the seal embraces the

---

[6]Diary, 1914-1922, p. 125.

[7]*Minutes of the Board of Trustees, 1893-1923*, p. 91.

[8]*Op. cit.*, p. 92. It should be noted that the Board followed a decision made sometime in 1901 to consider 1888 as the founding date of the college.

Regis Arms, the Jesuit escutcheon, and the motto of our Centennial State."[9]

This whole matter of the change in the name and the consequent adoption of a new seal and coat of arms was not achieved without special sadness on the part of some who cherished the old name. One man in particular was saddened by the new development—Dominic Pantanella was known for his great devotion to the Sacred Heart. Now, at the age of ninety, he had to accept a new name for the college that he, with the able assistance of Edward Barry, had built. A writer for *The Brown and Gold* captured the spirit of the change, combining some nostalgia with the acceptance of the inevitable when he wrote:

> Soon the name of Sacred Heart College will be changed to that of Regis College, in honor of St. John Francis Regis of the Society of Jesus. The reasons for the change are evident. Our old name was too sacred for the sport yells and athletic columns into which it was bound to enter. Our new name, that of a sainted college professor and zealous missionary priest of the mountains and plain district of France is particularly apropo (sic). It is not without regret that we abandon the name that has been so identified with *Alma Mater* through all these years, still there are many advantages in this step. The name of Regis will mean much to us. The change will go into effect immediately after the closing in June and when the Fall term comes we will return to greet Regis, Thou rulest the West.[10]

A second project high on the list of Kelley's priorities was his plan to apply for accreditation by the North Central Association of Colleges and Secondary Schools. Kelley knew that he had a better chance to obtain speedy recognition for the high school and that he could then work to bring the college into line with the fundamental requirements of the association. The separation of the two operations had been evolving for a number of years. The first mention of granting high school diplomas appeared in the catalogue for the year 1915-1916. In time a second section of the catalogue listed the high school faculty and the courses of instruction under a separate heading. By 1920 the historian of the house was able to record that it took four years of high school and four of college before a student could earn an A.B. degree.[11]

When Kelley became president he lost little time in applying to the North Central for accreditation for the high school. H. M. Barrett, a faculty member of the University of Colorado and the representative of the Association in the Rocky Mountain Region, visited the school, evaluated its pro-

[9]*The Brown and Gold,* vol. IV, No. 1, p. 2.
[10]*The Brown and Gold,* vol. III, No. 8, p. 2.
[11]*Historia Domus,* R.C.A.

gram, and sent his recommendation to the officials of the association that the high school be added to the list of accredited secondary schools. When the association held its annual meeting it voted, on March 17, 1921, to recognize the high school as a member. But Kelley's efforts to gain recognition for the college were not successful; still, in spite of known deficiencies, the president did not give up hope. A writer in *The Brown and Gold* wrote in the issue of April 1, 1921: "The day is now near at hand for the accrediting of our College Department, when we will take our place as a full-fledged standard college recognized throughout the country."[12] This prediction remained unfulfilled until 1952. The finalization of the division between the high school and the college raised the question whether there should be distinct names for the schools. The consultors considered this matter in a meeting on June 23, 1921; after some discussion they decided on the name "Regis High School."[13]

The change in the name of the college and the accreditation of the high school were milestones in the history of the institution. However, Kelley's plans for a building program distracted the attention of the public from appreciating their importance. At the time when they were being realized, Kelley announced a building program that must have staggered the imagination of the venerable Father Pantanella. On April 23, 1921, the *Post* published the announcement that the college envisioned a $2,500,000 project for the expansion of facilities. The plans called for a new residence hall for college students, a second residence hall for senior students of the preparatory school, a science building, a recitation building, a chapel, a library, an athletic stadium, a gymnasium for seniors, a central power plant, and the remodeling of the existing main building. The overall plan was "to fashion the Jesuit school into a symmetrical educational center, with beautiful harmonious grounds and Gothic buildings modeled after the famous structures at Oxford and Cambridge Universities and Boston College."[14]

To veterans who knew the local scene these aspirations and plans must have seemed far beyond the possibility of realization. Kelley, however, would not admit that he was dreaming but continued to take practical steps to work toward the achievement of his goals. Some months after the announcement, in November 1921, Kelley established the Regis College Building and Endowment Association and opened offices in the Cooper Building. Theodore A. Chisholm, a former student of the college (1909-1913), acted as secretary, undertook the revision of the alumni directory, and handled the necessary campaign correspondence and literature. The

---

[12]*The Brown and Gold,* vol. III, No. 7, p. 2.
[13]*Consultors Meetings,* 1888-1942, p. 44.
[14]*The Denver Post,* April 23, 1921.

association planned to mail a drawing of the new buildings to every alumnus. In an effort to assure uniformity in the development plans the school authorities retained a well-known landscape architect, Irvin J. McCrary, who was to work in conjunction with the building architect, Henry J. Manning. Together these men planned the new campus arrangements.[15]

Kelley realized that the closed society that had been characteristic of the college during the preceding decades should be exposed to the public and that he would have to make a concerted effort to bring the message of the college to the people. He set up a publicity bureau under the direction of Thomas Dermody, an experienced newspaper man. Dermody was assisted by Emmett Barry, Joseph Dooling, Arthur Rayhawk, and Joseph Neary. The members of this bureau were expected to handle publicity in the Denver dailies as well as in other papers of the state and region. It was up to the bureau to ''send out news items to the 'home papers' whenever a 'native son' carries off any honors of the school.''[16]

Planning for the future was one thing; solving an immediate problem was another. When Kelley assumed the burden of office he was soon well aware of the fact that the existing facilities of the college were inadequate. There had been a gradual increase in the number of students enrolled in the school. In 1919 there were two hundred sixty-one; a year later the total reached two hundred eighty-nine; in 1921 the number was increased to three hundred ten. The president and his consultors realized that something had to be done to meet the needs of a growing student body and resident faculty. They applied for permission to build an addition to the northeast end of the main building that would give the institution more adequate kitchen facilities, two dining rooms, one for the faculty and one for the students, and some private rooms for boarders. The proper Jesuit authorities approved the plan and authorized Kelley to borrow $50,000 to help finance the project; it was estimated that the addition would cost $78,000. Work on the addition began on May 29, 1922.[17] There was no attempt to match the stone facing of the original building, so the annex was hardly an architectural gem. It did, however, provide some essential facilities for an institution that was attracting more students.

While the addition was being built Kelley and his aides were working feverishly on plans to launch a major drive for funds to build a new residence hall. The immediate goal of the drive was the raising of one million dollars. The support of the more prominent men in the Denver community was enlisted to serve on the Citizens' Endorsement Committee. A writer in *The*

---

[15]*The Brown and Gold,* vol. IV, No. 3, p. 1.

[16]*Op. cit.,* p. 3.

[17]Diary, 1914-1922, p. 149 and 155.

Brown and Gold wrote about this phase of the preparations that the committee, under chairman John K. Mullen, embraced:

> . . . not only the community's leading businessmen, but city and state officials and those more prominent in educational matters. Of unusual warmth and sincerity are the public commendations of Dr. George Norlin, President of Colorado University, and of Ex-Governor Buchtel, Chancellor Emeritus of Denver University. Both of these men, in pleading our cause, recognize the proper situation and need of Regis College in Colorado's educational field. Most grateful is the very enthusiastic support of Rt. Rev. J. Henry Tihen and that of Colorado's priesthood.[18]

Besides the Endorsement Committee there was an Executive Committee made up of Bishop J. Henry Tihen, Robert M. Kelley, William P. Horan, and Rev. Hugh L. McMenamin. McMenamin had graduated from the college in 1897 and then studied for the priesthood. It was not long after his ordination that he helped to build the Cathedral of the Immaculate Conception and became pastor of the Cathedral parish. McMenamim generously supported the college whenever it was in need.

After all the preparations had been completed, the drive was launched with a parade. The "kick-off" dinner was held at the Shirley-Savoy Hotel, since demolished. The plan was to have a concerted drive during a week in October. Three hundred workers had been lined up to do the canvassing. Every effort was made to keep enthusiasm alive. A daily report was due on the progress of the campaign to be presented each day at a luncheon served at the Shirley-Savoy and addressed by such distinguished men of the community as Governor Shoup, Mayor Bailey, Rabbi W. S. Friedman, and of course Bishop Tihen.[19]

In spite of these concentrated efforts the drive failed to achieve the goal that had been set for it. The November 1st issue of *The Brown and Gold* published the figure of $350,000, some of it collected and some only pledged.[20] Fund raisers are not easily discouraged and Kelley, endeavoring to hide his disappointment behind a facade of optimism, outlined for the editors of the college paper a number of immediate gains of the drive. He pointed out that there were enough funds to finance a new residence hall of one hundred sixty rooms, that the drive made Regis well known locally and nationally, that Regis had gained a great many new friends, and finally that some persons had promised to repeat the gifts that they had given or to donate

---

[18]*The Brown and Gold,* vol. V, No. 1, p. 1.
[19]*The Brown and Gold,* vol. V, No. 2, p. 1.
[20]*Ibid.*

something in the future.[21]

The drive had generated enough interest to encourage Kelley to take yet another step. The day after the end of the official campaign, October 17, a Greater Regis Association was formed. The plan was presented by John F. Toner and received enthusiastically. Two hundred persons signed the charter. Godfrey Schirmer, general chairman of the fund-raising campaign, was chosen president by acclamation; John J. Sullivan, a 1915 graduate of the college, was named secretary, and A. H. Seep became treasurer. Each member pledged himself to pay a membership fee of $10.00 a year. It was hoped that one thousand members could be recruited in a year's time.[22]

Kelley hid his disappointment as best he could. He issued a statement: All in all, I am well pleased—commenting on the drive. We have real need of $1,000,000 to expand adequately so as to meet the demands put upon us. With what has been given and what will be given, we intend to build and expand into a Greater Regis. The support we have received from so many of the good, generous and broad-visioned citizens of Denver is a new motive to dedicate ourselves to the welfare of this city and state, to renew our consecration of our lives to God and country.[23]

But in retrospect it is easy to understand why this campaign failed to achieve its goal. The small Catholic community in Denver was far from affluent in 1922. Encouragement did not cost much; it was more difficult to make substantial donations. Denver was not an industrial city and it was far from the thriving cities of the Midwest. A few Catholics, such as J. K. Mullen, were well on their way to amassing fortunes, but in the early nineteen twenties they were not yet in a position to make large gifts to the Catholic organizations of the city and the state. The chances of a college that aspired to become one of the great Catholic educational institutions in the Colorado-Wyoming-Utah region were slim indeed. When one gets a look behind the facade of optimism that had to be presented to the public and sees the reality, he realizes what must have been the extent of Kelley's disappointment. Many years after the drive of 1922 someone on the staff of the president of the college compiled a report on the drives conducted by the institution over the years; his record for the Building and Endowment Campaign of 1922—Goal: $1,000,000; Raised: $147,316.00.[24]

Since the college was committed to build a new residence hall and it was practically impossible to withdraw from that commitment, Kelley had to look elsewhere for the necessary funds. Since Colorado was part of the

---

[21]*Ibid.*
[22]*Ibid.*
[23]*Ibid.*
[24]R.C.A.

Missouri Province of the Society of Jesus, it was natural for him to seek help in St. Louis, the headquarters of the Province. It is interesting to speculate on the contents of the correspondence that preceded the actual transaction of the loan that was made by the officials of the Lafayette-South Side Bank of St. Louis, but such documents are not available. Kelley needed the permission of the Province authorities to enter into such a transaction. He also needed the approval of the members of the Board of Trustees of the college. The Board met on May 1, 1923, and authorized the president to negotiate for a loan from the St. Louis bank. The resolution read in part:

Whereas, said Bank has signified its willingness to loan said sum upon the note, notes or bond of the College, secured by trust deed on its properties between Federal and Lowell Boulevards and 50th Avenue and City Limits, two and one half acres in Adams County Colorado; now, therefore, be it resolved, that the officers of the College be and they are hereby, authorized and directed to borrow from the said Lafayette-South Side Bank of St. Louis the sum of $235,000, or such portion thereof as they deem proper, and as evidence of said indebtedness to execute and deliver to said Bank such note, notes or bonds as may be proper, and to execute and deliver as security therefor a trust deed covering the property owned by the College as above set forth.[25]

Kelley had been busy in the meantime and had taken the initial steps to get the project underway. The work of architect Harry James Manning had been finished sometime earlier; all that was needed was attention to the necessary details concerning the first unit of the overall plans for a greater Regis. Two and one-half months before the Trustees approved the president's request to obtain a loan, Kelley had hired a contractor for the building project. William Tamming signed a contract on February 10, 1923, agreeing to supervise construction. The college pledged itself to pay $162,248 to the contractor. The agreement called for substantial completion of the building on or before the first day of September.[26] By April the work had progressed so well that it was possible to have a public ceremony of the blessing of the cornerstone. This took place on April 22, with Bishop J. Henry Tihen as the featured celebrant and Governor William E. Sweet and Mayor D. C. Bailey in attendance. At the construction site the cornerstone was blessed as rapidly

---

[25]*Minutes of the Board of Trustees, 1893-1923*, p. 95. It should be noted that the college had purchased forty acres in 1922. This property adjoined the original fifty acres and included the land east of the present stadium to Federal Boulevard and about a block and one-half north from 50th Avenue. The purchase was made possible by $24,000 obtained from the legacy of a Jesuit Scholastic, Raymond H. Mullen.

[26]R.C.A.

as possible, and the celebrants adjourned through a snowstorm to finish the ceremonies in the gym.

The dignitaries spoke words of praise and encouragement on this great occasion in the history of the college. John J. Sullivan, who had graduated from the school in 1915, spoke on behalf of the alumni; he had become a successful businessman in Denver and would continue to be involved with the institution down through the years. Father Kelley, in his role as president, announced that the new building would be named after John Carroll, a former Jesuit, the first American bishop and a cousin of Charles Carroll of Carrollton, a signer of the Declaration of Independence. In his speech on the occasion of the blessing of the corner stone Kelley concluded, ''Thus we wish to hold [John Carroll's] memory and his name up to our students as the ideal they remember as a true product of the education we seek to impart.''[27] The students, in their enthusiasm, took up a collection from the student body to pay for a memorial window honoring Carroll. The window graced the entrance to the hall until sometime in the sixties when it was badly damaged by some students who were equally enthusiastic, but about other things.

During the ensuing months work progressed on the building while costs increased. Great effort was expended in an attempt to collect as much of the pledge money as possible. Results were very disappointing and plans had to be adjusted. Consequently, no attempt was made to finish the interior of the east wing. By November 18 the rest of the building was ready and the college students moved in.

Fund raising and badly needed building facilities were not the only preoccupation of the president. Kelley had been disappointed when the North Central Association postponed action regarding the accreditation of the college at the time they had voted to approve the high school. In March, 1922, Dr. C. A. Duniway, president of Colorado College in Colorado Springs, made an official visitation for the association. Dr. Duniway made a favorable report commending the standard of work in the various departments. When the association held its annual meeting during March, the Committee on Education recommended that Regis be recognized as a junior college. This was less than what had been expected, but the dean of the college, William J. Fitzgerald, wrote optimistically:

With the growth of Regis' College department and the increase in numbers in all classes, we hope to have the senior college take its rank among the accredited institutions at an early date. I consider this the most tangible proof of the progress Regis has been making, and a solid

---

[27]*The Brown and Gold,* vol. V, No. 8, p. 2.

assurance of further and more rapid growth.[28]

The members of the association hesitated to give accreditation to a college that was laboring under a heavy debt, one that was to be greatly increased because of the building program that was just beginning to get under way. Since there was no endowment beyond the contributed services of the Jesuits, the association wanted more assurance of the viability of the institution. Moreover, the existing facilities in 1922 were inadequate for the type of program that the professional educators of the association expected of a four-year college. The faculty could not measure up to the standards that the North Central had set for the schools which it recognized. The roster of the college faculty for the academic year 1921-1922 was impressive in that it listed eight professors and one instructor out of a total of nine.[29] Anyone with knowledge of the procedures of the Jesuits would immediately note that four of the eight professors were scholastics, young men assigned to the school so that they could gain some experience in the classroom before they went on to complete their studies and be ordained. They had received a good education but it is doubtful that they would meet all the requirements that were established by the accrediting agencies. As early as 1902 John Brown notified the General of the Order that some of his teachers were inept and that he did not see any possibility of their improving.[30] Kelley also was aware of the problems regarding his faculty; he urged the Provincial to send him men who would improve its quality. His hopes were high in 1925 when he learned that the Province had decided to discontinue the college division of Campion in Prairie du Chien, Wisconsin. The beleagured president wrote to the Provincial that his hopes were raised ''for something resembling an adequate faculty.''[31]

During Kelley's first administration (1920-1926) he began to engage the services of laymen, a matter in which his predecessors had been cautious. Laymen had been added to the faculty only to teach music and occasionally the commercial subjects. When Kelley became president he hired Warren F. Shook to act as secretary and Floyd C. Shafer to supervise the physical education program. By 1924, in view of the fact that there was little hope of obtaining assistance from the Province, he added Frank A. LaMotte, professor of modern language, and Glenn L. Hackett, professor of biology. In the following year the faculty roster included Joseph B. Bianchi and Guilio S. Dina as instructor and professor of Romance languages respectively, George N. Kramer as instructor in history, Lawrence H. Brown as instructor

[28]*The Brown and Gold,* vol. IV, No. 7, p. 1.
[29]*Catalogue of 1921-1922,* p. 5.
[30]S.J.A., Rome.
[31]M.P.A.

in mathematics, and Achimme J. Sommaruga as instructor in French. It is significant that the faculty roster for 1925-1926 lists the degrees of the professors and gives a summary of the academic background of each member.[32] The salaries that were offered certainly seem minimal when compared to modern scales. The consultors of the house, in their meeting on March 4, 1925, discussed the matter of salaries for lay professors and "it was thought well to offer Mr. Hackett $2,000.00 and Mr. Brown $1,800.00."[33]

It is impossible to conceive of a college without students. Teachers, administrators, curricula are component parts of the operation, but they would have no meaning if there were not students to be taught, encouraged and disciplined. Discipline had been a watchword since the foundation of the college; it was usually paternal, always corrective, and perhaps helpful. The Prefect of Studies and Discipline, with the assistance of the younger Jesuits, took seriously the principle that had been the subject of considerable discussion in the 1960's, namely that the teachers stood *in loco parentis,* and their concept of this was that they stood in the place of an authoritarian father.

Kelley was obviously intent on turning the college around and made many changes during the first two years of his administration. He proposed another important change in the fall of 1922, the formation of a Student Conclave. A Jesuit scholastic, John L. Polski, was directed to inaugurate it. Polski informed an interviewer for *The Brown and Gold* that the organization would have four principal functions, to encourage and support athletics, to direct and sponsor social affairs, to participate in dramatic work, and to develop student government.[34] Another reason for the organization was the desire to solve the perennial problem of promoting better relations between the resident and non-resident students. Since the foundation of the college the official policy favored the boarders and merely tolerated the day students. A student conclave could bridge the gap and bring the two together. Polski stated that the basic purpose of the organization was "to bring these two divisions of college men under a real collegiate organization and such a one that can direct and support all college activities with a maximum strength."[35] It was a step in the right direction but it was to be sometime before anything resembling student government on the campus would become a reality.

Another area of Kelley's concern was athletics. Every boarding school

---

[32]*Catalogue 1925-1926,* pp. 6-9.
[33]*Consultors Meetings 1888-1942,* p. 58.
[34]*The Brown and Gold,* vol. V, No. 2, p. 1.
[35]*Ibid.*

had to provide some opportunity for out-of-doors activity. From its early day the College of the Sacred Heart had fielded a baseball team. In 1910 the students formed a soccer team and even joined a soccer league. After 1912 the students could use the newly constructed gymnasium. Football made an appearance during these years. In general, however, the college followed the pattern that existed in most colleges in the United States, a pattern that was described by Edward Power when he wrote, "Indeed, an interest in athletics among Catholic Colleges, both intramural and intercollegiate, did not really develop until the advent of the twentieth century; it most surely did not figure large in their formative period."[36] It is true that the college students had formed an athletic association, but its activities were somewhat limited before Kelley's administration. In his first year Kelley engaged Floyd C. Shafer, a one-time student and football player at Notre Dame (1911-1912), as director of physical education. With Shafer as coach a football team was assembled and a beginning made in the direction of setting up a more ambitious athletic program. Those concerned with this development had ambition and a vision of grandeur. A great team would need a great name, so the editors of *The Brown and Gold* announced a contest during October for the selection of a name for the school's athletic teams. A committee of the full athletic board, several members of the faculty and the editor of the school paper decided to adopt the name "The Rangers."[37]

In 1924 the college hired Thomas A. McNamara to coach football. McNamara had attended the Universities of Georgetown and Fordham and had been a member of the coaching staff at the University of Pennsylvania. The new coach had grandiose dreams of the future of the college as a power to be reckoned with in intercollegiate athletics. In an interview with a reporter for *The Brown and Gold* he reviewed the potential of his team and concluded that there was great promise for the future and summed the whole matter up with the words, "you can build a 'Notre Dame of the West.' "[38]

Kelley wished to establish a better organization for the athletic program. He named as Director of Athletics Floyd Shafer, who was to continue as coach of basketball and baseball, and Rev. Bernard Murray, S.J., as faculty moderator. No one ever doubted Murray's love for the college. His name was to become legendary in the history of the institution. He was never modest when he talked about the school and its potential for greatness, tending rather to exaggerate when he looked toward the future. When asked about the potential of Regis in athletics he responded, "Put Regis in the

---

[36]Power, *op. cit.,* pp. 181-182.
[37]*The Brown and Gold,* vol. IV, No. 1, p. 9 and vol. IV, No. 2, p. 8.
[38]*The Brown and Gold,* vol. VII, No. 1, p. 5.

Conference. . . we need not be satisfied with that. It's not wholly visionary to see the Ranger Stadium as the scene of coast-to-coast intersectional battles. . . as the training camp of the greatest team in the country."[39]

A great football team must have a great stadium, so the Knights of Columbus of Denver undertook to solicit funds to pay for a stadium with a seating capacity of 15,000. A glance at the architect's drawing published in *The Brown and Gold* February 1924[40] shows that Kelley and his advisers were riding the crest of the euphoria that characterized all of their planning before the harsh facts of reality finally brought them to earth.

Kelley did not expend all of his energies on introducing innovations. Traditional activities were continued, especially those pertaining to elocution, dramatics and debating. The college was never very successful in developing a debating team but it did make an effort in this field of endeavor. Elocution continued to be a major activity. The highlight of the year was the final elocution contest. Students vied in a highly competitive way to win a place on the final public program. Judges from various professions in the city were invited and the finalists might make their declamations before as many as a thousand people. Gold medals donated by benefactors were awarded to the winners.

Dramatics continued to be important. One major production was attempted each year, some with noteworthy success. In 1923 the Dramatic Club undertook to present a rather ambitious program under the direction of Rev. Michael A. Gorman who had come to Regis from Marquette University. Gorman was the author of a dramatic presentation based on the Passion of Jesus Christ entitled "Retribution." This version had been presented successfully in Milwaukee and Madison before Father Gorman undertook to have it performed in Denver. With the help of some of the alumni living in Denver the students gave three performances in the old Auditorium Theatre early in March. Reviewers in the local newspapers were generous with their commendations, and Mayor D. C. Bailey was impressed by what he read and heard. Writing to Father Gorman on March 14, he suggested that a fourth performance be presented on Good Friday. The mayor wrote:

I am much interested in having a more universal observance of Good Friday, and following my previous efforts in the same direction, will issue this year an appeal to all good citizens to pay reverence by ceasing activities from 12 o'clock noon to 3 P.M. on March 30, 1923.

It has been brought to my attention that for the sake of accentuating the significance of this holy day that a presentation of the Passion Play as

---

[39]*The Brown and Gold,* vol. VII, No. 1, p. 1.
[40]*The Brown and Gold,* vol. VI, No. 5, p. 3.

recently given would be invaluable as well as most appropriate.

If you could entertain such a suggestion and arrange with me the expense incident thereto, so that it would be possible to throw the doors of the auditorium open to the people without charge, I see, to my way of thinking, a great help to us in bringing about a universal practice of conscientiously observing Good Friday annually.

Cordially yours,

D. C. Bailey, Mayor[41]

One of the more interesting developments during Kelley's tenure was the gradual emergence of a department of commerce and finance. We have noted that since the days in Morrison the authorities had an ambivalent attitude toward the teaching of commercial subjects. The matter surfaced again in 1921 when the consultors considered the advisability of dropping the commercial courses at least temporarily. All present were in favor of doing so.[42] Three years later friends of the school proposed that a school of commerce and finance be established. After discussing this proposal on December 7, 1924, the consultors recommended further investigation of the experience of other schools where such a department existed.[43] Four months later Kelley sought the advice of the Provincial in St. Louis when he wrote on March 6:

> Several business men of the city have been urging on me the advisability of establishing a School of Commerce and Finance. I have been collecting data and I believe that it is practical and advisable. . . . my idea would be to start a night school with classes downtown and a day school with classes on campus. . . . my idea would be not to change the name of the College to that of University. I believe that we should have several professional divisions before this is done.[44]

The Provincial advised Kelley not to yield to these pressures stating that the school was not yet ready for that kind of development. The consultors agreed that further investigation into the matter was needed.

In the meantime steps were taken in anticipation of a favorable decision. Four basic courses in accounting were offered during the academic year 1925-1926. Everett S. Bailey, a graduate of the University of Colorado who held a bachelor of arts degree and a diploma in commerce, was appointed instructor in economics. Bailey laid the foundation for one of the more successful departments in the history of the college. To promote a feeling of cohesiveness he, together with Joseph A. Ryan, dean of the college, estab-

---

[41]*The Brown and Gold,* vol. V, No. 7, p. 1.
[42]*Consultors Meetings 1888-1942,* p. 58.
[43]*Op. cit.,* p. 55.
[44]M.P.A.

lished the Delta Sigma Commerce and Finance Club in the fall of 1926 and had it incorporated under the laws of the State of Colorado. Students who had passed the first semester examinations in their freshman year and maintained a degree of excellence in their studies were eligible to join the club. The purpose of the organization was:

. . . to provide social entertainment for its members and to foster a deeper study of current business problems. The club meets once a month and conducts a program of semi-monthly talks on live business topics by prominent leaders in the commercial world.[45]

Incidentally, another club was established at about the same time, the Lambda Tau Club which had as its purpose the promotion of social activities on the campus. The members of this organization committed themselves to act as a unit for the advancement of any movement that would benefit the college. Two years later the club was one of the strongest organizations on the campus.[46] The late twenties were marked by a high tide of school spirit fostered by the Razzer Club that had been organized in September, 1923. Membership in the club was limited to fifty students who pledged themselves to boost Regis enterprises. Members were required to undergo a period of probation during which they qualified for membership by their attendance at Regis activities, "scholastic, forensic, and athletic."[47]

Kelley was president of the college for six years, the average term for most presidents of Jesuit colleges since they were also religious superiors. He had endeavored to create a better public image for the college in the city of Denver and the state of Colorado. He had established good relations with other college presidents; in fact, he had been invited to be one of the speakers at the banquet following the inaugural ceremonies of George Thomas, the new president of the University of Utah in Salt Lake City. He had initiated the practice of conferring honorary degrees when on May 31, 1922, he bestowed the Degree of Doctor of Laws *Honoris Causa* on Rear Admiral William S. Benson, a member of the United States Shipping Board who had been Chief of the U.S. Naval Operations during the First World War. He had expanded the facilities when he built the addition to the main building as well as Carroll Hall. This last was essential if the college division was to develop its own identity. He took steps to beautify the campus. He inaugurated an ambitious athletic program that seemed at the time to be essential. With the accreditation of the high school he launched that division on a course toward

---

[45]*Catalogue 1926-1927,* p. 72.
[46]*The Ranger,* 1928, p. 92.
[47]*Op. cit.,* p. 90.

becoming one of the best Catholic high schools in the city of Denver. His dream of getting the same recognition for the college as a four-year senior school was not realized in his time.

Kelley also improved the faculty. Since it was difficult to obtain more Jesuits, he began to engage the services of laymen. The names of the faculty members were listed in the 1925-1926 catalogue with their academic degree noted along with a summary of their academic background and teaching experience. Course offerings were improved; in fact, every effort was made to bring the college up-to-date in all departments so that it could measure up to the claim of being an institution of higher learning.

The price Kelley had to pay was high for an institution with no endowment and with such limited resources. The legacy of debt was to haunt Kelley's successors until 1945; it almost caused the closing of the college. John J. Brown, who was living in Cleveland, kept an eye on the developments in Denver and was anxious to hear all the news about the school that he had governed for eighteen years. He also kept up his contacts with members of the Old Mission who had returned to their native Italy when the mission was dissolved. On December 10, 1928, he wrote to an old friend who had become Provincial of the Province of Naples, Japhet S. Jollain, and informed him:

> Regis came very near going under financially last year. Could not even meet current expenses, I heard, due to a back breaking interest. They are some $300,000 in debt, I believe. This year they seem to be doing a little better and have hopes to keep afloat. Fr. Kelley knew not the value of a dollar and spent every one within his reach, a great many needlessly, as, v.g., on sunken gardens, lawns, waterpipes, etc., etc. Carroll Hall cost over $200,000 and one third is not yet plastered inside, even so.[48]

No doubt Brown looked back with nostalgia to the reasonably quiet days of his administration when every effort was made to pay off the debt that had been contracted when the main building was constructed. He may have had an unconscious resentment against Kelley with his bold plans because they constituted a threat to the very existence of the college. In the same letter Brown wrote that ''Fr. Joe Ryan is the salvation of the place so far. Kills self working for it. Scarcely any old mission men now remain. Every year one is taken away.''[49]

It was hardly an ideal situation for the fifty-nine year old Aloysius A. Breen, who became the eleventh president of the college on September 20, 1926. Breen, a seasoned administrator, had been president of St. Mary's

---

[48]P.N.A., Italy.
[49]*Ibid.*

College (1907-1914), Rockhurst College (1914-1919), and managing editor of the Queen's Work (1919-1926), an organization that promoted the works of the Sodality of the Blessed Virgin Mary. There was a marked contrast between Breen and his predecessor: Kelley had an imposing physical appearance; Breen was of ordinary build and did not present a very forceful image; and whereas Kelley was bold and imaginative, Breen was mild and quiet, in fact reminiscent of John J. Brown with his unassuming conservatism.

Breen inherited a college faculty of sixteen, most of them known for their competence as teachers rather than their professional standing as scholars. These men taught one hundred forty-four students under the direction of the dean of the college, Joseph A. Ryan. The high school, which by 1926 had definitely become a separate division, had a faculty of twelve and a student body of one hundred ninety-six. Bernard J. Murray was principal. He and Ryan had been members of the New Mexico-Colorado Mission and missed the old order of things, but both were dedicated and forceful men.

The new president found that the institution that he was to govern was carrying a burden of debt that amounted to some $300,000. Ordinary income was not sufficient to meet the demands of day-to-day expenses or even pay the interest due on the debt. It is true that the charges for attendance had been raised during the preceding years. By 1926 tuition had been increased to $150 for a school year, including library and athletic fees. The charge for board and tuition was $495 for the year. Of course, there were other incidental fees such as the $15 laboratory fee for chemistry and biology. If all this money had been collected it still would not be enough to help pay off the debt. Breen ordered that a study be made of the pledges that had been made during the campaign to raise funds for the building of Carroll Hall. The report was disappointing. The diarist wrote on February 24, 1927, "It is announced that about two-thirds of the people who pledged themselves during the drive for Regis have become unable to pay up. Many have died, changed residence or become impeded in many ways."[50]

The consultors deemed it advisable to commission the president to approach Bishop J. Henry Tihen and ask for assistance. The bishops of Denver, Joseph P. Machebeuf and Nicholas Matz, had been vigorous supporters of the college since it moved to that city, but their responsibilities toward the diocese understandably took precedence. Breen asked the Bishop to approve his request to present to the prominent wealthy Catholics of Denver the financial needs of the college. The Bishop's attitude was not

---

[50]*Diary 1923-1928,* p. 105.

encouraging. The minutes of the consultors for March 6, 1928, recorded:
Very Rev. Father Rector summarized the reply of the Bishop. In his
reply his Lordship discouraged the plan of approaching the wealthy
Catholics of Denver as futile. He regretted the plight of Regis and
expressed his willingness to cooperate in every possible way to come to
its assistance. He could however suggest no definite course of action.[51]

The seriousness of the financial situation is reflected in the subsequent
proposals of the consultors. Having learned from the president that the
authorities in St. Louis had not formulated plans regarding the future of
Regis, the consultors drew up their recommendations for the consideration
of the Provincial. They suggested that the high school be discontinued and
the college boarders be transferred to the rooms that were occupied by the
high school students in the main building. Carroll Hall would then be offered
to the Provincial as a house of studies for a hundred Jesuit seminarians. The
college would ask the Province to pay $60,000 for the building. If this
proposition was accepted Regis would discuss the problem of the unfinished
condition of Carroll Hall.[52] Unfortunately, the record of the Provincial's
response is not available.

Frustrated at every turn, Breen called a meeting of the Board of Trustees
and informed the members that it was imperative that the debt be refinanced.
The board directed the president to do whatever was necessary to achieve
this goal.[53] Breen went to St. Louis where he met with the officials of the
Lafayette-South Side Bank and Trust Company and they agreed to refinance
the debt. Breen then called a special meeting of the board on November 6,
1929, and presented the legal papers setting forth the details of refinancing
over a period of five years and each member of the board signed the
agreement.[54]

A major reason for the financial woes of the college was the athletic
program. It has been noted that Kelley inaugurated an ambitious athletic
policy that envisioned Regis as an athletic power. The golden formula of a
great coach with outstanding athletes playing before large crowds in a
spacious stadium simply had not worked out. The architect's plan for a big
stadium had to be set aside for a more modest playing field with exposed
stands for the spectators. In 1925 some forty men, prominent in the business
and professional life of Denver, formed the Regis Athletic Association.
These charter members pledged themselves "to promote clean athletics at
Regis College as well as any other activity which serves the upbuilding of the

---

[51]*Consultors Meetings 1888-1942*, pp. 71-72.
[52]*Op. cit.*, p. 72.
[53]*Trustees Meetings 1887-1934*, p. 94.
[54]*Trustees Meetings 1887-1934*, p. 95.

College. The officers of the association representing a membership which is to be statewide will help in directing the athletic policy of the school."[55]

An ambitious athletic policy demanded a well-paid coach, athletic scholarships, and all of the business transactions necessary to outfit a team and to make arrangements for it to play against teams good enough to attract a profitable number of paying customers. Every effort was made to arrange a representative schedule for the Rangers. At first the athletic department had to be content to play against the teams of the state. In September, 1924, the new stadium was dedicated with a great deal of fanfare; the occasion was honored by the presence of Governor William E. Sweet, who raised the flag during opening ceremonies. The first game was played against the Colorado School of Mines, with the Miners winning 7 to 0. A brief perusal of the account of the game in *The Brown and Gold* gives the impression that a new era was dawning in the history of the college.[56]

In the subsequent year or two the athletic program became more and more ambitious and games were scheduled with teams outside of Colorado. There was no end to enthusiasm on campus but the response of the public did not measure up to expectations. Expenses exceeded income and as early as November 29, 1926, the consultors of the college became alarmed. In a meeting on that date it was announced that the secretary of the Regis College Athletic Association reported a deficit of $5,000 for each of the past two years. Breen asked the members of the board if the association should be continued. In light of the willingness of the association to continue at least for another year "because of favorable outlook," the board voted in the affirmative.[57]

Matters did not improve as far as finances were concerned during the subsequent months. The association simply could not raise enough money to cover expenses. In May, 1928, the officers of the Athletic Association met with Breen and made its needs known to him. It is interesting to note that the author of the consultors' minutes used the word "demand" when he recorded that "The association demands $7,500 in some shape or form as a yearly loan in order that it may continue."[58] The consultors agreed that the athletic fee of $10.00 should be set aside for athletics, fully realizing that the maximum from the fee amounted to only $2,000 per year.

In view of the fact that the college was working on refinancing it is understandable that it was necessary to take a hard look at the current athletic policy. The matter was discussed in a number of meetings of the consultors.

---

[55]*Catalogue 1925-1926*, p. 65.
[56]*The Brown and Gold*, vol. VII, No. 1, *passim*.
[57]*Consultors Meetings 1888-1942*, p. 62.
[58]*Op. cit.*, p. 73.

On September 6, 1930, the consultors recommended that a complete report be made on the record of the athletic department for the past five years. In January, 1931, the board voted unanimously against the continuance of intercollegiate football as it was being conducted at Regis. When it came to vote on whether the college should withdraw from the Rocky Mountain Conference, the vote was three to two in favor of withdrawal. The next question considered by the board followed logically: should Regis discontinue intercollegiate football at least temporarily? Joseph A. Ryan and John J. Driscoll voted to discontinue; Francis X. Hoefkens and Gerald P. Walsh voted against dropping the sport. The president decided to take the matter up with the Provincial in St. Louis. At the next meeting of the board, February 11, 1931, the members decided to discontinue intercollegiate football. When the consultors met on March 6 the minutes of the meeting on January 7 were amended to show that Breen had voted against intercollegiate football.[59] In the light of the careful recording of the votes in the minutes of the consultors it is interesting to note that both *The Denver Post* and the *Rocky Mountain News* had announced the end of intercollegiate football at Regis on January 20, 1931.

Football was not the sole preoccupation of those interested in an athletic program. Regis continued to field a representative baseball team and steps were taken to improve basketball. There was an ephemeral interest in boxing due to the presence of a student from Alamosa, Pedro Quintana, who was proficient in the ring as a lightweight boxer. Quintana, fighting under the name of Eddie Mack, compiled a respectable record in the ring. The editor of *The Ranger* for 1928 described his achievements:

> During his very successful boxing career, Eddie fought every lightweight contender the matchmakers could obtain, losing but one fight, that to Caponi, on an accidental foul. The climax of his boxing career was reached when he held Red Chapman, claimant of the world's lightweight title, to a draw. Eddie was the aggressor throughout this bout. An encounter with Sammy Mandell, present holder of the lightweight crown, was denied Eddie when the title holder, through illness, was unable to appear and defend his title.[60]

Mack organized a boxing club and coached some thrity-five students who were interested in the sport.

Wrestling was introduced and became a popular part of the athletic schedule during the 1926 and 1927 seasons. The coach, Francis J. Farrell, was well qualified to develop a wrestling team and was making progress in

---

[59]*Op. cit., passim.*

[60]*The Ranger,* 1928, p. 144. Incidentally, Eddie Mack was business manager of *The Ranger* for 1928. He was acknowledged as one of the most popular students on the campus.

his attempt to build a squad capable of participating in intercollegiate contests. Unfortunately, Farrell was seriously injured during an exhibition match sponsored by the Lambda Tau Club. After this incident, interest in the sport dissipated and the promise of a successful wrestling squad never became a reality. Hope for the future continued; the editor of *The Ranger* wrote:

The work that Farrell started so well has not been in vain. It has been delayed, but will be taken up again in the near future, and will move forward to the goal aimed at by the young coach.[61]

Breen's later years as president were not all dark. The department of accounting which had such a tenuous beginning was gaining stature. In 1931 the department offered a major requiring a minimum of twenty hours. Qualified laymen were recruited to teach the courses: Joseph W. Thompason, C.P.A., lecturer in advanced accounting, Thomas R. Young, C.P.A., lecturer in auditing, Edmund L. Mullen, LL.B., lecturer in business law, William B. Paul, C.P.A., instructor in accounting, and Stephen J. Donoghue, M.B.A., professor of accounting and director of the department.[62]

The man behind the growth of the department was Joseph A. Ryan who had entered the Society of Jesus in 1909. When he had finished his course of training as a Jesuit he returned to Regis in 1926 as dean of the college. Ryan was a man of foresight, determination, persistence, and vision. He was convinced that the college should have a department of commerce and finance. With characteristic thoroughness he decided that he should become proficient in accounting. He spent the summer of 1927 as a student at Marquette University and the summers of 1933-1935 at Creighton University. Under his competent guidance the department, of which he was chairman from 1933 to the year of his death from a stroke in 1957, won recognition as one of the most successful departments in the history of the college.[63]

Another department was to achieve stature in due time, namely, chemistry; it began to emerge under the direction of Francis P. Keenoy, who had the assistance of the scholastic A. H. Hoenemeyer. In 1931 the department offered a major with a minimum of twenty-six credit hours. The students responded with enthusiasm and organized the only honorary scholastic club

---

[61]*Op. cit.*, p. 146.

[62]*Catalogue 1931*, pp. 6-8.

[63]Father Ryan, a stern man, was an exacting teacher. No one doubted his dedication. Many of his students gained stature in the business community. As a Jesuit of the old school he inspired a deep feeling of loyalty to the college. It was a true measure of the man that after the death of Everett Bailey's wife, Ryan persuaded his sister Margie to take care of the five Bailey children and to see to it that they received an education.

on campus to stimulate extracurricular activity and interest in chemistry. Members pledged themselves to discuss topics that would help stimulate interest in the class lectures and laboratory work. They inducted the president of the college and A. W. Forstall into the club as honorary members.[64]

School spirit was high during the late twenties and students were eager to participate in the affairs of the college. They revived the student council and established it as the student governing body of the college. The council formulated a complete outline of student activities and supervised the student assemblies. The administrative council was made up of four seniors, Charles J. Stubbs, president, Adrian W. Maguire, John K. Murphy, and Eddie Mack (Pedro Quintana); four juniors, Joseph F. Sobeck, Thomas E. Carey, Thomas A. Doran and Joseph J. Cella; sophomore representative William T. Sweeney and the freshmen agent T. Raber Taylor.[65] This was an auspicious beginning for student government.

Obviously the early thirties were years of great difficulties because the Great Depression was in full swing. Surprisingly, the enrollment figures for these years for the high school and the college held up quite well in spite of the depression; in 1930 there were 451 students. There was a significant drop in 1932 when the total was 391. The lowest total for these years, in 1935, was 304; after 1935 there were significant increases over the succeeding years. Regis survived while another Jesuit college, St. Mary's in St. Marys, Kansas, was discontinued as a boarding school for young men and was converted into a seminary for young Jesuits who were preparing themselves for ordination to the priesthood. The closing of St. Mary's made it possible for Regis to obtain some good men for its faculty, for example, John F. Bannon who was a great asset to the school during the single year he taught there. By 1932 the faculty numbered thirty-two men, some of whom were to give many years of dedicated service to Regis.

In 1930 the high school acquired a very promising young Jesuit, Gerald P. Walsh, who was appointed to succeed Joseph P. Mentag as principal on September 26th. Walsh was dynamic and very personable. He lost little time in initiating a Mother's Club for the high school. Since its foundation on December 1, 1930, this organization has given invaluable assistance to the school. It is still flourishing and is a tribute to the generous women who have contributed their services over the years. As principal of the high school, Walsh became a member of the Board of Trustees and was elected secretary. On July 31, 1931, he was appointed the twelfth president of the college to succeed Father Breen. With a young man of thirty-five years in charge of the

---

[64]*The Ranger*, 1929, p. 98.
[65]*The Ranger*, 1929, pp. 84-85.

administration there was hope for the future. Unfortunately, illness and complicated personal problems forced Walsh to give up his office in less than two months. On September 23, 1931, John J. Driscoll was appointed acting president until a successor could be found.

During these years of crises certain events took place that deserve to be recorded. For example, the authorities wished to widen the base of operation and introduce a night school and Saturday classes. The history of the efforts to establish a viable evening division shows a record of tentative beginnings usually ending in failure. Some years earlier an attempt had been made to provide an opportunity for the Catholic nuns who were teaching in the Denver area to obtain college credits; the catalogue for 1925-1926 published a list that included the names of the students who were enrolled for the academic year, and among them were fifteen Sisters.[66] There are references to the night school and to Saturday classes for the Sisters in some of the documents through these years. The effort seemed to have been too much for an overburdened faculty. On September 13, 1932, the diarist states with annoying simplicity, "This year there is no night school nor Saturday classes."[67]

Benefactions to a private independent college are necessary for survival. In the course of the history of Regis certain benefactors came to the aid of the college at critical times. Donations of money are essential but there are other gifts that are worthy of note. Two valiant women who were to give many years of service appeared on the scene to give secretarial help; it is true that they received some remuneration for their work but their devotion went far beyond the financial return for their work. These women were Mary Ryan (after her marriage, Mary Peck) and Alice O'Connor. Mary Ryan was the niece of one of the most dedicated Jesuits at Regis, Joseph A. Ryan. Mary worked for many years in various offices such as the business office, as well as those of the dean and the president. Mrs. O'Connor was to act as secretary for years in the office of the dean.

Other benefactors included the Cozens family who owned many acres in the mountains near Fraser, Colorado. Over the years the Jesuits had found a welcome on their summer vacations at the Cozens Ranch. In time the family dwindled to one surviving member, William Cozens. Cozens never married and in his later years found companionship with his Jesuit friends. In his declining years he resided at the college. In appreciation for the many years of friendship he deeded his Fraser property to the Jesuits. The diarist noted on August 4, 1931, that William Cozens was "our benefactor by giving to

---

[66]*Catalogue 1925-1926*, p. 73.
[67]*Diary 1930-1933*, p. 184.

this College the Fraser Villa with 400 acres of pine land.''[68]

Services and grants of property are important contributions. Financial aid by way of donations for the purpose of establishing scholarships is of even greater and of more immediate value. The college's experience with a scholarship program is far from impressive. Certainly the authorities were aware of the necessity of having scholarships; for years an appeal was printed in the yearly catalogue. Scholarships became a reality by 1932 when the college was finally able to offer financial aid to qualified and usually needy students from funds donated by various benefactors. The earliest recorded scholarship was set up in 1901 and designated The Sacred Heart Scholarship. Others followed: The Desaulniers, 1912; George F. Cottrell, 1928; William J. Scholl Memorial, 1939; Joseph T. Ward Memorial, 1931; and The Frederick G. Bonfils Foundation, 1931. Two benefactors established funds that were considerably more generous than those already mentioned. The John K. and Catherine S. Mullen Benevolent Corporation donated $15,000 in memory of Reverend Dominic Pantanella; the annual income from this fund was to be made available in perpetuity to needy and deserving students to be applied to the expense of tuition. A second generous donation was the one made by the sisters and heirs of Eugene Henry Rourke, La Junta, Colorado, of $15,000; it, too, was to help cover the cost of the tuition of needy students in perpetuity.[69]

A major benefaction was made at this time by John O'Connell of Las Animas, Bent County, Colorado. The immediate donation of $7,000 was only a beginning since O'Connell changed his will leaving half of his estate to the college; this was to become effective after his death. O'Connell was an unpretentious man who owned a considerable number of acres in Bent County. Accounts of the preliminaries to this bequest indicate that John O'Connell had intended to give his estate to the Diocese of Denver for the support of St. Thomas Seminary, but for some reason not easily traceable he became somewhat disenchanted with the authorities of the diocese and decided to leave half of his estate to Regis. Legend has it that when he called at the college he looked so unimpressive that the man on duty hesitated to contact Father Breen, for whom O'Connell had asked. Breen, who was approaching the end of his term as president, agreed to see the visitor. Some years later he recalled the events of that day and related them to Raphael C. McCarthy, who had been appointed president of the college on June 10, 1947. McCarthy committed to writing Breen's account. According to it, O'Connell told the president that he had decided to change his will and make

---

[68]*Diary 1930-1933,* p. 80.
[69]*Catalogue 1932,* pp. 19-20.

Regis a beneficiary of half of his estate, the other half was to be given to the seminary. When Breen heard the word seminary he asked for some time to think the matter over; he thought it prudent to gain time so that he could consult Bishop J. Henry Tihen. Evidently the Bishop had not been impressed with Mr. O'Connell. He asked Breen, "Is that fellow bothering you too? Go ahead, get what you can, but neither Regis or the diocese will ever get anything." When Breen saw O'Connell again he said that it would be all right for him to make a new will. Breen must have had great satisfaction when he visited the Bishop later and presented to him a check for $7,000 and said, "Here's your share."[70] Under the date of July 14, 1931, Breen received a letter from the law office of Smith, Akolt and Campbell notifying him that John O'Connell had made a will leaving "all the property which he may own at the time of his death in equal shares to the College and Seminary." The college and the seminary were to wait some four years, until 1935, before this bequest became a reality. This account has been included with some detail because without O'Connell's benefaction the college most likely would not have survived the crisis of 1935 when the authorities of the Missouri Province gave serious consideration to the question of closing Regis College and High School.

In the meantime, John J. Driscoll administered the affairs of the institution. During his brief tenure of three and one-half months the initiative in formulating plans to raise money to assist the college passed into the hands of a dynamic leader of the diocesan clergy, Hugh L. McMenamin, pastor of the Cathedral of the Immaculate Conception. In October, 1931, McMenamin, a graduate of the class of 1897, called on his fellow priests to carry on a fund-raising campaign to collect $30,000 for the college. He was ably assisted by another legendary figure among the diocesan clergy, William O'Ryan. Both of these men were enduring friends of the Jesuits and they encouraged their fellow priests to do as much as possible to come to the aid of the financially troubled college. To encourage other priests these two men donated $500 each to get the campaign started.[71]

About two and one-half months later, Joseph A. Herbers took over as the fourteenth president on January 6, 1932. Herbers came to Regis from Creighton University in Omaha, Nebraska, where he had held the office of Dean of Men since 1926. Previous to his experience at Creighton he had been Prefect of Studies and later dean at St. Mary's College in Kansas. The new president was not temperamentally suited to be the chief officer of an educational institution that was in deep financial trouble at a time when the

---

[70]*Letter in Regis Archives.*
[71]*Diary 1930-1933*, p. 101.

whole country was in the grip of the Great Depression.

Herbers discovered that the friends of Regis had been busy preparing for a fund-raising campaign. McMenamin had called the attention of the new bishop of Denver, Urban J. Vehr, to the plight of the college. The bishop promised to support the efforts that were being made to alleviate the financial needs of the Jesuit institution and approved the request that appeals be made in the parishes. Herbers had little time to assess the problems facing him, but he accepted the challenge and immersed himself in the preparations that were being made to launch the fund drive.

The planners for the campaign adopted the slogan "Save Regis—Regis Shall Not Close." The campaign started with a luncheon at the Argonaut Hotel on January 19, 1932; workers learned that the goal for his endeavor was $125,000 to be raised over a period of five years. The Regis Jesuits were authorized to go to the parishes and explain the necessity of saving the college to the people at Sunday Masses. It should be noted that among those who first subscribed to support the campaign was Bishop Vehr. Forty-six of the diocesan priests followed his example and together they pledged $6,000.00.[72] In spite of great enthusiasm and hard work the campaign was not a success. Perhaps it was foolhardy to try at that time, and the move to do so must have been born of desperation. The economy was on the verge of being turned around, but it was to take time for the changes to take effect. The report on file in the records summarizing the history of fund raising by the college indicates that this campaign fell far short of the goal, the total amount raised being only $41,749.00.[73]

In spite of difficulties the college kept its doors open. There was a gradual decline in enrollment, which fell from 456 in 1931 to 304 in 1935. As if matters were not difficult enough there was trouble with the officials of the North Central Association. The association had given accreditation to the high school in 1921, but accredited the college only as a junior college. The officials of Regis decided to ignore the implications of the North Central's decision and continue as a four-year college empowered to grant degrees. The association objected to this, requesting Herbers to accept the status of a junior college and to stop granting degrees. Correspondence was carried on between the college and the association until the facts of the situation were made crystal clear by the secretary of the association, George A. Works, who wrote on January 12, 1934:

You must meet the requirements as a senior college, or must cease to

---

[72]William H. Jones, *The History of Catholic Education in the State of Colorado* (Washington, D.C., The Catholic University of America Press, 1955), p. 316.

[73]R.C.A.

give senior college work and drop back to the rank of a junior college if
you are to remain in the Association. As your indebtedness is greater
than your endowment, under a strict interpretation of the regulations it
would be necessary for you to have a survey if you are to remain on the
junior college list. I do not know what the action of the Board of Review
would be; but it is possible that they would be willing, in view of the fact
that you had a survey last year, to continue you as a junior college on the
basis of that report.[74]

The correspondence shows that Herbers was not to be easily deterred from
continuing his efforts to operate Regis as a four-year college. Works was
equally persistent in presenting his request that the last two years of college
be discontinued; he told Herbers that if he did not do so, Regis would be
dropped from the list of accredited junior colleges. Finally, in a letter dated
`ril 25, 1934, the president was notified that Regis was no longer recog-
niz. as an accredited junior college because it had "failed to meet the
standards for four-year institutions."[75]

As a result of this action the college's credits were not recognized by other
institutions so that students who transferred from Regis had to accept the fact
that they would have to start over again. Some of the Colorado institutions,
however, gave Regis a vote of confidence. The catalogue of 1935-1936
published this statement: "Regis College is recognized by the University of
Colorado and by other State and Private Colleges and Universities in Colorado."[76] Herbers' disappointments were made bearable by the support he
secured from his fellow Jesuits who discovered ways of coping with the
problems resulting from the Depression. The treasurer, Francis X. Hoefkens, one of the kindest men in the community, managed to keep creditors
from taking drastic action against the school by distributing his limited funds
as carefully as possible. Joseph Ryan supplemented his excellent work as
acting head of the department of accounting by raising ducks and rabbits to
provide food for the table. John P. Stanley, a lay brother, took care of the
chicken coop. But in spite of this support Herbers was a disheartened man.
He lost interest and withdrew from participation in public affairs as much as
possible. As a general rule presidents of Jesuit colleges could expect to
remain in office for six years but Herbers' days were numbered. After three
years and two months he was replaced by Robert M. Kelley who returned to
serve a second term beginning on February 21, 1935.

During the nine years of his absence from Denver, Kelley held various

---

[74]R.C.A.
[75]*Ibid.*
[76]*Catalogue 1935-1936.*

positions in the Missouri Province, most notably that of president of Loyola University, Chicago (1927-1933). He returned to Regis as a seasoned administrator and lost little time in addressing himself to the most pressing problems at hand, the perennial problem of reducing and, hopefully, liquidating the debt. He discovered that the college had been in default since November 1, 1933. It was imperative that something be done to rectify this situation. The members of the Board of Trustees met on February 26, 1935, and again on March 6 to consider a course of action. The president was instructed to ask for an extension of time on payments due on the debt and to proceed to formulate a plan to refinance the bonded indebtedness.

There was no doubting the seriousness of the financial crisis but an even greater one had to be faced in 1935. In May of that year Daniel O'Connell, the National Secretary of the Jesuit Interprovince Educational Society, submitted a report to Samuel H. Horine, Provincial of the Missouri Province, recommending that Regis College and High School be closed. The General of the Society of Jesus had sent out an instruction ordering an evaluation of all the Jesuit universities, colleges, and high schools in the United States. O'Connell visited the various schools and wrote a report to the Provincials informing them of the recommendations he intended to send to the General.

His suggestion regarding Regis was that it be closed and the Province take over its debt. The Province would find compensation in the fact that it would gain some thirty-nine Jesuits. O'Connell was of the opinion that even if Kelley were successful in his efforts to refinance the bonded debt he would never be able to make the interest payments when they were due. He wrote with surprising frankness that Regis should default and not even try to borrow any more funds. Recording the academic qualifications of the members of the faculty, O'Connell pointed out that there was only one man with the Ph.D. degree. Another important weakness was the lack of accreditation. He mentioned that the North Central had objected that some professors taught in diverse departments. Moreover, the library was sadly deficient; it lacked sufficient reading areas and needed more space for the stacks. The picture was not all black. O'Connell admitted that in general the teaching seemed to be done well; he praised the work of Bernard S. Karst, the principal of the high school, and the work and cooperation of Theodore J. Schulte. His conclusion was that in view of the shortcomings and weaknesses as well as its hopeless future he would ask the General if he would consider means of withdrawing the Jesuits from Regis.[77]

There is no doubt that this report was a serious blow to the administration

---

[77]R.C.A.

and faculty of Regis College and High School. The members of the Board of Trustees met with the president and together they determined to do everything in their power to save the school. Kelley formulated answers to O'Connell's objections and presented them to the Provincial and his consultors when he met with them on August 17, 1935. He acknowledged the validity of some of the objections raised by O'Connell, asked for a few years' grace to give him time to rectify the situation, and concluded, "My position then in regard to closing Regis is that it would be inadvisable to do so unless and until it is convincingly clear that Regis is unable to meet the reasonable standards we set for our schools taking into account the territory served and the circumstances of the times."[78]

Happily for Regis, Father Provincial Horine agreed with Kelley's request. Horine assembled some cogent arguments against closing the school; understandably, one of his more important and telling reasons was the fact that the Province was not able to assume the Regis debt since its own debt was so burdensome. Horine's letter to the General concluded:

The Fathers Consultor of Regis and also those of the Province agree unanimously that closing Regis this year will be a hasty and not sufficiently warranted action. Father Rector (Kelley) must in all fairness to himself, to the Society, and to such benefactors as Regis has had, be given further opportunity to achieve yet more success in his untiring efforts to salvage the institution. His refinancing of the bonded debt was excellently done. He now waits for definite word as to the future of Regis that he may undertake plans to secure students and to reduce debts. As for the future, the Fathers Consultor of the Province agree that in view of Regis' past history and work, of the Society's reputation locally and in this country, we must not run away from difficulties or burden the Province probably to the extent of injuring its credit.[79]

Father General Wlodmir Ledochowski took some time to consider the whole matter. After discussing the documents submitted by Kelley and Horine with the American Assistant, Zacheus J. Maher, he decided to give Regis some time to find a solution for its problems. In a letter to the Provincial, March 31, 1936, he wrote that he had sent a telegram on March 9th giving permission for Regis to continue at least for the time being (*saltem ad tempus continuari posse*).[80]

There are at least two reasons that explain this favorable decision. The first is that Kelley had succeeded in his efforts to get the bonded debt

---

[78]*Ibid.*
[79]M.P.A.
[80]*Ibid.*

refinanced. He had called upon the officials of the Eckhard and Peterson Company of St. Louis and negotiated with them a new arrangement for paying off the debt. This company had bought out the bonding business of the Lafayette-South Side Bank of that city, which had made the loan for building Carroll Hall possible in 1923. Kelley was successful in arranging new terms, namely, an extension on the maturity of bonds to the year 1945 at three percent for past due interest, three percent from 1935 to 1940, and five and one-half percent from 1940 to 1945. The officials of the company were successful in obtaining the consent of nearly all of the bondholders to the new terms.[81]

The second and probably decisive reason was the prospect of realizing a considerable sum of money from the estate of John O'Connell. When the will was probated after his death on June 4, 1935, the college and St. Thomas Seminary received equal shares of 2,600 acres of land, 500 of which were valuable agricultural lands and the rest grazing lands along the Arkansas River, Las Animas, Colorado. Besides the property there was a trust fund which the two institutions would share. In December, 1935, the trust department of the Colorado National Bank distributed part of the trust fund; the college received $24,000 without restriction. By August 1, 1936, Regis had received money amounting to about $37,000. The college and seminary undertook the joint administration of the property that was deeded to them; each of the parties could expect $1,400 a year from the rental of the land. Obviously, this turn of events was deeply appreciated by the Jesuits at Regis. Kelley paid $11,000 on current debts and bought up, at face value, $10,000 in outstanding bonds.[82]

Some events in the history of an institution remain inexplicable. One such event took place on April 17, 1935, when Kelley announced that the college would resume participation in intercollegiate football. Given the circumstances of the times, the Depression and the financial status of the college, this decision seems to have been foolhardy. It is even more difficult to understand when it is recalled that Kelley as president of Loyola University in Chicago had dropped football from the athletic program. It is true that he envisioned a modest participation, at least in the beginning. He appointed a Jesuit scholastic, Jerome R. Boyle, as moderator of athletics. Boyle had been a credit to the team in the middle twenties, then had entered the Society of Jesus and in 1935 was teaching at Regis High School. Another former star

---

[81]M.P.A.

[82]*Report* of Rev. Augustine Walters. *M.P.A.* Walters conducted an impartial review of the financial status of Regis College and High School in 1937. His eight-page report, submitted to the Provincial of the Missouri Province, is very helpful because it states clearly the principal facts regarding the finances of the institution in concise, understandable language.

at Regis, Adrian Maguire, was appointed coach. Maguire had been the coach of the Regis High School team until the time of his appointment to the college.

Perhaps one of the reasons for the resumption of intercollegiate football was the hope that an athletic program would help improve the public image of the school. Kelley was much more aware of the public than his predecessors had been. Soon after the institution was given a chance to work out its problems Kelley submitted a plan to the Provincial and asked approval for a lay advisory board for the college. He had had some experience with a lay board during his term of office as president of Loyola University in Chicago. In 1936 the president and board of trustees went on record as being in favor of a board of advisors ''to whom they may refer every problem in which the experience and wisdom of the lay mind may be helpful.''[83]

The trustees envisioned a board of laymen that would help to give the college an efficient financial administration such as would create public confidence. Another function of the board would be to establish a business policy that would have continuity. One of the more important roles would be ''to assist the College in rendering a more effective service in the field of public welfare, and to form closer contacts with men and women in public life.''[84] The tentative statement in identifying the specific functions of the board reads like a policy statement for a lay board of trustees, allowing, of course, for complete control of the Jesuit president. Provincial Samuel H. Horine thought that this proposal was reasonable and accordingly wrote to the General on April 14, 1936, requesting approval for such a board.[85] Rome approved and Kelley began to enlist the leaders of the Catholic community of Denver, asking them to serve on the board.

The response of the friends of Regis was prompt and Kelley was able to announce the formation of the board on February 2, 1937. The group was to meet twice a year but would hold extra sessions for the consideration of particular problems when necessity required. Committees were formed to consider finance, ways and means, public relations, and building and grounds. The college would seek the advice of these men regarding policies concerning student aid, the refinancing of the bonded debt, and the collection of unpaid pleges of the Regis good-will campaign. The advice of the members would be sought regarding the reorganization of the alumni, publicity, advertising, and improvements in the buildings.[86] This plan was a

---

[83]

[84]*Ibid.*

[85]*Letter* in M.P.A.

[86]*The Denver Catholic Register,* Feb. 11, 1937 (In Diary 1934-1938, p. 187).

presage of a new era in the history of the college but it was destined to be stillborn if one makes a judgment based on the available evidence.

Another question came up for serious consideration at this time, namely, the wisdom of trying to operate an adequate college while trying to maintain a first-class high school for boarders and day students. On March 29, 1937, the president submitted to the proper authorities a tentative plan regarding the future of the high school. After consulting the Prefect of Studies of the Missouri Province, the Bishop of Denver, and two diocesan priests, the president proposed that Regis High School be phased out of existence by dropping the first year during the school year 1938-1939 and one year each in the succeeding years so that in 1942-1943 there would remain only a four-year college. Kelley outlined seven reasons against closing the high school and thirteen in favor of discontinuing the effort to maintain both divisions. Among the reasons for closing the high school one finds the statement that unless a higher rating was obtained Catholic higher education would not have the prestige it should have in the Rocky Mountain region. It was also noted that without unexpected financial and academic aid it seemed impossible to develop both high school and college. If there were additions to and improvement in the faculty, the college could do excellent work. In the event that there was only a college there could be a concentration of educational efforts. Finally, Kelley pointed out that Regis High School was not necessary since the educational capability of the Diocese of Denver, with seven Catholic high schools in the city of Denver and three or four outside the city, was sufficient to care for the secondary school needs of the Catholic community in the region.[87]

This matter was considered important enough to be submitted to the authorities in Rome. The American Assistant to the General, Zacheus J. Maher, wrote to Kelley in May, 1937, and advised caution. He agreed that it would be desirable to separate the two operations but questioned the wisdom of closing the high school. Maher asked for more information about the high school enrollment, specifically the number of boarders and of day students. He wanted to know about tuition and whether or not separate accounts were kept. Admitting that he did not have a clear idea of the physical setup in Denver, he nevertheless suggested that the possibility of building a plant for the high school be thoroughly explored. Finally, he advised more study of the question when he wrote:

> In view of the lateness of the school year, of the time it will take to have proper data presented to His Paternity, and of the coming of Father Provincial to Rome, would it not be well not to think or speak of closing

---

[87]*Memorandum Regarding Future of Regis College, Denver, Colorado.* M.P.A.

even the first year of High School during the academic year of 1938? This more particularly so since you need the revenue. Let us take the academic year of 1938-39 to study the problem more deeply and delay any action until 1939.[88]

The suggestion of Maher was accepted and Regis High School got a reprieve, at least for the time being.

Evidently, the proposal to phase Regis High School out of existence was not taken seriously by Bernard S. Karst, principal of the high school since 1933. In May, 1937, Karst was successful in his efforts to engage Clarence H. Kellogg as coach. Previous to this move the athletic program had been conducted on a hit-and-miss basis. For example, the football and basketball coach for the 1936 season had been Joseph Loffreda who took time off from his regular job to coach on a part-time contract. Karst engaged the services of "Kelly" Kellogg as coach for football, basketball, baseball and track. Over and above his coaching duties Kellogg was to teach American history. This decision of Karst laid the foundation for an excellent athletic program in the high school. Kellogg had played football at St. Mary's School, conducted by the Christian Brothers in Moraga, California. After his college career he played professional football with the Chicago Cardinals. At the time he agreed to come to Denver, he was completing work on his Master's Degree at the University of California at Los Angeles.[89] "Kelly" was to compile an enviable record as a coach at Regis High School and College, since he chose to remain with the institution for many years.

Father Kelley was indefatigable in building up the public image of the college. After careful preparation he organized a Regis Men's Club. About two hundred laymen held their first meeting in the main building on May 10, 1937, to hear Daniel A. Lord, a Jesuit who was gaining a great reputation throughout the Midwest as a leader in the Sodality movement and as a very successful speaker at special functions. The leaders of the Catholic segment in Denver gathered together to encourage the Jesuits in their work. Graduates and friends showed a great deal of enthusiasm on the occasion. Two enduring friends of the Jesuits who remained loyal in spite of many frustrations, John J. Sullivan and Edmund Mullen, lauded another effort of the authorities of the college to win support from the Denver community. Mr. Sullivan, the president of the Alumni Association, stressed in his talk the mutual benefits to be gained through participation in the athletic and cultural interests of the college. Mr. Mullen introduced the officers of the newly established club. The president, Thomas J. Tynan, came to Denver

---

[88]Maher to Kelley, R.C.A.
[89]*The Denver Catholic Register,* May 5, 1937.

from New York, where he had become acquainted with the Jesuits at Fordham University; he was to become one of the more loyal friends of Regis College and High School and his generous support of every effort to improve the institution has been carried on by members of his family. Other officers were Joseph Schmittling, secretary, and Joseph J. Cella, treasurer. Besides these officers there were a number of vice-presidents who were to serve in an advisory capacity, Ferman Bischofberger, Captain Frank Campbell of the Regis Retreat League, Charles Smith of the Parent-Teachers' Association, John Walsh of the Regis Guild, and John J. Sullivan of the Alumni Association.[90]

While all these developments were taking place time had to be found to start planning for the Golden Jubilee in 1938. At the time those who were familiar with the history of the college were accustomed to considering 1888 as the founding date; the decision to do so had been made some thirty-seven years previously. In January, 1938, Kelley announced that Bernard J. Murray had been appointed chairman of the committee in charge of making preparations. Father Murray, an alumnus of the school, had been a member of the former New Mexico-Colorado Mission and few could match his love of and loyalty to his Alma Mater. Many suggestions were made for a gala celebration. The final plans opted for a greater emphasis on the religious aspect, including a parade, a rally, the renewal of the Holy Name pledge, and an outdoor Mass and Benediction. A banquet and an open-house party were to conclude the festivities.[91]

The climax of the Jubilee Celebration was a Pontifical High Mass with the Most Reverend Urban J. Vehr as celebrant. Among the dignitaries present were Bishop Anthony J. Schuler of El Paso, Texas, a former president of the college (1903-1906), Bishop Francis M. Kelly of Winona, Minnesota, Abbot Leonard Schwinn, O.S.B., of Holy Cross Abbey, Canon City, and Very Rev. Peter A. Brooks, S.J., Provincial of the Missouri Province. The choir of Montezuma Seminary in New Mexico sang the Mass, the Most Reverend Charles F. Buddy of San Diego, preached the sermon. Bishop Buddy was very generous in his praise of the Jesuits and their contributions to education through nearly four hundred years. The sermon was long and the sun was hot, but few who were present could forget the occasion. The religious celebration was followed by a banquet for the clergy. The Rev. William O'Ryan, one of the most loyal friends Regis had, gave a principal talk made memorable by his sparkling Irish wit.

The Jubilee furnished an opportunity for a fund-raising campaign. The

---

[90]*Op. cit.* (cf. p. 99. Diary 1934-1938).
[91]*The Ranger,* 1939, p. 34.

college did not have an enviable record in this field of endeavor but such an occasion could not be passed up. After careful preparation the drive was launched under the title of The Greater Regis Jubilee Campaign at a dinner held at the Albany Hotel on March 19, 1939. This time the goal was more modest and realistic, a mere $100,000. A layman, Charles C. Seidenstricker, was the key man for the college. He rented offices downtown so that he would have closer contact with the business community. In spite of a well-planned and coordinated drive this effort was not a complete success. The amount collected and pledged was $60,000.[92]

All things considered, the financial status of the institution was greatly improved by the end of 1938. Kelley was tireless in his efforts to establish a solid financial basis for the college and high school. In September, 1939, he negotiated an extension agreement with the Eckhardt-Petersen Company of St. Louis. In a letter to Provincial Peter A. Brooks dated October 13, 1939, Kelley explained that he had gained an extension for four and one-half years, from May 1, 1945, to November 1, 1949, and instead of paying five and one-half percent interest, he would be paying only three percent. He explained to Brooks that the reason for choosing the dates agreed upon was "that they feel surer of the bond market at the present time than they would have felt,—say if it were dated from May 1, 1940 to May 1, 1950."[93]

Encouraged by his success in negotiating an extension agreement that gave promise of providing a better financial base for future operations, Kelley prepared to apply to the North Central Association for accreditation. He knew well that finances were not the only obstacles impeding the hoped-for recognition. There was need of modernization of the departmental structure. Accordingly, the departments were grouped under four divisions: language and literature; philosophy, religion and social sciences; natural sciences and mathematics; and commerce and finance.[94] The revision reflects the thinking of the academic community in the United States at that time. Kelley was also aware that the North Central visitors would make a careful investigation of the library. The college was fortunate in having Emmanuel T. Sandoval as librarian. He had been appointed to that position in 1925 and had built up a representative library which by 1941 contained approximately 46,500 volumes. Sandoval was not a healthy man but he was an indefatigable worker and a man of determination. He promoted interest among the friends of the school by establishing the Regis Library Association and initiating the Regis college review service. He contacted eighty-six

---

[92]*Op. cit.*, p. 37.
[93]M.P.A.
[94]*Catalogue 1936-1937*, p. 32.

publishers who were willing to use the service to promote their books. By 1935 he had obtained $2,740 worth of books for the library.[95]

A third necessity was an improved faculty especially men with the doctorate degree. Some success had been achieved in this matter by 1938, when there were three members of the faculty who had Ph.D. degrees and one Ph.D. candidate. There was need, moreover, for a better balance in the matter of rank. In 1938-1939 there were eleven full professors, one associate, two assistants, and five instructors, four of whom were scholastics beginning their teaching careers. Due to the cooperation of Peter A. Brooks, Provincial of the Missouri Province, there was considerable improvement in the faculty in 1941-1942, when Regis could list in its faculty roster seven men with the doctorate. Better balance was evident in the matter of rank, with nine full professors, three associates, one assistant, seven instructors, and four lecturers.[96] Some of the new faculty members were promising young men; these were Edward A. Conway, instructor in religion, who had a doctorate degree from the Gregorian University, Rome; Joseph P. Donnelly, instructor in history, with a Ph.D. from St. Louis University; and Leo C. Brown, instructor in economics, who had a doctorate from Harvard.

Kelley applied to the North Central for a review of the status of the college and the officers of the association agreed to send examiners to evaluate the situation in Denver. This was to take place in January, 1941, and it is understandable that there was an optimistic anticipation of the visit of the examiners. Kelley wrote American Assistant Zacheus J. Maher that Regis stood "a good chance of making the grade."[97]

The men who visited the college seemed to be favorably impressed and indicated that they would recommend accreditation. When Kelley went to the annual meeting in Chicago he was optimistic about his prospects for gaining the approval of the association—but the officers of the North Central were not impressed. It seems that the men who were on the commission may have been a bit weary of reviewing the application of Regis College for accreditation, especially since they continued to think that the college was far from having financial stability. Kelley wrote to Maher on July 5, 1941, "Our financial status seems to have been the chief reason why we failed to secure our objective, I believe that the adverse decision was arrived at previous to my appearance before the Commission. Four only of the Commission were present when I made my apperance, three of them being absent."[98]

---

[95]*The Brown and Gold,* Jan. 15, 1935, p. 1.
[96]*Catalogues for 1938-1939 and 1941-1942, passim.*
[97]Kelley to Maher, R.C.A.
[98]*Ibid.* (Kelley to Maher, R.C.A.).

This frustration was somewhat compensated for by the good showing that was made by the high school. Ever since the early nineteen twenties the high school had been finding its own identity. It had been accredited by the North Central Association in 1921, and, although it occupied the same campus as the college and shared some common facilities, it continued to maintain a high rating among Denver secondary schools. A number of excellent principals from B. J. Murray to Bernard S. Karst had directed the affairs of the school in such a way as to enhance its reputation. Bernard Karst, especially, kept up an excellent association with Dr. Arthur C. Cross of the University of Colorado, who was one of the main contacts in the state with the North Central. Not long after the association had rejected the college's request for accreditation, the State Committee of the North Central made an evaluation of Regis High School and rated it "excellent to superior in nearly every department."[99]

Both college and high school began to see better days ahead. This was noted by Zacheus J. Maher, who visited the institution in October 1940. He reported to Provincial Peter A. Brooks that the years of uncertainty had passed and that seemingly insuperable obstacles had definitely been removed. Maher accounted for this turnabout in these words:

First of all, there has been the careful financial management of Father Rector (Kelley). Next, the appointment of several good faculty executives, men devoted to the school and determined to have it take its merited place among the duly recognized colleges of the North Central. In their work they are being encouraged as well as helped by the Ph.D's, whom your reverence in your prudence has assigned to Regis this year, and by the work of other younger Fathers who are endeavoring to bring Regis before the public in a dignified and academic way.[100]

Enrollment in each division held up in the years 1939 through 1942. In the former year there were two hundred and forty-eight in the college and two hundred and seventy-one in the high school. There was a slight drop in 1940 but an increase in 1942. In due time World War Two had an effect on registration in the college; in 1943 there were only seventy students enrolled, and in 1944 only sixty-six. The high school, however, registered an increase—it stood at three hundred sixty-six in 1944.

During Kelley's administration two distinct honors were conferred on a member of the faculty, Armand W. Forstall, who had become an institution during the course of his career at Regis. Forstall had joined the faculty at

---

[99]Flanagan to Maher, R.C.A.

[100]Maher to Brooks, M.P.A. (Note: this letter was written before the North Central voted on Regis' request for accreditation.)

Morrison in 1885; he spent the next two years at Las Vegas in New Mexico. When the college opened in Denver in 1888, Forstall was there. After two more years he went on to complete his studies in preparation for ordination at Woodstock in Maryland. After various assignments to Georgetown, Holy Cross, and Woodstock in Maryland, he returned to Denver in 1905 and was to remain there for the rest of his life. He was a good teacher of mathematics, physics, and chemistry. His teaching did not deter him from branching out to other fields of endeavor. Over the years he assembled a collection of mineral specimens from the Rocky Mountains, a collection that is still useful for the courses in geology taught by Dr. William S. Levings. Each "rock" was carefully identified, labeled and placed in a cabinet. Forstall frequently reviewed the "rocks" in his collection; from time to time he would enlist the help of some unsuspecting student who happened to pass by, asking him to bring specimen after specimen and identifying each in turn.

For years Forstall helped many miners who brought him specimens of the ore that they had discovered in their mines for an assay. He tested the ore and informed the anxious miner whether he had anything of value. He was interested in radium and with Charles Paulot became the co-discoverer of carnotite, a deposit rich in radium. In 1912 Forstall published a short article under the title "Carnotite a Supply of Radium" in the *Twelfth Biennial Report of the Bureau of Mines of the State of Colorado for the years 1911 and 1912* (pp. 47-51). Forstall was not provincial in his outlook; he sent samples with his preliminary finds to Mme. Marie Currie's laboratories in France and must have been greatly satisfied when the experts in France supported his findings and agreed with him in asserting that Colorado ore was the peer of any in the world.[101]

Father Forstall received public recognition for his many accomplishments in the various fields of science. In 1935 the authorities of the University of Denver awarded him the Degree of Doctor of Science, *honoris causa*. The next year Forstall's work was recognized by the Ministry of National Education of the Government of France. French Consul General Yves Meric de Bellefon, had suggested that Dr. E. B. Renaud nominate Forstall for the academic distinction of "Officier d'Academie" with the purple ribbon and silver "Palmes Academiques." Renaud wrote to Kelley, "Since I personally consider Father Forstall as the most deserving science teacher, and most outstanding scientist and scholar in this region, I wished to have the honor of presenting his name for this much sought after distinction."[102] The nomination was forwarded to Paris and in due time approved. Renaud, as the representative of the government of France, awarded the academic distinc-

[101]Bill Wood, *Rocky Mountain News,* April 2, 1948.
[102]Renaud to Kelley, R.C.A.

tion at a memorable ceremony at Regis on October 14, 1936, in the presence of some four hundred distinguished guests and friends.[103]

Another Jesuit, Conrad Bilgery, attracted the attention of scholars in the field of paleontology. Bilgery joined the faculty in 1926 as professor of mathematics. He came to Denver after gaining experience at Jesuit colleges in Cleveland, Toledo, and Omaha. Mathematics, however, was not his sole preoccupation; he considered himself a proficient geologist. In his spare time he began to examine the areas of the Platte River and north Denver ranging over the territory to the base of the foothills. He found a response from interested students who accompanied him on his expeditions. He decided to offer introductory courses in geology, and the interest he created in this field led to a significant discovery of the bones of ancient mammoths in 1932. One of his students, Michael P. Ryan, the son of a station master for the Union Pacific Railroad at Dent, Colorado, saw some interesting bones that had been exposed by an excavating machine. Ryan decided to examine the site. Accompanied by Father Joseph A. Ryan and his brother Dan, Bilgery went to Dent to evaluate the discovery. After a preliminary investigation he was convinced that further exploration was justified. With the help of his students he began to explore the site more thoroughly. By the end of November, 1932, the workers had unearthed parts of at least six or seven individual mammoths. Winter put an end to these endeavors. In the meantime, Jessie D. Figgins, director of the Colorado Museum of Natural History, was convinced that this find was significant. With the help of personnel from the museum, excavation was resumed. The final result was that parts of fourteen individual mammoths were found. The staff of the museum assembled the bones of two mammoths. One of these was given to the Carnegie Museum in Pittsburgh, the other was displayed in Denver.[104]

Kelley's administration during his second term in the office of president was reasonably successful. The developing national crisis took its toll of the college but the high school remained alive and well. The financial status of the institution had improved notably; as Kelley informed Zacheus J. Maher in August, 1940, $25,000 had been paid on the debt with $20,000 of the bonds taken up. He had, moreover, paid off a $5,000 loan at a local bank. He must have had great satisfaction in being able to inform the

---

[103]The diploma of officer of the French Academy and the decoration of the silver academic palms was framed and for years adorned a wall opposite the chemistry office in Carroll Hall. It was moved to the quarters of the department in the science building. Unfortunately it has been defaced; souvenir-hunting students absconded with the silver palms.

[104]Father Bilgery wrote a preliminary report, "Evidences of Pleistocene Man in the Denver Basin." A copy is in the files of the physics department of the college. The author is again indebted to Rev. Joseph V. Downey, S.J., for the opportunity to use this report. (Note: In 1957 the directors of the Denver museum sent the Dent mammoth to Cleveland.)

American Assistant that he had been authorized to build a chemistry department on the first floor of the east wing of Carroll Hall, a part of the building
which he had been forced to leave unfinished during his first term in 1923.[105]

The last two and one-half years of Kelley's second term as president were
considerably brighter than most of the others. One reason for this was the
acquisition of competent young men for the faculty. Not the least cause of
optimism was the new dean of the college who took over in that office in
August, 1939. John J. Flanagan had his work cut out for him when he
became dean of a small college on the eve of the outbreak in Europe of World
War II, but he was equal to the challenge. Flanagan, a native of Paton,
Iowa, gave up the prospect of a career in law when he entered the Society of
Jesus in 1926. Ten years later he was ordained. After the completion of his
training he was appointed assistant dean of the College of Arts and Sciences
of St. Louis University. After a year of experience he was assigned to Regis
College as dean and registrar. His first major task was to prepare for the visit
of the team representing the North Central Association. This was a time-
consuming operation and Flanagan shared the frustration of all the Jesuits at
Regis when the officials of the association voted against accreditation.

A second major problem tested the abilities of the dean. The future of the
college became even more precarious as the international crisis was developing. Enrollment held up through 1942 but it was seriously endangered as
soon as the Congress of the United States passed the first peacetime conscrip-
tion in the history of the country in 1940. Flanagan planned to meet the
problem by offering the facilities of the school available to the armed forces
for the training of young men for the various branches of the services. Early
in 1942 the president of the college, Kelley, attended a meeting of the
National Conference of College and University Presidents in Baltimore.
When he returned to Denver he announced that Regis College would accel-
erate its program and make it possible for students to finish their college
course in three years and receive their degree before entering military
service.[106] Flanagan had to make the necessary adjustments and plan for
initiating a summer session. In March, 1942, the Navy Department approved
the Regis curriculum for the Navy V-I Program that made it possible for
young men of the ages seventeen to nineteen to enlist in the reserves and to
continue at Regis until the end of the sophomore year.[107] After two years and
seven months of intense activity and planning as dean, Flanagan was
appointed the sixteenth president of Regis College and High School.

[105]Kelley to Maher, R.C.A.
[106]*The Denver Catholic Register.*
[107]Flanagan to Brooks.

Las Vegas College—1878-1888.

Joseph P. Machebeuf, First Bishop of Denver—donated land and building in Morrison.

The College of the Sacred Heart—Morrison, 1884-1888.

Main Hall under construction in Denver in 1887.

The College of the Sacred Heart, Denver, c. 1895.

Main Hall c. 1949.

Main Hall c. 1965.

Salvatore Personè, President of Las Vegas College, 1878-1883; 1884-1888.
President of The College of the Sacred Heart, Denver, 1888-1892.

124

Dominic Pantanella, President of The College of the Sacred Heart, Morrison 1884-1888; Builder of Main Hall in Denver.

Lake east of the Main Building, c. 1890.

Part of Faculty 1899-1900. Standing, Aloysius A. Laur. Back Row, L. to R., John B. Hugh, Francis X. Hoefkens, Alphonse J. Lebeau, Robert F. Spirig, Charles A. McDonnell. Front Row, Augustus Forster, Sebastian A. Mayer, Edward J. Burrows, Edmund S. Behiels, Eugene J. Montell.

Statue of the Sacred Heart donated by parents of J. Brisben Walker in 1890.

Gateway–symbol of seclusion.

Faculty, 1911-1912. Back Row, L. to R., Eugene J. Montell, Aloysius L. Scheid (Layman), Francis D. Stephenson, Edward S. Johnson. Middle Row, Eldridge S. Hyde, Sebastian A. Mayer, John M. Floyd, John B. Hugh, George A. Keith, David J. Guthrie, Charles A. McDonnell. Front Row, Joseph M. Minot, Francis X. Hoefkens, C. Marion Garde, John J. Brown, Armand W. Forsall, John X. Peters (de Pietro).

Front Entrance, c. 1890.

Robert M. Kelley, President, 1920-1926, and 1935-1942.

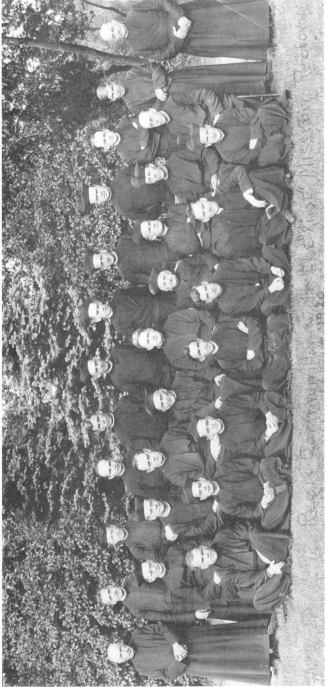

Jesuit Community 1920. Back Row, L. to R., Brother Ben Tovani, Br. Anthony M. Uliano (Julian), Br. Vincent Buehler, Br. Leo Beriault, Mr. Ignatius J. Davlin, Mr. Bernard C. Zimmerman, Mr. Eugene P. Murphy, Mr. Joseph A. Ryan, Rev. William J. Fitzgerald, Rev. Robin S. Shea, Br. William Auberer, Br. Celestine Arechaga. Middle Row, Rev. Francis X. Hoefkens, Rev. Leo N. Krenz, Rev. William F. Robison (Guest), Rev. Dominic Pantanella, Rev. Robert M. Kelley, Rev. Francis X. Gubitosi, Rev. John M. Floyd, Rev. Sebastian A. Mayer, Rev. Armand W. Forstall. Front Row, Mr. Joseph M. McAndrews, Mr. Charles Palacio, Mr. Francis A. Bautsch, Mr. Bart N. Quinn, Mr. Gerald J. Ellard, Mr. Raymond F. Bellock, Mr. John B. Gerst.

North Entrance to Carroll Hall.

Joseph A. Ryan, Professor of Accounting.

Bernard J. Murray, Recruiter and Spiritual Counselor.

Stephen R. Krieger, Mathematics teacher in High School.

Bernard S. Karst, Principal, Dean of Students, Associate Professor of Education.

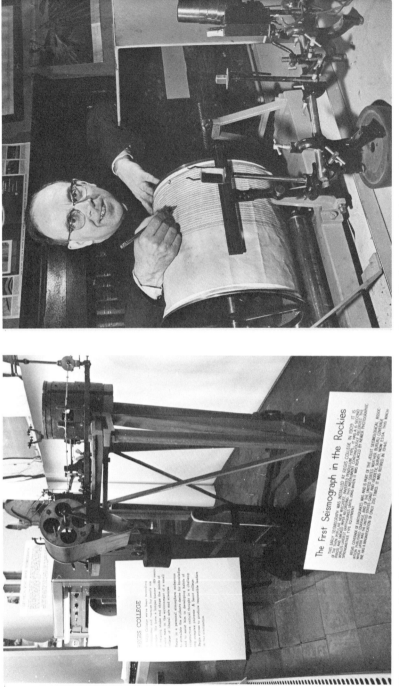

Joseph V. Downey and the new Seismograph.

First Seismograph in Rocky Mountain Region.

Aerial View of the campus c. 1945.

Dedication of new Shrine in memory of Brother Ben Tovani, 1950.

John J. Flanagan, President, 1942-1947.

Raphael C. McCarthy, President, 1947-1953.

Richard F. Ryan, President, 1953-1968.

O'Connell Hall completed in 1957.

Fieldhouse completed in 1960.

Dedication of Fieldhouse. L. to R. John J. Sullivan, Bishop Bernard J. Sullivan, S.J., Stephen L. R. McNichols, Archbishop Urban J. Vehr, Richard F. Ryan.

Student Center, Enlarged in 1963.

DeSmet Hall completed in 1964.

Science Building completed in 1966.

142

L. to R., Frederick T. Daly, S.J., Walter F. Simon, Richard F. Ryan, S.J. Father Daly is holding a citation for excellence in design of the Science Building and Dayton Memorial Library.

Dayton Memorial Library completed in 1966.

143

Louis G. Mattione, President, 1968-1971.

Thomas James Casey, Acting President, 1971-1972.

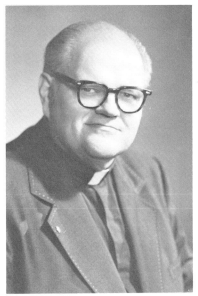

David M. Clarke, President, 1972. . .

144

West Hall completed in 1972.

New Regis High School completed in 1976.

Aerial View of campus, 1964.

Chapter 5

Stabilization and Growth

By the time John Flanagan was installed in the office of president, March 19, 1942, the United States had been at war for some three and one-half months. It had been a period during which the war had gone badly for the American people and was hardly a propitious time for a man forty-one years old to assume the burdens of directing an institution that had enough difficulties without having to face the prospect of a sharp drop in the enrollment of the college because so many young men were being called to the service of their country. The new president could find some hope for the viability of the institution in the fact that the high school was in good condition. Bernard Karst, principal, had received a favorable report from the State Committee of the North Central Association shortly before Flanagan took office.

In spite of the restrictions necessitated by the war the new president and his colleagues planned to have a public reception. Flanagan was fortunate in having Edward A. Conway on the faculty. Conway was a very personable individual with a flair for public relations. He was also a good organizer, and in due time he had the friends of the college working with enthusiasm for the inaugural reception for the sixteenth president of Regis.

Flanagan inherited a faculty that had a number of very competent men. Out of twenty-six members, seven had earned the degree of Doctor of Philosophy and one, Florence J. Mahoney, was a candidate for that degree. Three of those who held the doctorate, Edward A. Conway, Leo C. Brown and Joseph P. Donnelly, were men of great promise. Two scholastics, Robert J. O'Sullivan and Walter J. Ong of the English Department, were to achieve distinction in their chosen field of English. Due to the circumstances of the time, however, these men were not to have the opportunity to exert their influence on many students since the student body in the college was being decimated. The president realized that every effort should be made to balance the loss of students in the college by making every effort to increase enrollment in the high school. He had limited success in this endeavor. From two hundred ninety-seven in 1942 the student body in the high school increased to three hundred sixty-six by 1944.

Flanagan exerted every effort to arouse the interest of the officials of the Armed Services in the facilities of the institution. He elicited the support of the United States Senators from Colorado, Eugene Milliken and Edwin S.

Johnson, in his efforts to secure a government contract. With the assurance of political support, Flanagan's hopes rose. He wrote to Peter A. Brooks, the Provincial in St. Louis, and informed him, "We have been told from reliable political sources that Regis will definitely be given a training unit."[1]

The optimism of the Regis president was based on his assessment of what could be made available to the Armed Services, namely a modern fireproof building with eighty-five private rooms in which two hundred fifty to three hundred men could be accommodated. There was, moreover, adequate classroom space in the same building. The dining facilities in the Main Building were rather optimistically estimated as sufficient to provide for five hundred men.[2]

The high hopes of obtaining a government contract were not realized. The representatives of the Armed Services who evaluated the facilities found them inadequate for their purposes. A disheartened Flanagan reported to Zacheus Maher, the American Assistant to the Superior General of the Order, on January 25, 1943:

> We have been very much disappointed in our efforts to obtain a contract
> with the government for specialized military training. The institution
> has been surveyed four times by different branches of the Armed
> Services, but always we were found to be too small.[3]

Some five months after this discouraging news the gloom was suddenly and unexpectedly dispelled. In the intervening time the University of Denver had been awarded a contract by the government for the training of servicemen. When the details had been worked out, the officials of the university realized that they needed assistance. They negotiated with the owners of El Jebel Masonic Temple, some eight blocks west of Regis College, for the use of their building. It was soon realized that even more facilities would be needed and the officials of the University of Denver proposed that Regis participate in the project in the role of subcontractor. If this proposal was acceptable to the Regis authorities, it was suggested that they undertake the task of educating engineering students for the United States Army. This offer was welcomed by Flanagan and his consultors, especially in view of the declining enrollment in the college. There were only seventy students in 1943 and there was every prospect that the number would dwindle even more as the weeks and months passed.

The Army sent men to evaluate the facilities for the fifth time and a favorable report was submitted. Flanagan wrote to Brooks on June 28, 1943:

---

[1]Flanagan to Brooks, M.P.A.
[2]M.P.A.
[3]Flanagan to Maher, R.C.A.

We had a very encouraging survey of our facilities last Friday by a representative of the Headquarters of the Seventh Service Command. It was in conjunction with the proposed joint program to be sponsored by Regis College and the University of Denver. The Major made favorable comments on our Physics, Chemistry and Biology equipment.[4]

On July 1, 1943, Flanagan met with the members of the Board of Trustees to discuss the forthcoming agreements with the Army and the officials of the University of Denver for a specialized training unit to be quartered in Carroll Hall. Evidently the members of the Board of Trustees were unwilling to approve a completely subordinate role for Regis in this project. They approved the plan, provided certain conditions were met. They specified these conditions:

1) The enterprise was to be understood as a joint program in which the College and the University participated as equals—the Administration, however, was to be in the hands of the University since the University was to have the principal contract.

2) Regis College was to participate in the teaching program to the extent of furnishing at least 25% of the teachers.

3) All publicity about the program was to be submitted to the president of the college for approval before being given to the newspapers or otherwise published.[5]

The summer of 1943 was a hectic one. Some improvements in the facilities of Carroll Hall were mandatory; for example, bathrooms and shower baths were inadequate to take care of some two to three hundred men. The necessary adjustments in Carroll Hall were made in record time, but the work in the Masonic building had not progressed as quickly. That building was not ready when two hundred twenty-five foreign-language students were due to arrive. When they appeared on the scene, Regis offered them temporary quarters. In due time the language students moved into the El Jebel Temple and the engineers took over in Carroll Hall. Everything was in order and classes began on August 9, 1943.[6]

In the meantime the military personnel had moved with expected efficiency and established the necessary chain of command to provide for the training and provisioning of the 4767th Service Command Unit of the ASTP. The unit was under the command of Lieutenant Colonel Willard L. Smith, a veteran officer who had eight years of experience instructing men in the ROTC unit at the University of Virginia.

---

[4]Flanagan to Brooks, M.P.A.
[5]*Trustees' Meetings, 1935-1956*, p. 48.
[6]*The Denver Catholic Register*.

The academic program was under the direction of Dean Clarence Knudson who headed the list of University of Denver faculty members who taught in the Regis classrooms. Members of the Regis faculty who participated in the program were: Conrad Bilgery, John Gibbons, William Stackhouse, Edward Wintergalen, Joseph McCallin, Louis Keenoy, Joseph Downey, Louis Bloomer, and Edward Conway. Bernard J. Murray acted as liaison between the military and the college and served as unofficial chaplain for the unit.

The students were divided into twelve sections. The training was intensive. Twenty-four hours a week were spent in the classroom and laboratory; the same number of hours were given to supervised study. Five hours of military instruction and six of physical training were crowded into the schedule. Somehow they found time for social activities that were graced with the presence of young ladies from Loretto Heights and Colorado Women's College. The soldiers formed a student council and a band. They were even able to field a basketball team wearing the Regis uniform. A show was prepared for broadcasting over radio station KOA. Finally, a group of eager students overcame the objections of Colonel Smith and published a yearbook as a memento of their experiences.[7]

The Army program lasted some seven months, from August 9, 1943, to March 16, 1944. The program seems to have been satisfactory. By March the military authorities changed their overall plans. The invasion of Normandy was only two and one-half months away and it would seem that all available manpower would be needed. The project at Regis was terminated and the soldiers were transferred to Fort Logan, Colorado. The diarist wrote under date of March 16, 1944, "It was announced that 162 of the ASTP students here will leave on next Monday for induction into the Rainbow Division."[8]

The participation in the Army Training Program was a unique experience for the Jesuits and students of Regis College and High School. The main building was crowded because all available space in Carroll Hall was needed by the military. The Jesuits had to be housed and the high school students accommodated; at the time the number of young men in the high school reached three hundred thirty. Somehow everyone survived and the strain did not prove to be too much. A very important result of this whole arrangement was that the financial situation at the institution was greatly improved. The income provided by the government for the room and board of the soldiers

---

[7]The yearbook was published with the title "All Present"; it was dedicated "with appreciation and admiration" to Regis College.

[8]*Diary, Aug. 1943-Oct. 17, 1951,* p. 30.

and the salaries of the teachers paid through the University of Denver were most helpful. Flanagan wrote to Maher in January 1944 that the "arrangement has worked more smoothly than we had anticipated and has been of the greatest financial assistance to the college."[9]

When Flanagan assumed the responsibilities of the office of president he was well aware that he was inheriting an albatross because of the debt. Kelley had refinanced the bonded debt in 1940 and had some success in purchasing a number of the bonds. Flanagan proposed to discontinue football as soon as it was feasible. Consequently, he was in a good position to continue to work toward retiring the debt. Soon after becoming president he wrote to the Provincial (Brooks), "We can let football die a natural death next year."[10] In the meantime, Flanagan made a concerted effort to collect the pledges made to the college during the various fund-raising efforts, especially the Golden Jubilee Fund Campaign. Next, he engaged the services of a collecting agency and in time certain debts owed the college began to be paid. He wrote to Brooks on April 27, 1943, "We have had an account in the hands of a collecting agency for some time. . . our collections in general have been very good. We have almost $20,000 in the bank at the present time."[11]

In retrospect it seems that it must have taken a great deal of courage to launch a fund-raising campaign in the early months of the year 1944. It is true there were signs that the tide of the battle in the war might be reversed, but it was hardly a propitious time to make a concerted effort to go to the people of Denver with a request for money. Friends and alumni, for example Thomas J. Tynan and Edward A. Hanifen, urged the president to organize a group of one hundred fifty men to contact fifteen hundred people in Denver to try to persuade them to purchase a war bond for the college because in doing so they would help the government and Regis. No doubt because of the restrictions caused by the war, the campaign was to be launched in a quiet way "without the customary expense of advertising or public dinners."[12] The campaign was planned to coincide with the fourth war bond drive. Potential donors received a letter dated February 1, 1944, explaining the plan and informing the recipient that he or she would be contacted "in the interest of a project to reduce the debt of Regis College, and to help prepare it for its place in postwar education."[13]

To elicit interest in the project, Flanagan published a progress report that

---

[9]Flanagan to Maher, R.C.A.
[10]Flanagan to Brooks, M.P.A.
[11]Flanagan to Brooks, M.P.A.
[12]R.C.A.
[13]*Ibid.*

was very informative regarding the financial status of the college. The report read in part:

Regis entered the last ten-year period (1934-1944) with an indebtedness of $300,000. Gifts, drives for funds, increased income from larger enrollments, have reduced this indebtedness to $183,000. The remaining indebtedness, however, is still so great that it forces the institution to operate on a margin that is too small. It is also an impediment to higher accreditation for the College Department, since the best accrediting agencies demand that the stability and future of member institutions be not threatened by financial hazards. Fortunately, Regis is rapidly approaching the status demanded by these agencies. A further reduction of $50,000 on the present debt will assure Regis of the requisite security.[14]

The statement included information regarding enrollment, new classrooms, laboratory facilities and the library. Flanagan also spelled out the future needs, specifying the need for a new and larger high school building, a new library and chapel, and the renovation and modernization of the Administration Building.[15]

The goal of the war bond campaign was a rather modest $35,000, and the drive seemed to have been reasonably successful. Some bequests helped to narrow the margin on the debt, and Flanagan was able to write to Maher on September 10, 1944, that the total indebtedness stood at $138,000. In fact the tone of this letter was optimistic. It reports that the first floor of the Administration Building had been completely renovated with the result that the high school had been given respectable quarters for the first time in years. Because of the war the enrollment in the college had dropped to fifty students. The high school enrollment, however, was the best in its history, having reached 379. The recruiters had been able to persuade parents to send their boys to board at Regis; as a consequence Carroll Hall, recently vacated by the army, was completely filled. A final bit of good news was the announcement that the institution had received $10,000 from the estate of Michael J. Burke of Edgewater, Colorado.[16]

Such benefactions encouraged Flanagan to find other means of support. In 1945 he inaugurated an annual bazaar. With the assistance of two veteran Regis Jesuits, Bernard S. Karst and Stephen R. Krieger, he elicited the support of the Denver community for such a venture. Karst and Krieger were well known in Denver; the former had been principal of the high school since 1933, the latter was an excellent, if exacting, teacher of mathematics in

---

[14]*Ibid.*
[15]*Ibid.*
[16]R.C.A.

the same division. They were successful in organizing the various groups such as the Regis High School Mothers' Club, the Regis Guild (made up of relatives of Jesuits from the Denver and surrounding area), the Regis College Parents Association, and Regis alumni and friends. Members of these organizations had sponsored events, for example, card parties, to help the institution. The new plan called on the members to join forces in planning and carrying out one large benefit affair for Regis.[17] The first bazaar was quite successful and the event became an annual affair for almost a decade.

Another possible source of money was the estate of John O'Connell. Since the death of Mr. O'Connell in 1935, the college and St. Thomas Seminary maintained an agent who looked after the property for both institutions. The acreage was a good distance from Denver and the administration of it constituted a problem. Flanagan consulted with authorities of the seminary and they agreed that it would be practical to try to sell the land. Proper authorization was given and some of the acres were sold; both institutions benefitted by the sale.

By 1945 Flanagan had succeeded in reducing the indebtedness of Regis. In ten years the debt was cut from some $300,000 to about $140,000. At this point Flanagan made a bold move; he asked the authorities of the Missouri Province to help Regis wipe out the debt. He was a persuasive man, and succeeded in convincing the Provincial and his consultors to help Regis to refinance the debt through the Province. The Provincial, Joseph P. Zuercher, agreed to help Regis liquidate the debt. An agreement was reached between the Missouri Province Educational Institute and the Regis College Community. One of the more important stipulations between the parties stated:

> The Province will advance $100,000 to Regis College for the purpose of calling outstanding bonds against the College. So far as the records of the College will show, this advance will be considered as an outright gift thereby placing Regis in position to be debt free and thereby improving their position with the North Central Association and also placing them in a better position to make appeals to possible benefactors for positive improvement since it recognized that it is very hard to get money for the purpose of paying debts.[18]

It was with a great deal of satisfaction, to say the least, that Flanagan announced in April, 1945, the complete liquidation of the debt. The story was featured in *The Denver Catholic Register* on April 26, 1945. The *Register* reported:

---

[17]R.C.A.
[18]M.P.A.

The complete removal of the indebtedness of the College is the result chiefly of several large bequests made to the College in the past few years. Outstanding among these was a bequest from the estate of the late John O'Connell of Las Animas. Regis received a cash legacy from this estate and title to a large tract of real estate in Southern Colorado. It was the disposal of this land that supplied the final impetus to the debt-removal drive. In all, the College received a total of more than $80,000 from the O'Connell estate.

Other large bequests were received from the estates of Michael Burke of Edgewater and Julia Clifford of Denver.

A financial drive being conducted by friends of Regis College in the past year netted $25,000. Numerous other large contributions have been made by friends of the Jesuit school who prefer to remain unnamed.[19]

Among the many happy consequences of Flanagan's accomplishments was his ability to make a final payment to the Belgian Jesuits, who needed every dollar they could get to help them to overcome the ravages of the Second World War. The Belgian Province of the Society of Jesus had come to the assistance of Regis a number of times since the relocation of the college in Denver. Dominic Pantanella had borrowed a substantial sum of money in 1887. In 1910 the college borrowed $15,000 at four and one-half percent interest, and in 1925 another $12,000 at five percent.

When the Germans invaded Belgium in May, 1940, the Provincials of Belgium sent the Reverend Alphonse B. Verhoosel to the United States with the charge that he was to take care of the interests of the two Belgian provinces during the duration of the war. Verhoosel took up residence at Georgetown University where, besides looking after the interests of the mission of the Belgian Jesuits, he taught in the School of Foreign Service. The issue of *The Denver Catholic Register* which printed the news of the liquidation of the debt at Regis came to Verhoosel's attention. He wrote to Flanagan on August 27, 1945, and inquired about the amount of money that Regis still owed to the Belgian Jesuits. Verhoosel presented his question rather delicately. After introducing himself and giving references that would help identify him, he wrote:

May I please ask you Rev. Father, in the name of both Belgian Provinces, to be so kind as to give me some information of the amount of

<hr>

[19]*The Denver Catholic Register,* April 25, 1945, p. 1. It should be noted that there was no public acknowledgement of the role of the Missouri Province in the process of the liquidation of the debt. The diarist noted under date of April 22, 1945, "Fr. Rector announced that the generosity of 'anonymous' friends had made the drive so successful that all outstanding Regis Bonds are being called in, paid off, and Regis is out of debt." *Diary, August, 1943-October, 1951,* p. 81.

dollars still to be paid to Belgian [sic] so that we might be able to plan more or less the reconstruction of our Provinces.[20]

After verifying Verhoosel's standing, Flanagan wrote the Belgian Jesuit on September 7, 1945, that the Regis Jesuits owed the Belgians $15,000 plus the interest, due from 1940 to 1945 and amounting to $2,475.00. It must have given the president of Regis a great deal of satisfaction when he was able to write, "We can arrange to pay this amount as you shall request on rather short notice. Please let me know when you will want this money and how it is to be sent."[21]

Finances are not the only concern of a college president, and Flanagan certainly was thinking about the future and planning for the challenges of the postwar period. As early as February 22, 1945, he sought the approval of higher superiors for his project of opening a downtown branch. He wrote to Maher on February 22, 1945, "I believe it is time to ask for permission to establish a Regis College Extension in downtown Denver. The center would be used for late afternoon and evening classes."[22] Approval was given in April, 1945, and Flanagan made the necessary preparations for the downtown school. He leased the second floor of a building on the corner of 17th and California Street. By August 2, 1945, Flanagan wrote to Maher, "We are announcing the opening of the downtown school this week. Classes to begin September 28th."[23]

In the meantime, matters of academic administration were of great concern for the president. In spite of the report of the State Committee of the North Central Association in 1942 that gave Regis High School a good rating, there were problems that needed to be addressed. Bernard S. Karst had directed the affairs of the high school in a highly commendable way since 1933. Karst's health was not good. Moreover, he was not a man to rely on records. He kept a great many things in his head, and because he had a phenomenal memory he was able to give the high school a good administration. However, his administration was not regarded highly by Wilfred M. Mallon, the Prefect of Studies for the Missouri Province, who made an evaluation of the high school in 1944 and reported that it was the poorest high school in the Missouri Province. Flanagan agreed, and wrote to Father Provincial Zuercher on June 6, 1944, "I can well believe this and we just can't go on that way."[24]

Evidently the Provincial had been aware of this matter because in the

---

[20]R.C.A.
[21]*Ibid.*
[22]M.P.A.
[23]*Ibid.*
[24]M.P.A.

assignments published on June 16, 1944, he designated Paul F. Distler to be the principal of Regis High School. Distler had just completed a crash program of training for this task. He was young and methodical and assured the high school of a more orderly administration. Karst was a genuine, warm person. His rather severe countenance was somewhat frightening to many young students, but when they became aware of the warmth of his personality they learned to love him. He was always just in his dealings with the students, and elicited the devotion of their parents. It is probably true that there was need of more orderly procedures and better supervision by the principal.

With the prospect of an end to hostilities brightening after the surrender of the Germans, Flanagan concentrated his efforts on the hope of obtaining a dean for the college. John J. Gibbons, a former member of the New Mexico-Colorado Mission, had taken over as dean when Flanagan become president of the college and high school. Gibbons' administration as dean was mostly a holding action since the college had few students. He was a dedicated Jesuit and gave many years of useful service to Regis until he was transferred to Rockhurst College in Kansas City, Missouri. Flanagan was planning for the post-war period, and begged the Provincial to send him a man who could meet the demands that would be made when the college would get a new start after the war. He wrote to Zuercher on May 14, 1945, ''We really need a Dean very badly and soon. . . would there be any chance to have Father Kessler (if he is to be the man) come to Regis by June 15 or July 1?''[25] EugeneH. Kessler arrived at Regis on July18, 1945, took over as dean of the college and director of the downtown division, and diligently began to get things in order for the academic year. Besides his duties on campus, he had to prepare for the opening of the school in the city where classes were to commence on September 28th. Kessler, like Distler, was a hard-working and methodical man and he got down to business as soon as possible. Due to the foresight and planning of Flanagan, the college was well on its way to being ready for the influx of students that would come when the returning servicemen would be taking advantage of the G.I. Bill.

The college was fortunate in acquiring the services of Thomas E. Kelly, who came to Regis in the summer of 1946. Kelly was appointed executive secretary to the president. A vivacious, persuasive, energetic man, Kelly returned to the scene of his former labors—as a young Jesuit in training he taught at Regis High School from 1933 to 1936. He knew Denver, and lost little time in making contacts and becoming acquainted with the policy of the United States Government regarding the disposition of what had become

---

[25]M.P.A.

surplus supplies. Working with the administrators of war surplus, Kelly acquired desks, chairs, file cabinets and other equipment. In anticipation of an increasing enrollment, the college purchased an army barracks 135 x 60 feet from the authorities at Fort Logan, an army post just south of Denver. It took about two months to prepare for the foundation of the structure; on November 21, 1946, the contractor was ready for the building.[26] When the work was finished, Regis had eight new classrooms and three offices. The building was hardly an architectural masterpiece but it was functional and filled a need at a time when the enrollment in the college was increasing. In 1945, 131 students were enrolled; in 1946, 438; and in 1947, 527. The downtown division accommodated 180 students. The high school showed a decrease, no doubt because there was an increasing demand for rooms in Carroll Hall for returning veterans.

Flanagan took steps to improve the main building, where the first-floor corridors and classrooms were badly in need of renovation. With the funds realized from the bazaars, which became more successful each year, an extensive renovation was undertaken on the lower floor. Another noteworthy step was taken when Flanagan decided to remodel the front entrance of the main building. The original doorway was massive and quite formidable; the remodeling called for the replacement with glass panes and two doors that presented a more inviting welcome to visitors and gave the area a brighter appearance.

Flanagan was aware of the importance of establishing a good public image for the college and the high school. The improved financial status of the corporation justified his hiring a man who could take care of publicity. Flanagan made a good choice in Mr. Ed Williams, who was proficient in this field of activity and a personable man very much at ease in meeting people. He carried the message of the college to the public and began a new era with a concerted effort to make Regis better known in Denver, the State of Colorado, and the surrounding region. Flanagan cooperated in this area of endeavor; he was chosen as chairman of the regional unit of UNESCO in May, 1947, and was also active in promoting better relations with the diocesan clergy in Denver. He wrote to Provincial Peter A. Brooks, "Archbishop has noticed our consistent attendance at functions over which he has presided. He told one of our friends in the Diocesan clergy that we were evidently becoming more 'Diocesan minded.' "[27]

---

[26]*Diary, Aug. 1943-Oct. 17, 1951*, p. 147 and p. 156.

[27]M.P.A. Relations between the Jesuit Community and Urban J. Vehr had become somewhat strained during Kelley's second administration. The reason for this is not clear. Flanagan made a definite effort to restore better relations and was successful. Denver was raised to the status of an Archdiocese in 1941.

The academic year 1946-1947, Flanagan's last as president, was a hectic year. In the first place, a polio epidemic forced the postponement of the opening of the high school. In November, 1946, a national coal strike further disrupted the schedules of both high school and college. The difficulty of operating with coal in short supply was further compounded by a change in the weather that brought heavy snow. To cope with the emergency, the president decided to give the students an extended Thanksgiving holiday. He announced that classes were suspended and would be resumed on December 30. The decision was not popular because it would deprive the students of the New Year holiday with their families and friends. Somehow the crises were weathered and the situation was normalized during the month of January.

Flanagan's term of office was terminated on June 10, 1947. He had served as president for five and one-half years and he had successfully directed the institution through the critical years of the war. He deserves a great deal of credit because he put the college and high school on a firm foundation and left them in an improved position to meet the challenges of the post-war period. His greatest single accomplishment was the liquidation of the debt which had been a burden since 1888. His vision of a successful downtown school was not destined to be fulfilled, but he bequeathed to his successor a college and high school in good financial condition with more than competent facilities ready to meet the needs of those who sought a sound education in the Jesuit tradition.

Flanagan left his successor another legacy that was to bring the college some renown, the decision to concentrate the resources of the institution on building a creditable basketball team. The experience of the school in trying to field a first-class football team had been less than rewarding. In his planning for the postwar years Flanagan decided to use the resources of the college for building an outstanding basketball team. He engaged the services of Larry Lee Varnell as an instructor in English and athletic coach. Varnell had had experience as athletic director at the National Business College in Roanoke before he entered military service. One of his assignments brought him to Colorado, and when the hostilities were ended he learned about the possibility of joining the faculty of Regis College. Varnell had been successful as a coach of basketball, and was able to persuade some of his former players to enroll at the college. Two of the more outstanding athletes, Harvey E. Moore and Robert E. Fisher, provided a good foundation for a representative team. Varnell built well, using all the available talent at hand. His first season was not spectacular; Regis won nine games and lost ten. But the coach was pleased with his team and planned to undertake an ambitious schedule for the 1947-1948 season. The list of opponents included teams representing the universities of San Francisco, Montana, Creighton, Iowa,

DePaul and Marquette. Regis, with a roster that included Bob Fisher, Harvey Moore, Bryce Heffley, Jerry Simon, Tom Waters, Jim Sheehan, Phil Antonelli, Bob Wallace, Jerry Coursey, John Kilpatrick, Bob Burns, and Dick Petry, compiled a record of eighteen victories and five defeats. Success engendered a lively school spirit and elicited the nickname of "The Buzz Boys" for a team that had a bright future. The hopes generated by the success of the 1947-1948 season were realized in a striking way during the next basketball season. With the acquisition of Pete Berney, Varnell had a well-balanced team that won thirty-six games, losing only three. The team won first place in the first annual National Catholic Intercollegiate Tournament held in Denver. In April they had finished second in the tourney under the auspices of the National Association of Intercollegiate Basketball in Kansas City, Missouri, that attracted a field of thirty-two teams from many parts of the country. Bob Fisher was named a member of the first all-tournament team. Three men, Moore, Fisher and Heffley, made the first team of the N.C.I.T. Denver and Colorado responded generously with congratulatory messages and the General Assembly of the State of Colorado passed a resolution of appreciation of the accomplishments of the team in winning national recognition for the state.[28]

Flanagan did not neglect the academic. He recruited some very competent laymen for the faculty. Outstanding among these were: George E. Bechtolt for modern languages; John V. Coyne, business administration; Joseph J. Gonzales, English; Fred R. VanValkenburg, history; Ralph G. Verdieck, chemistry.[29] This group was one of the more significant additions of laymen to the college faculty. Of these five men, two, Gonzales and Verdieck, would remain on the faculty only a few years. The other three were to give many years of dedicated service. Bechtolt was an invaluable asset in the department of modern languages, while VanValkenburg was a tower of strength in the department of history. Coyne has given over thirty years of service in the department of business administration. Over and above his teaching duties he was, in time, appointed director of the Evening Division, and gave the evening program some of its most successful years. He rendered great service to successive deans and served as assistant dean from time to time. Flanagan, of course, did not foresee how valuable these men would prove to be, but they were a credit to his ability to select men who were able to carry on their work in conformity with the Jesuit tradition.

During Flanagan's tenure there was a change in the college newspaper. The difficulties caused by the war had forced the authorities to suspend

---

[28]*The Brown and Gold* and *The Ranger, passim.*
[29]*Catalogue, 1947-1948,* pp. 7-12.

publication of *The Brown and Gold*. After the lapse of a year, it appeared as a magazine designed to keep the alumni in the armed forces informed about the activities taking place at Regis. The editor and business manager of this new venture was Aldo G. Notarianni. After some two years, the school paper once again was published as a newspaper under the guidance of Louis A. Bloomer who was appointed moderator.

After five and one-half years, John Flanagan was appointed executive secretary of the Catholic Hospital Association. Considering the disturbed conditions of the times during his term of office and the difficulties of a small college during the war years, his accomplishments must be considered monumental. He established the institution on a firm financial foundation and prepared it for the challenges of the post-war years. Flanagan was a worthy successor of Marra, Brown and Kelley.

Flanagan had the distinction of having two bishops in his community, Anthony J. Schuler, retired Bishop of El Paso, and Bernard J. Sullivan, retired Bishop of Patna, India. Both of these men had been members of the New Mexico-Colorado Mission. As Jesuits they had the right to choose their place of residence after they retired from their dioceses. Bishop Schuler joined the Regis community in 1942 after twenty-seven years as Bishop of El Paso. Although he belonged to the Province of New Orleans, he preferred to spend his last years at the college he had governed for three years, 1903-1906. Bernard J. Sullivan had been assigned to the Mission of Patna, which he governed as bishop from 1929 until he resigned in 1945. He, too, preferred to return to the field of his early labors and joined the Regis faculty in 1946. He chose to set aside the insignia of a bishop and to assume the duties of an instructor in English, philosophy and religion. The catalogue of the Missouri Province has the interesting entry after his name: "Lecturer in Philosophy and Religion in the College, fourth year of teaching, Spiritual Adviser of the junior and senior students."[30] Bishop Sullivan discovered a second career and proved to be a great asset to the college.

On June 10, 1947, John Flanagan left for his new assignment with the Catholic Hospital Association. His successor, Raphael C. McCarthy, became the seventeenth president of Regis College and High School. McCarthy was no stranger to Regis. He had attended Sacred Heart College before he entered the Society of Jesus on August 14, 1906, as a member of the New Mexico-Colorado Mission. After the initial stages of his Jesuit training, he returned to Denver in 1913 and taught the classics, mathematics and biology for some four years before resuming his studies in preparation for ordination to the priesthood. He was ordained by Archbishop (later Cardinal) John J.

---

[30]C.P.M., 1947, p. 7.

Glennon on June 27, 1920. His superiors, impressed by his capabilities, sent him to London to study for a doctorate in psychology at King's College, University of London. He received his Ph.D. in 1925 and returned to St. Louis University where he joined the faculty with the rank of Associate Professor of Psychology. He filled various positions there until he was appointed president of Marquette University in Milwaukee in 1936; he successfully directed the affairs of that university during the difficult years of the war. In June, 1947, at the age of fifty-eight, he succeeded John Flanagan as president of Regis College and High School.

McCarthy, the first president of the college to hold the doctorate, had a wealth of experience in administration. It was fortunate for him that he inherited an institution that was relatively debt-free and that he did not have the major worry of his predecessors in the office of the president. He was free to plan the necessary expansion of facilities to meet the needs of returning veterans. The high school was prospering. Distler brought more order into the administration. The faculty had some outstanding men. The main problem that proved to be somewhat of a thorn in the principal's side was providing adequate facilities for boarding students. When Carroll Hall was practically empty during the war, the high school boarders moved in. But the end of the hostilities made it possible for many college students to return. An increasing college enrollment forced retrenchment in the number of high school boarding students and Distler began to plan the phasing out of the high school boarders. The principal's office finally acquired secretarial help when Mrs. Joseph Price, a delightful woman, was engaged as secretary. "Mom" Price became an institution; she was to give many years of dedicated service while she lightened the burden of the principal and made it possible for him to give his time to planning improvements in the high school.

McCarthy had to make some immediate decisions regarding the main building. Flanagan had made some necessary improvements on the first floor and had completely altered the main entrance. When it was realized that the porches on the north side of the building were causing a strain on the stone walls and weakening the structure, McCarthy ordered the porches removed. At the same time officials of the Denver Fire Department were taking a dim view of the lack of adequate safety provisions and ordered that another exit be placed on the east end of the building at the second-floor level, with a set of steel stairs allowing for a quicker evacuation in case of necessity. These matters needed immediate attention and were finished in due time.

One of McCarthy's major concerns during the first years of his administration was the matter of arriving at a decision regarding the continuation of the high school. The concern was shared by the Provincial, Zuercher, who wrote to the president on December 31, 1947, ''We would very much like to have a complete study of the High School question at Regis both as regards the boarding scholars and also the further question of continuing the High School at all.''[31] A detailed report was submitted to the authorities in St. Louis in January, 1948. It recommended that boarders were no longer to be accepted and that the high school be discontinued. Accordingly, Zuercher informed McCarthy on February 3, 1948, that he could arrange to take no first-year high school boarders for the next school year. Furthermore, he recommended that no public announcement be made that would lead the people to think that the high school might be closed. This precaution was necessary because such action could not be taken without the approval of the General of the Society of Jesus.[32]

On February 6, 1948, Zuercher wrote to the General in Rome and explained why this action was recommended. The Provincial's overriding concern was for the college; he thought that if the high school were closed, the college would stand a better chance of gaining recognition by the North Central Association. He concluded his letter to the General with the words:

> Since therefore it seems proper and necessary to the Consultors of the Province, to the present Rector and to the former Rector of Regis College, to the Province Prefect of Studies, and to myself, I formally ask Y.P. to permit the closing of Regis High School according to the plan outlined above.[33]

Distler, the principal of the high school, lost little time in sending a letter to the parents of the boarders informing them that boarders would be phased out. As principal, he had been concerned about the difficulties of running a boarding school. He thought that the necessity of having someone on duty around the clock drained the energy of the young Jesuits who had a full schedule of teaching and moderating activities. Consequently, Distler was very much in favor of terminating boarders in the high school.

The advisability of closing the high school entirely remained under consideration through the remaining months of the year 1948. On October 27, 1948, the Provincial met with the board of trustees and discussed the high school question. He said that the reason for considering such action was to help the college in its application for recognition by the North Central Association. He informed the board members that the General in Rome thought that the conclusion to close the high school was a prudent one. The

---

[31]M.P.A.
[32]*Ibid.*
[33]*Ibid.* Note: the initials Y.P. stand for Your Paternity.

Provincial then suggested that the president contact the Archbishop and the Pastors of the parishes from which a goodly number of students came and test their reaction.[34]

McCarthy obtained an appointment with Urban J. Vehr, Archbishop of Denver. The Archbishop informed the president that he did not think that he could provide enough facilities to take care of the growing Catholic population in the city and that the closing of Regis High School would be a calamity since the Jesuits took care of a definite clientele in the city. The Archbishop asked for help in solving the educational problem.[35] Consequently, no definite action was taken and Regis High School got a new lease on life.

When McCarthy became president he soon realized that it was of the utmost importance to provide more facilities. The high school and college were experiencing an increase in enrollment. It is true that there was a slight decrease after the peak year for the college in 1947 when 527 students were enrolled. The high school was showing a decrease from 366 in 1944 to 341 in 1947. Although the institution was relatively debt-free, McCarthy knew that he could not build without again going into debt, and it was hardly possible that he would receive approval for such a move. In such circumstances his fertile brain dreamed up some chimerical alternatives. In the Spring of 1948 an old landmark in downtown Denver, the Public Market building was being dismantled. McCarthy had made the acquaintance of Mr. Kollie Barnett, who supervised the dismantling of the building. Barnett offered the college any materials they would choose to select. McCarthy and his consultors agreed to take sixteen trusses of laminated wood for which Barnett asked only $5,000.[36] He also agreed that if Regis could not use the material he would remove it without charge.

McCarthy was enthusiastic and he wrote to Father Provincial Zuercher on April 4, 1948, explaining that if this material was acquired it would:

> . . . give Regis a basketball court seating over 4,000, an auditorium 80
> x 125 with a twenty-five foot ceiling and behind that two floors of 7500
> square feet apiece, the bottom floor for recreation facilities, the upper
> for classrooms, dormitory or some other useful purpose.[37]

Unfortunately, union officials intervened and prevented the material from being hauled across town. McCarthy was not easily disheartened. Within six months he was talking about acquiring some buildings from Fort Logan. He discussed with his consultors the possibility of obtaining a two-story wooden building that could serve as a college dormitory. He could get this for

---

[34]*Minutes of Consultors Meetings, 1944-1963*, pp. 9-10.

[35]*Op. cit.*, p. 12.

[36]*Op. cit.*, p. 8.

[37]McCarthy to Zuercher, M.P.A.

$3,600. He also saw the possibility of acquiring a one-story building that could serve as a clubroom or recreation center for the college students.[38] There is no further information about this matter and we must conclude that this plan was abandoned.

McCarthy was somewhat more successful in his efforts to get a chapel that could serve the needs of both the high school and the college. The existing chapels were far from adequate for the number of students attending each division. The high school had outgrown the chapel on the third floor on the west side of the main building; the small chapel on the lower floor of Carroll Hall could accommodate only some twenty-four college students. At a meeting with his consultors on October 27, 1948, McCarthy suggested that they consider the possibility of acquiring a Quonset or Butler prefabricated building to be used as a chapel. At a meeting on November 25, 1948, Francis X. Hoefkens moved that the president should proceed with the building of a chapel.[39] The president must have been confident of the approval of his superiors, since ground was broken four days later. McCarthy decided to put up a Butler building with a vestibule of brick. The capacity was somewhat optimistically estimated at 550. The pews were donated by various individuals, mostly members of the Regis Retreat League. The carpeting was donated by a Mr. Bernard Lynch of the Retreat League, the communion rail by Mr. and Mrs. J. Phelan. The total cost of the building was $28,000 plus $5,000 for the furnishings; the first figure was later revised upward to $29,360. The profit realized at the bazaars, some $17,500, was used to pay for the building. The chapel was duly dedicated by Archbishop Urban J. Vehr on April 25, 1949, and served a pressing need for many years until it was gradually taken over by the drama departments of the college and high school in the early seventies.

The next item on McCarthy's agenda was his determination to construct a classroom building. With this and other projects in mind, the president initiated a quiet drive for funds. Accustomed as he was to a generous response for such projects while he was president of Marquette University, McCarthy had a rude awakening. The response from the Denver community was less than enthusiastic. He wrote to Father Provincial Zuercher on July 4, 1948, "I never saw a place where there is such lack of enthusiasm, and even of interest, as this. We have tried all this last year to build up alumni spirit and our efforts have been practically sterile. I am told that this is the story over a long stretch of years."[40] Two years later he reiterated this impression

---

[38]*Minutes of Consultors Meetings, 1944-1963*, p. 14.
[39]*Op. cit.*, p. 10 and p. 11.
[40]McCarthy to Zuercher, M.P.A.

when he wrote, "This is a fierce place to raise coin."[41]

In spite of the setbacks, McCarthy was not easily discouraged. In May 1950, he prepared for a major drive. His goal was $500,000. The objective was to raise money for a classroom building. He elicited the support of Archbishop Vehr, who gave $1,000 to the drive and sent his regrets that he could not be present at the kick-off ceremony. The drive was somewhat more successful than previous ones but fell far short of the goal. Some $215,600 was realized, and work was begun on the construction of a classroom building. The fate of the drive might have been influenced by the fact that the United States was involved in the Korean War that began in June 1950. In spite of many problems, such as the difficulty of obtaining steel, work progressed on the structure from October, 1950, until the students moved in for classes on October 26, 1951. The usual discussions were held to decide on a name for the third major building erected since 1887. Out of the discussions there surfaced two names, "Loyola Hall" and "Assumption Hall"; the consultors chose the former designation.[42] The college had a building with twelve classrooms and four offices. After considerable discussion McCarthy decided to use the southeast wing for the college library. He had hoped to make it a chemistry laboratory but found that the cost was prohibitive. DeSmet Hall—the barracks building—was remodeled and converted from a classroom building into a recreation hall with a music room and offices set aside for the use of the staff of *The Brown and Gold.*

The retirement of the debt and realization of a much-needed classroom building cleared the way for yet another bid for recognition by the North Central Association. Flanagan had hoped to make this move soon after the debt had been paid off. The authorities of the North Central, however, had suspended any consideration of accrediting schools for the duration of the war and for some time thereafter until things had settled down and there was a return to normalcy. With the prospect of having a new classroom building ready by the first semester of the academic year of 1951-1952, McCarthy began serious preparations to apply to the North Central for accreditation. It was fortunate for him and the college that Flanagan had the foresight to obtain the services of Wilfred M. Mallon, Province Prefect of Studies, who had experience as an examiner for the North Central Association. As early as March 13, 1946, Flanagan had written to the Provincial, Zuercher, "Father Mallon is giving us some valuable help in the work of reorganization to the college."[43] Mallon undertook a study of the college in 1947-1948 and again

---

[41]M.P.A.

[42]*Minutes of the Consultors' Meetings, 1944-1963,* p. 25. Note: it should be remembered that the Dogma of the Assumption was defined in 1950.

[43]Flanagan to Zuercher, M.P.A.

for a week in 1949-1950, concluding with a review that took ten days in 1950-1951. During this last period he gave invaluable help to the members of the various committees that were preparing a self-evaluation in support of the application for accreditation by the North Central Association.

The college was indeed fortunate in having the assistance of Mallon who was very knowledgeable about the procedures of the association. The self-evaluation was thorough in covering every facet of the operations of the school, and it facilitated the work of the examiners, Donald M. Mackenzie, dean of Blackburn College, Carlinville, Illinois, and Rev. Martin E. Schirber, O.S.B., dean of St. John's University, Collegeville, Minnesota, who visted the college in February, 1952. The examiners reported to the board of review of the Commission on Colleges and Universities that the school was average in most areas, but above average in the quality of the advanced education which it offered. In support of this conclusion they pointed out that two students in the department of accounting placed first and second in the nationwide tests of the American Institute of Accountants. Furthermore, they called attention to the fact that graduates with chemistry majors had been placed in graduate and professional schools and that a significant number had qualified for fellowships, and that in two years chemistry students had ranked well above average on the American Chemical Society Quantitative Chemistry test and the American Chemical Society Organic Chemistry test. The library was rated as entirely adequate with a record well above average in expenditures for library materials.

The examiners were not blind to weaknesses and frankly enumerated them. The more obvious weak points were: the lack of a written constitution for faculty organization, no program for fine arts, failure to provide a well-planned program of academic counseling, and the need for an adequate health service.[44]

Once the preliminaries were over, the officials of the North Central Association acted on the application for accreditation on April 2, 1952, and gave a favorable decision. After thirty-one years of frustration the college was in a position to inform its students that their credits would be recognized by colleges and universities across the land. Much work had gone into the effort to present the college's case to the association. The success in gaining accreditation was due in great part to the special efforts of five men who worked indefatigably to attain that long desired goal: John J. Flanagan, Joseph A. Ryan, dean Louis G. Mattione, Wilfred M. Mallon, and Raphael C. McCarthy. The latter's relief is evident in the telegram sent to Provincial

---

[44]A copy of the report is kept in the office of the dean.

Daniel H. Conway with the laconic message, "Regis admitted to North Central April, 1952."[45]

The eleven years from Kelley to McCarthy were important for the development of the college and high school, and Regis emerged from them in good condition to meet the challenges of the fifties and sixties. The beginning of the new phase in the development of the institution witnessed the end of an era in the loss of two stalwart men of the former New Mexico-Colorado Mission who had given much over the years. On June 15, 1949, Francis X. Hoefkens died; he had joined the mission in 1892 when he left his native Belgium. He followed the regular course of training for a Jesuit in the Midwest, making his novitiate and juniorate at Florissant and studying philosophy at St. Louis University. He then spent four years at Sacred Heart College, Denver, where he was initiated into the procedures of the office of treasurer as an assistant to Father Dominic Pantanella. In 1902 he returned to St. Louis to study theology in preparation for his ordination to the priesthood. He returned as a priest to Denver, where he was destined to spend the rest of his life with the exception of the one year which he spent making his tertianship in Cleveland. After his return to Denver, he resumed his duties as assistant treasurer until he relieved the aging Pantanella of his duties in 1918.

Hoefkens was a kind man and a dedicated Jesuit. No one knows with certainty how many students he helped in his quiet, paternal way as he performed his duties as treasurer of the institution. He never lost his interest in athletics and was a familiar presence at all the games played on the campus until declining health forced him to restrict his movements. It is regrettable that he did not leave a summary history of the finances of the institution. After a brief and final illness, he died on June 15, 1949.

A year and one-half later, November 14, 1950, another veteran of the mission, Benjamin Tovani, was taken in death. Known affectionately as "Brother Ben," Tovani came to Colorado in 1885. He made his novitiate at Morrison. As a lay brother he had many tasks to perform, such as cook, tailor, and infirmarian. His performance in the latter office was the most remembered by the many boarding students whom he treated, not always in a professional manner. Much of his time over the years was given to his labor of love, the building of his shrine. Motivated by an ardent devotion to the Blessed Virgin Mary, Brother Ben built a Lourdes shrine and adorned it with whatever material he could collect, including broken glass and bottle caps. In the course of the years he added other shrines dedicated to his favorite saints and sequestrated them in a labyrinthine maze amidst trees and bushes. Visitors from many parts of Denver came to pray and admire the ingenuity of

---

[45]M.P.A.

Brother Ben's handiwork. Time exacted its price on the shrines and on the builder, and Brother Ben witnessed during his last days the demolition of his life's work. McCarthy called upon the Rev. James Hannon, whose hobby was the building of simple but beautiful shrines, to erect one near the spot of the largest of the old ones; it stands there today as a memorial to the work, life, and devotion of Benjamin Tovani.

During the postwar period there were some notable changes in personnel. Thomas K. McKenney replaced Distler as principal of the high school. His relaxed style was a great contrast to his predecessor's intensity, but he was transferred after two years in the office. McKenney was followed by James R. Eatough, under whose regime the high school was to prosper.

There were some significant changes in the college. A new dean, Louis G. Mattione, directed the faculty through the self-evaluation that was a necessary preliminary to the effort to gain accreditation by the North Central Association. The Chemistry Department was significantly strengthened when Francis J. Ozog and George M. Tipton, both with doctorates, joined the faculty. These men gave invaluable service in the building of a premedical program that was to establish an enviable record in preparing students for medical schools. The History Department was enhanced by the acquisition of William B. Faherty, a successful author who had recently finished his studies for the doctorate. The Sociology Department was strengthened when Lucius F. Cervantes, Ph.D., joined the faculty.

The president of a Jesuit institution has many duties other than the academic. He is the superior of the Jesuit community and is responsible for the maintenance of the physical plant as well as the appearance of the campus. Time was taking its toll on the main building and engineers advised the removal of the cupola that crowned the building. McCarthy ordered it removed, an order that resulted in removing the strain on the walls and depriving North Denver of a very familiar landmark. Other decisions had to be made, such as terminating sporadic attempts to farm some of the land. Through the years, the college had engaged in the farming business, raising crops such as corn and alfalfa. Father B. J. Murray has been quoted as saying that some of the best alfalfa in North Denver was raised on the land now occupied by the Student Center. Father Joseph A. Ryan had been engaged in the project of raising rabbits and ducks to help supplement the supply of meat for the dining rooms during the depression. Brother John P. Stanley was quite successful in raising chickens. Pigs also were kept. McCarthy gradually put an end to these activities. There is something incongruous about a college president meeting with his consultors and discussing the momentous question dealing with a decision to dispose of pigs. On February 7, 1949, the consultors considered this matter and the minutes record, ''It was moved by

Father Heavey, seconded by Father Mattione, and agreed to by all that we should sell all of them just as soon as they are ready for market and keep no more pigs."[46]

It is a tribute to McCarthy's foresight that he persuaded the Provincial to assign Brother A. Albert Knoll to the Regis community. Knoll was no amateur gardener. Before he entered the Society of Jesus, he had taken courses in horticulture and floriculture at the Missouri Botanical Gardens (Shaw's Gardens) in St. Louis. He earned a diploma and went into business on his own. A few years later he decided to become a lay brother in the Society of Jesus. During his novitiate he had charge of the grounds of the seminary in Florrisant. This background and experience fitted him perfectly for the work that McCarthy had in mind for him. Without modern equipment, Knoll undertook the task of making the Regis campus one of the most attractive in the Rocky Mountain region. Before his arrival the groundskeeper had to depend on horses, ploughs, and rakes to get his work accomplished. McCarthy changed this when he acquired a tractor, the first step in the acquisition of the equipment that would make the attainment of Knoll's goal possible.

One of the projects that needed attention was the removal of the trees that lined the road leading from 50th Avenue to the Main Building and provided an impressive entrance to the college grounds. Unfortunately the trees were dying. Because the Denver Tramway Company had replaced its old streetcars with trolleybusses and destroyed the conduit that brought water to the campus from an irrigation ditch, the trees could not survive. In spite of the objections of many they had to be cut down. The removal of the trees opened up a vista that provided a challenge for a landscape gardener. Knoll accepted the challenge, but it would take some years before his dream would become a reality. He acquired a detailed knowledge of the campus which made it possible for him to attain his goal through an opportunity provided when McCarthy's successor undertook a major building program.

A college cannot exist without students. After the war there was a significant change in the composition of the student body. Before the war the highest number of students registered was 281. Within two years after the end of hostilities 527 students chose to enroll at Regis College. It is difficult to assess the spirit of a given student body. The prewar students manifested a lively school spirit, loyalty, and a great respect for their teachers. These qualities remained even though there was a sharp increase in numbers. Some former students returned after the war, while a significant number of veterans who had been stationed in the Denver area came to Regis to resume

---

[46]*Minutes of Consultors' Meetings, 1944-1963*, p. 12.

their studies. There was a good balance between those who had left the armed services and the younger men who came from high schools. The boarders adjusted themselves to rather cramped living conditions. Army surplus provided the college with double-decker bunks so that two students could be placed in each of the small rooms in Carroll Hall. Regis was fortunate in having Bernard S. Karst, the former principal of the high school, in charge of the hall. Father Karst had an uncanny ability to size people up and he was seldom wrong in his judgment about a man's character. He was an ideal man to preside over the transition. Stern of visage, kind of heart, he understood young men and their problems. He provided the right amount of flexibility without sacrificing essentials; consequently, the students had few complaints.

During the early postwar period a lively school spirit developed and it was sustained by the enthusiasm generated by a successful basketball team. Old organizations were revitalized and new ones formed. There was one club that did not survive the war and that was the MACE and MITRE Club which had inspired some excellent men devoted to the furtherance of Catholic Action. Traditional organizations such as the Sodality of the Immaculate Conception, the Student Council, the Choral and Dramatic Clubs and Delta Sigma, continued to attract members. A new spirit was manifested in organizations such as the Chemistry Club (Rho Chi Sigma), Mathematics, Biology, International Relations, the Aquinas Academy, the Nebraska and Milwaukee Clubs, a Ski Club, a Veterans' Club, and the Joint Committee for Student Action.

During this period there was a definite break with the parochialism of the past. A group of enthusiastic students applied for affiliation with the Alpha Delta Gamma fraternity, the only national Catholic social fraternity in Catholic colleges devoted to increasing student spirit and promoting activities, while aiding existing student organizations in carrying out their programs.[47] The charter members of the Iota Chapter were Bob Druding, Jerry Coursey, John V. Crowe, Mike McGreevy, Con Curran, Bob Gebken, Gene (Dennis) Daly, George Schorie, John Borgerding, Chuck Sillstrop and Andy Martelon. Three of the charter members, Bill Reedy, Don Powers, and Joe Stengele, transferred to Notre Dame soon after the formation of the chapter. It is not without significance that Bernard S. Karst was the moderator of the fraternity. ADG was destined to have a stormy career and did not survive the opposition that it generated.

Other evidences of a revitalized enthusiasm were found in the decision to resume publication of the annual, and in the inauguration in 1946 of the

---

[47]*The Ranger,* 1950, p. 72.

Coronation Ball, destined to become the highlight of the social activities. More attention was given to student involvement in government. Under the direction of John J. Quirk, dean of men, the Student Council became more active. In 1948 the council sent Jack O'Brien, Bill Diss, Phil Antonelli and Frank DeLorenzo as delegates to a constitutional convention of the Rocky Mountain Region of the National Students' Association that met at the University of Colorado in Boulder. [48]

The evening school remained viable during McCarthy's regime. In fact enrollment increased from 131 in 1946 to 322 in 1952, and the president was forced to reassess the future of the evening school. His problem was complicated when the owners of the building raised the rent. Under the circumstances, McCarthy decided to transfer the whole operation to the Regis campus. The evening school had had reasonable success in spite of the fact that it had been treated somewhat like an unwanted stepchild. It was technically under the direction of the dean of the college, but the dean was a busy man trying to cope with a rapidly expanding student body. Various directors were appointed to work under the dean but the turnover in this department was great and it was impossible to develop a consistent policy. One of the principal reasons for the survival of the evening school was the dedicated work of Joseph A. Ryan, who kept a sharp eye on the accounting and business administration programs. These were the most popular courses offered because Ryan recruited good teachers for them. An example of Joe Ryan's interest in his students is found in the fact that he established a Beta Chapter of the campus organization of Delta Sigma. The new chapter admitted only women students who had successfully completed one semester in a commercial course. Father Ryan had built up his department over the years since the late twenties so that it had become the envy of most of the other departments of the college. Ryan's reputation for turning out excellent graduates was recognized by the American Institute of Accountants when the officers of the organization certified him as a professional examiner. [49]

An increasing enrollment in the high school and college made it necessary to expand the staff in the various offices. Traditional caution regarding the presence of women in secretarial positions was overcome and more women were employed. Marie Schrempf, Dolores Mueller, and Lucille Gargaro joined the veterans, Alice O'Connor, Mary Peck, and Adelaide Price. Most of the more recent additions to the staff did not remain very long; they found husbands and became housewives or found some other employment. Lucille Gargaro alternated as secretary between the offices of the dean and the

---

[48]BG, vol. XXXII, no. 2, May 7, 1948, p. 1.
[49]BG, vol. XXXIII, no. 6, Jan. 14, 1949, p. 1.

president. These valiant women served Regis well over the years.

It took some time to modernize the telephone service. Father John Brown hesitated to expand this means of communication but eventually other telephones had to be obtained. At long last, in 1932 a switchboard was installed. Mrs. Sophia Clair was engaged as operator of the system. Mrs. Clair was cheerful and conscientious in the performance of her duties. She was patient but persistent in her efforts to transmit messages to the Jesuits who were generally busy about many things. The paging system was less than perfect, but she saw to it that messages were delivered. In 1952, Mrs. Clair celebrated the twentieth anniversary of her service to the high school and college.

Another individual who served the institution well over many years was Oreste Graiff. ''Rusty'' could repair anything from a broken light switch to a burst water main. Few could match his knowledge of the location of pipelines and electrical wires. He was indispensable to an institution that had to operate on such a limited budget, and few realized how much money he saved for the school by his ability to repair or replace broken items or advise the professionals when it was necessary to call on them.

Finances remained a big worry for McCarthy. It is true that he inherited an operation that was practically debt-free. But essential needs had to be provided for and sources of income discovered. Jesuit presidents of colleges felt obliged to keep tuition charges down to a minimum but they found it necessary to review the policy from time to time. In 1950, McCarthy commissioned Joseph V. Downey of the department of physics to conduct a study of the tuition charges in other Catholic colleges that were about the same size as Regis. Downey discovered that the college's tuition charge of $135.00 per semester was almost the lowest among more than thirty Catholic colleges in the United States. The report was presented to the members of the board of trustees on June 5, 1950. After due consideration, the board decided to change from the flat sum per semester and to charge $10.00 per semester hour. It was decided further to increase laboratory fees from $5.00 per semester in science courses to an annual rate of $15.00 for chemistry, $12.00 for physics and the same for biology.[50] Two years later the trustees considered raising the tuition from $10.00 to $11.00 per semester hour; this time the increase was rejected by a vote of three to two.[51]

Jesuits have always found friends who, although unable to help by making substantial monetary donations, have been willing to give helpful advice in matters of business and fiscal responsibility. McCarthy became acquainted

---

[50]*Trustees' Meetings 1935-1958*, p. 85.
[51]*Op. cit.*, p. 100.

with two businessmen, Emmett J. Dignan, a banker, and Martin T. Griffith, an automobile distributor. Both men were knowledgeable and very willing to promote the interests of the school. They recommended that the president propose to the members of the board of trustees that they establish a tax-free corporation called the Regis Endowment Fund which would be administered by laymen who would be trustees of the fund. The reasoning behind this suggestion was the fact that businessmen in Denver had told Dignan and Griffith that they did not like to contribute to Regis because "the Jesuits don't know how to handle money."[52] The members of the board thought that there might be some difficulty because of Jesuit rules and regulations. The matter was submitted to Rev. Adam Ellis, an expert on Canon Law, who suggested some changes in the wording of the document that would allow for the dissolution of the corporation if the process of state law were followed or if a majority vote of the board of trustees of Regis College should so decide. Otherwise, according to Ellis, the constitution for the proposed corporation presented no difficulty.[53] McCarthy appreciated the interest of Dignan and Griffith and publicly acknowledged their contributions by conferring the honorary degree of Doctor of Laws on each of the two men at the commencement exercises in 1953. Incidentally, these were the only honorary degrees, save one, that McCarthy conferred during his term of office.[54]

After six years, Raphael C. McCarthy was ready to make way for a younger man. He left the college and high school in good condition. The college was healthy and the high school's reputation as one of the better Catholic secondary schools in the Rocky Mountain region was beyond question. It had not been difficult to maintain high standards in the high school even though there was a frequent turnover in the personnel of the faculty. Regis was fortunate in that a goodly number of very capable scholastics were assigned to the high school faculty. Continuity was somehow preserved, even though there were few priests who remained on the faculty for a long time. Some few did, for example, Theodore J. Schulte who was a tower of strength, and Stephen R. Krieger, who became a legend in the school and the city of Denver. The soft-spoken and always kind John F. Bergin spent many years at Regis. The two brothers, Francis P. and Louis T. Keenoy, gave many years of service. Others who strengthened the high school faculty were Michael L. Hindelang, Hugo J. Gerleman, Joseph W. Poeckes, John F. Lyons, and Aloysius S. Hahn. Father Hahn, besides being an excellent teacher of Latin, was a champion on the makeshift handball

---

[52]*Minutes of Consultors' Meetings, 1944-1963,* p. 29.

[53]*Trustees' Meetings, 1935-1956,* p. 103.

[54]In 1948 Regis granted an honorary degree to the Most Reverend Hubert Newell, an alumnus of the college, who had been named Bishop of Cheyenne.

court, and many students learned to respect his ability. The scholastics could expect to remain at Regis for only three years, but traditions were so solidly established that continuity was assured. The tradition of excellence in forensic activities was perpetuated and the students of Regis High School performed well in the numerous speech meets held in the region. C. H. Kellogg built an athletic dynasty that kept Regis in the headlines of the sports pages of the daily papers. Regis High School kept its accreditation with the North Central Association and few would question that it fulfilled the requirements of a solid secondary school in the Jesuit tradition.

Chapter 6

Expansion
and Modernization

Richard F. Ryan became the eighteenth president of Regis College and High School on July 1, 1953. A mature man of forty-one, he inaugurated a new era in the history of the school. He held a bachelor's degree from the University of Wisconsin, Madison, and a master's degree from St. Louis University. After he finished his course of training as a Jesuit he was appointed assistant dean of the school of arts and sciences, St. Louis University. Three years later he was designated successor to McCarthy as president of Regis.

The new president was more fortunate than most of his predecessors since he did not inherit a burdensome debt. Moreover, McCarthy had built a chapel and a classroom building without noticeably increasing the school's liabilities and bequeathed a college to his successor that had finally won accreditation from the North Central Association, a recognition that the high school had enjoyed since 1921.

There were, however, some matters that needed immediate attention. For example, there was a pressing need to replace the original water pipeline from the corner of 50th and Lowell to the main building. Orestes Graiff, the faithful maintenance man, assured the trustees that the line was probably as old as the building and he was certain that it had not been replaced during his thirty-two years as handyman.[1] A second project that had to be completed was the remodeling of the second floor in the east wing of Carroll Hall, converting classrooms into living quarters for college boarders. Ryan was not happy about this undertaking because the cost was much higher than McCarthy had anticipated, but he realized that the alterations were necessary because the number of boarders was increasing each year.[2]

As Ryan familiarized himself with his assets and needs, he decided to take his fellow Jesuits into his confidence, giving periodic reports on the financial condition of the institution and briefing the members of the community on his plans for the future. This was a welcome departure from the practices of previous presidents and the informative talks were well received. It became clear from these reports that Ryan had three major objectives on his list of

---

[1]*Minutes of Board of Trustees,* 1935-1956, p. 107.
[2]Ryan to Conway, M.P.A.

priorities: a building program for the college, the acquisition of a new location for the high school, preferably in another part of the city, and the improvement of the public image of Regis in the Denver community.

Since Ryan inaugurated a new era in the development of Regis, it will be more convenient to record the achievements of his administration in a topical rather than in a chronological order. The president realized that there should be long-range planning if a building program was to be implemented. To achieve this end he appointed Fr. Frederick T. Daly chairman of a campus development committee and requested Frs. Christian L. Bonnet and William H. Steiner, and Mr. John V. Coyne to assist him. Ryan asked David Hoene, recently appointed assistant to the president, to serve as secretary for the committee. To facilitate their work, Ryan engaged Emmett Meehan to conduct a survey of the property and make a plat of the grounds.

In the meantime the president investigated the possibility of obtaining a loan from the Housing and Home Finance Administration while he sought the necessary approval from the Jesuit authorities in St. Louis and Rome. The latter overcame their proverbial slowness; Vice-Provincial Louis J. Hanlon sent his request, dated October 19, 1955, to the general and received a letter of approval dated October 27 from Vicar-General of the Society of Jesus.[3]

Daly was an excellent troubleshooter. He efficiently supervised all the necessary preparations and kept a sharp eye on every phase of the building program. Work began on the dormitory in October, 1956, and on the center in April, 1957. The dormitory was ready for occupancy in 1957. It was fitting that the residence hall should be named O'Connell to honor the man who had been the most generous single benefactor up to that time.

The center proved to be a special boon since the kitchen facilities in the main building had been overtaxed for some time. It was now possible to serve meals to some 350 students in rather pleasant surroundings, a far cry from the crowded conditions in the dining hall in the main building. Moreover, the center included a bookstore, a faculty dining room, a game room, meeting rooms, an office for the manager, and storage rooms. Finally, there was a well-appointed lounge which the president could use for the entertainment of important guests and potential benefactors. The completion of the two buildings was an auspicious beginning to the most ambitious construction program envisioned for the college since Kelley's dream of a campus filled with Gothic structures.

While work progressed on the two buildings, Ryan had been busy plan-

---

[3]M.P.A.

ning his next project, the building of a fieldhouse. The decision to proceed with this undertaking was not an easy one to make. Influential members of the faculty hoped that a science building would be next on the agenda. The members of the science division had established an enviable record of preparing premedical and predental students for acceptance by the professional schools. Although the facilities of the science departments were far from inadequate, more modern equipment would help the science teachers to enhance the reputation of the college. On the other hand the school was still riding high on the accomplishments of the basketabll team. Everyone was aware that the athletic facilities were inadequate. The old gym was shared by the college and high school teams and inevitable tensions developed. Moreover, it was impossible to provide sufficient space for spectators in the old gym and it was necessary to rent facilities that were available in the city, for example, the Auditorium Annex. Paying rent for such facilities and meeting the obligations of hosting noteworthy teams on a "home" floor required an outlay of money that could be balanced only if large crowds of people would pay to watch the games; these crowds had not materialized. It is not surprising that the members of the board of trustees, taking all these factors into consideration, decided that a fieldhouse was the more pressing necessity. The minutes of the meeting of the board for September 20, 1958, are concise beyond belief; they read: "Fieldhouse before Science Building. All favor immediate inception."[4]

Once the decision was made to build a fieldhouse, Ryan had to find the means to finance the project. He learned that a loan from the government was not forthcoming. There was some money on hand because in December, 1955, Regis had received a gift of $232,000 from the Ford Foundation.[5] Ryan proposed to use $40,000 of this money, supplemented by $25,000 from savings accounts, $60,000 from annual giving, $20,000 from future annual giving, and $35,000 from unrestricted securities, to get the project under way.[6] He realized that he would need canonical approval to borrow the rest of the necessary money. He was so confident of his ability to liquidate the debt in due time that the authorities approved his request to borrow from $250,000 to $300,000.[7]

After all the preliminaries were taken care of, ground was broken on April 27, 1959. Within a year construction was finished and the building was dedicated on May 2, 1960. It proved to be an excellent addition which

---

[4]*Trustees' Meetings, March 1957-September 1963*, p. 4.
[5]*Diary, Oct. 1951 to July 1, 1961*, p. 117.
[6]*Ibid.*
[7]Ryan to Fisher, M.P.A.

included a gymnasium with a seating capacity of 2200, a swimming pool, a lecture hall popularly referred to as "Fieldhouse Five," four classrooms, an office, and the conveniences one would expect in such a building. The fieldhouse provided facilities that had been needed for a long time. The basketball team finally had a home court far superior to that in the old gym and the swim team was qualified to host intercollegiate meets. Moreover, there was adequate space for baccalaureate services and commencement exercises. It would no longer be necessary to rent buildings in the city for these events.

Ryan was determined to liquidate the debt that had been contracted to make this building possible. Since coming to Regis he had won the confidence of a few bankers and through judicious management of his finances he was confident that he could pay off the loan in two years.[8] He did so well that he was able to report to the Provincial, under date of November 14, 1960, "We have been able to whittle down the debt on the Fieldhouse to $68,000, and will have that paid off next year."[9]

Ryan's success was due in part to the fact that he had resources that his predecessors had not enjoyed: students were paying more for their education. The Trustees had finally abandoned the caution that governed their decisions regarding increases in tuition. When Ryan came to Regis, students paid $10 for a credit hour, $220 for board, and $50 per semester for room. If a student preferred a private room he paid $87.50.[10] Gradual increases had been approved in the years 1953-1959. In 1960 tuition was raised to $300 per semester for those who carried twelve to eighteen hours; a student taking fewer than twelve or more than eighteen hours was charged $17.50 per semester hour. The charge for board and room was increased to $400 for students wishing a private room; otherwise the charge was $375. The president was successful, to a degree, in formulating policies that improved the collection of monies due the college. With more money and more students, 775 full-time in September 1960, Ryan had considerably more money than his predecessors. Incidentally, the operations of the business office had expanded so much that more space was needed for the staff. Consequently, a two-story cinder block addition was built on the north side of the main building to provide classrooms for the high school and adequate accommodations for the business office.

Ryan was not content with these accomplishments; more needed to be done. The record of his financial administration was so successful that he

---

[8]Ryan to Fisher, M.P.A.
[9]Ryan to Fisher, M.P.A.
[10]*Catalogue, 1951-1953*, p. 30.

decided to initiate the next phase in his building plans by applying for a second loan from the Housing and Home Finance Agency. He reported to Provincial Linus J. Thro in June, 1962, that he had requested a loan of $1,153,878 for a new residence hall and the enlargement of the student center.[11] After he had received preliminary approval from the government, he applied through the provincial for approval by the authorities in Rome. After the necessary arrangements were made, ground was broken for the new dormitory on the site of old DeSmet Hall and preparations were made for the enlargement of the center. In due time both building projects were completed. The trustees voted unanimously to name the new dormitory in honor of the Jesuit missionary Peter DeSmet. A rather jubilant dedication took place on May 4, 1964.

There was reason for jubilation. While work was progressing on the two buildings, Ryan received word that Regis had been named a beneficiary in the will of Mrs. Elizabeth Dayton, who had died on March 12, 1963. The will named a number of individuals and a few organizations who were to receive bequests, but bequeathed the major part of the estate to Regis College. The lawyer for the Dayton estate informed Ryan that the executor, the First National Bank Trust Department, estimated that Regis would expect something around $750,000. In the light of future developments, it is interesting to note that Ryan wrote the provincial, "He [the lawyer] cautioned me not to make mention of this at this time for 'you might wish to hold this as the start for a fund drive.' "[12]

The bequest, the largest in the history of Regis, came as a complete surprise. No one at the college knew Mrs. Elizabeth Dayton nor did anyone have reason to suspect that she had any special interest in the school. Mrs. Dayton, a widow of some forty-two years, led a rather sequestered life after the death of her husband, a prominent lawyer in Denver. The only known contact with the college was made some three years before her death when her lawyer, Marmaduke Holt, visited with Ryan and asked him questions about the school. Later Holt explained that Mrs. Dayton had been impressed by the signs of vitality at Regis and had expressed surprise at the small endowment of the institution.[13] The generosity of the donor was manifested in the terms of the will which allowed the money to be used at the discretion of the trustees of the college.

---

[11]Ryan to Thro, M.P.A.

[12]Ryan to Thro, M.P.A.

[13]*The Regis Roundup,* August 1963, p. 4-5. The author is indebted to Philip E. Gauthier, sometime director of public information for the college, who published the article about Mrs. Dayton without the credit of a by-line.

The Dayton gift came at a most propitious time. Ryan had been planning a capital fund drive since March, 1962. In that year the college had engaged John Paul Jones as consultant to study the possibility of the project. Detailed preparations had been made to launch a major attempt to raise $2,250,000 over a period of three years to pay for the construction of a science building and a library. The case for the college was published in an attractive brochure, ''A Call from Regis College.'' After the usual historical introduction and the presentation of the problem and the needs of the college, the brochure included a financial statement comparing the assets and liabilities of the institution for the fiscal years 1954, 1959, and 1964.[14]

Without a doubt, the campaign was the most effective effort to raise money in the history of the college. It was well planned and carried out under the leadership of the following: William T. Blackburn, general chairman, Alfred E. Ellerby of the Regis Directors, Walter F. Imhoff and Stanley M. Hall for the alumni, and Patrick Coursey of the national Regis Club board. A letter dated November 29, 1964, informed the provincial that Regis was geared to start a fund campaign sometime in March. Ryan's confidence is reflected in his request for approval of his request to proceed with the construction of a science building and a library.[15]

Actually, the fund-raising campaign was not announced until May 9; the response through the spring and summer was so encouraging that Ryan decided to have groundbreaking ceremonies on July 23. By August 15, gifts and pledges from alumni, parents, and friends amounted to $160,000; $240,000 was forthcoming from firms, corporations and foundations. The most heartening news came from the government: the Department of Health, Education and Welfare, through the Higher Education Facilities Act, made a matching grant of approximately $740,000.[16]

In January, 1966, fifty-two per cent of the construction was completed and there was high expectation that the buildings would be finished in early June. Fred Daly was in charge as building coordinator. The architects, Walter F. Simon and Robert Husmann, won recognition for the excellence in design of the two structures when the architects received an award from the Society of American Registered Architects during the annual convention held in Cleveland.[17]

---

[14]Incidentally, the brochure was awarded a first honorable mention in the American Alumni Council's competition for direct mail publications at the Council's meeting in Atlantic City, New Jersey. *Regis Roundup,* Aug., 1965, p. 6.

[15]Ryan to Thro—a carbon copy of the letter is included in *Trustees' Meetings, 1963-1965.*

[16]*Regis Roundup,* Aug., 1965, p. 6.

[17]*Regis College Report,* Jan., 1966, R.C.A.

The dedication of the two buildings provided a fitting climax to ten years of intensive planning and resulted in six edifices that not only enhanced the appearance of the campus but provided excellent facilities for a growing institution. The ceremonies began on March 17 and ended with an open house on March 19. On the 17th the buildings were blessed by the retiring Archbishop of Denver, Urban J. Vehr, who was assisted by the auxiliary Bishop of Denver, David M. Maloney, and Hubert M. Newell, Bishop of Cheyenne and a graduate of the college. The blessing was followed by benediction in the fieldhouse with Bishop Charles A. Buswell of Pueblo preaching the sermon. A reception and dinner honoring Archbishop Vehr was held in the Center. Saturday, March 18, was a busy day, beginning with the presentation of the buildings by architect Robert Husmann and James W. Pinkard of the construction company. This ceremony was followed by an honors convocation at which the honorary degree of Doctor of Humanities was conferred on Eugene A. Dawson, president of Colorado Woman's College; Doctor of Laws on James W. Naughton, S.J., a graduate of Regis High School who came from Rome as the personal representative of Pedro Arrupe, Superior General of the Society of Jesus; and Doctor of Laws on Edward J. Vollmer, O.S.B., Abbot of Holy Cross Abbey, Canon City. A Doctor of Science degree was bestowed on an alumnus of the college, Gilbert M. Castellan, professor of Chemistry, Catholic University of America. Father Naughton conveyed the best wishes of the Jesuit General to Father Ryan and to the Jesuits as well as to the friends and benefactors of the college. The academic part of the program was highlighted by seminars held on the afternoon of March 18, one on questions of science with R. G. Gustavson, professor of chemistry, University of Arizona, as the featured speaker, and another on humanities led by Stanley Ghosh of the National Foundation for Arts and Humanities, Washington. The printed program featured portraits of Mr. and Mrs. W. L. Dayton in whose honor the library was named.

The members of the planning committee had done their work well. The center and circle drives had been eliminated and a mall created between the main building on the north and the library on the south, which has its main entrance to the north. Planners intended to exclude traffic from the center of the campus and to provide ample parking space on the periphery. This was an excellent decision because it gave ample opportunity for Brother Al Knoll to exercise his considerable expertise in landscaping. By judicious planting of bushes and flowers, Knoll enhanced the appearance of the campus and made it one of the most beautiful in the area.

Among Ryan's many concerns, improvement of the faculty was high on his list of priorities. He had inherited a good faculty, one that had been rated about average for colleges the size of Regis by the examiners for the North Central Association in 1952 who reported:

> There are favorable qualities which do not show up in the objective ratings; among these should be included a genuine enthusiasm for teaching and a fine spirit of cooperation among faculty members and between the faculty and the administrative officers. It is apparent that the faculty and administration work together as a team, constantly exchanging advice and suggestions.[18]

When Ryan became president the faculty consisted of twenty-two Jesuits and nine laymen; eight professors held doctorates. Two priests, John J. Gibbons and Joseph A. Ryan, had belonged to the New Mexico-Colorado Mission. The former had done excellent work in the Registrar's Office, making sure that the records were in good order. The latter had become a legend in the Rocky Mountain region, especially among accountants. He was an honorary member of the Colorado Society of Certified Public Accountants and a member of the educational committee of the National Association of Cost Accountants. He also served on the board of governors of the Catholic Accountants' Guild. In 1954 some of his former students established and incorporated a foundation "to provide financial assistance primarily for the furtherance of accounting and business education at Regis College in the form of scholarships, grants-in-aid, chairs for learning, professorships, instructorships, and fellowships."[19] Joseph A. Ryan had established and fostered the development of one of the strongest departments in the college. The third faculty member who had belonged to the Mission was Bernard J. Sullivan, retired bishop of Patna, India. He was a gracious and kind man who filled in wherever he was needed. Two other members of the old Mission, Bernard J. Murray and Brother Anthony M. Uliano, were living examples of the Jesuit spirit that inspired the members of the Neapolitan Province.

Father Murray served in a number of capacities in the Missouri Province from 1927 to 1936. He returned to Regis as director of public relations and moderator of the alumni. In 1945 he was assigned to other work in the province but resumed his position as director of the alumni in 1951. He spent the next twenty years of his life in various occupations, some of which involved him in college activities and others pertained to the requirements of the Jesuit community. For many years he was a mainstay in the laymen's retreat league. For many people in Colorado and Wyoming "B.J." was Regis. Uliano, "Brother Julian," was assigned to the community in 1906 and he served it well as porter and tailor until his death in 1965. In his

---

[18]Report to the Board of Review—on file in Dean's Office., p. 1.
[19]Letter of Paul L. Schmitz.

younger days he taught young men not to challenge him on the handball court in the old middle gym. Many younger Jesuits marveled at Julian's ability to provide for their needs; over the years he had established a rapport with individuals in department stores and through them he obtained basic items of clothing at very reasonable prices. Brother Julian was indeed a great asset to the Jesuit community for many years.

Three natives of Germany, formerly of the Buffalo Mission, made significant contributions to Regis. Conrad Bilgery has been mentioned; his colleague Philip Froebes taught physics and mathematics in the college but he had been reassigned before Ryan became president. The other member of this trio, Henry P. Hecken, served on the faculty as professor of physics from 1931 to 1963. He also supervised the classes in engineering drawing until his retirement in 1963. Hecken rendered invaluable service to the school and the religious community. Other Jesuits who served the college well but were destined to be reassigned to other schools were Lucius F. Cervantes, sociology; William B. Faherty, history; Charles F. Kruger, librarian; George M. Tipton the co-builder of an excellent department of chemistry. Six former Jesuit members of the faculty of 1954 have departed this life: John J. Quirk, J. Clement Ryan, Thomas F. Singleton, Ervin A. Stauffen, and Elmer J. Trame. All of these men contributed much to the college-in-transition during the administration of McCarthy. The last named, Trame, was instrumental in making the department of biology a worthy co-partner with chemistry in preparing students who wished to go into medicine or dentistry. He came to Colorado for his health in 1937 after he had earned his doctorate at St. Louis University. He used his considerable talents to build a solid department of biology. Without a doubt, he contributed considerably to the success of the premedical and predental programs. Being a very personable man, he made many friends for the college until poor health forced him into retirement.

Ryan inherited a dean, Louis G. Mattione, who had been in that office since 1948 and was destined to have the longest term as dean, twelve years, in the history of the college. Mattione was forthright in the way he directed the academic affairs of the college. He was not strong in following protocol but there was no doubt that he was in control. His office was open to faculty members and students alike. He listened to objections and complaints, then made decisions and stood by them. The examiners for the North Central had made a good assessment of Mattione's style when they wrote in their report, "It is apparent that the faculty and administration work together as a team, constantly exchanging advice and suggestions."[20]

---

[20]*Op. cit.,* p. 1.

The college was fortunate in recruiting competent laymen to complete the faculty roster. A few of these men remained at the college for many years. George E. Bechtolt was a mainstay in the department of modern languages, and Peter A. Rotar lived up to the standards established by Joseph A. Ryan in the department of accounting and business administration. The history department had a tower of strength in Fred R. Van Valkenburg, who also helped to stabilize the department of education. Unfortunately, he had a serious difference of opinion with the president and decided to pursue his teaching career elsewhere. John V. Coyne had joined the faculty in 1946 to teach in the department of business administration. He was destined to remain at the college for many years during which he served in a number of capacities—director of the evening division, assistant dean, director of academic services, and professor of business administration. Another layman, Francis J. Ozog, proved invaluable in making the department of chemistry one of the most respected in the college.

Ryan had indeed inherited a good faculty and he was determined to make it better. He broke with the all-male tradition in 1956 when he engaged the services of Ann Laughlin as lecturer in sociology. Miss Laughlin had been with the State Department after the second world war and had traveled extensively in Europe and Africa. During the few years she was on the faculty she was in demand as a speaker on Communism and related topics. In due time the authorities realized that it would be difficult to retain her on the faculty because she did not have the necessary academic qualifications.

In the meantime Ryan continued to strengthen the faculty. He used his considerable persuasive powers to influence the provincial to assign capable men to the college and high school, and enlisted competent lay instructors to stengthen the departments. In 1955 there were thirty-two faculty members in the college, eight of whom held doctorates. Ten years later there were fifty-seven teachers, twelve holding the doctoral degree. Undoubtedly, Ryan charted a new course for the faculty. Due to the changing times, the balance between Jesuits (21) and non-Jesuits (32) altered significantly and more women were recruited. In 1965 there were five women on the faculty roster, two of whom were nuns, Sister M. Antonia Anthony, O.S.F., and Sister M. Cecilia Linenbrink, O.S.F.[21] An assessment of Ryan's efforts to build a good faculty will have to wait for a future historian who will have a better

---

[21]For some time the Franciscan Sisters of Marycrest Convent sent their postulants and novices to pursue their studies in the college. A number of the Sisters continued their studies and earned the bachelor's degree.

perspective.

In 1960 Ryan decided that it would be most helpful if he had a very clear understanding of the status of the plant and all the operations of the college. Accordingly, he established these five *ad hoc* committees: academic, financial, development and public relations, student services, and property survey. The respective chairmen were Harry E. Hoewischer, Eugene A. Donohoue, Martin C. Kelly, Glen O. Stocking and Bernard S. Karst, and Frederick T. Daly. Under date of November 16, 1960, the president addressed a very detailed mandate to the members of the steering committee which specified areas of inquiry for each, such as the purpose of the college, the curriculum, the students, the faculty, academic organization, the library, plant facilities, and so forth. After two years of work, some of it intensive, the results were collated and incorporated in a report "Regis College Self-Study 1950-1960." The final draft was edited by John Gribben of the English Department. It is an impressive and thorough study and anyone who wishes to acquaint himself with the status of the college in 1960 will find the answers to most, if not all, of his questions.[22]

In the early 1960's some of the laymen decided to join the American Association of University Professors. They planned to establish a chapter of the AAUP on the campus. Ryan was concerned about the consequences of such a development. He took the matter up with the trustees in a meeting on September 23, 1961. The president pointed out that there was a difference between joining the association and establishing a chapter.[23] The minutes do not record a decision regarding this question but Ryan took steps to assure Jesuit participation if the movement should gain momentum. He asked a number of the Jesuits to join the association and declared that the administration intended to follow the guidelines of the AAUP. The movement did not gain much support from the faculty. It did, however, make Ryan aware that the laymen were concerned about the salary scale and it was imperative that he take steps to adjust the scale and pay salaries comparable to those offered by similar schools in the area. Harry E. Hoewischer prepared a report on the matter of salaries but did not have a chance to complete his study since he was removed from the office of Dean. His replacement, Robert F. Houlihan, made specific proposals for an adjustment in the salaries offered laymen to a startled Ryan in January 1964. The president wrote to Provincial Linus J. Thro on the 26th, "He [Houlihan] bowled me over with the size of the requested increases for the lay faculty, but I am going to go along with him."[24]

---

[22] A copy of the Study is in the office of the Dean.
[23] *Trustees' Meetings, 1957-1963*, p. 12.
[24] Ryan to Thro, M.P.A.

The perennial problem of discipline was studied and reassessed in the light of the changes that were taking place in the country. It was no longer possible to rely on the traditional paternal, almost casual, approach to discipline. Bernard S. Karst, as director of Carroll Hall and a member of the committee on discipline, was responsible for the maintenance of order. He was excellent when he had a manageable group of young men. The presence of a greater number of students required a more formal approach to the problems of supervision, especially at a time when there were demands for more freedom from restraints. McCarthy had responded to the need of adjusting to new circumstances by appointing John J. Quirk dean of men in 1951.[25] Quirk had many excellent qualities but he tended to be inflexible in matters pertaining to discipline. This was an admirable quality but hardly one that would facilitate his dealings with young men who were developing new concepts of life-styles. The fact that Quirk suffered from ulcers complicated matters, and McCarthy had to find someone who was more amenable to existing circumstances. The president appointed Francis J. Malecek dean of men, an office he administered from 1952 to 1960.

Soon after he became president, Ryan realized that the statutes of the college needed overhauling. Such a revision was made by October 1954. The amended statutes specified that the dean of students was the chief officer of the college in matters of discipline, housing, student activities, and social life among the students. Furthermore, he was the executive officer of the committee on student life, approved all events and meetings of student organizations, and was responsible for the supervision of all student social events.[26]

It was quite obvious to Ryan soon after he became president that the student council as it existed in 1953 was inadequate to meet the needs of a growing student population. He appointed an interim committee to study the problems connected with student participation in government. After some consideration the members recommended that a constitution be written which would establish guidelines for student government. Such a document was prepared and approved in 1957; it provided an "opportunity for college men of Regis to exercise judgment and initiative in assisting the administration and faculty in their task of student development."[27] The constitution established a student senate composed of the entire student body, a general assembly of twenty voting members to act as a legislative body, and an executive board to act as the chief coordinating and regulatory body of all

---

[25]*Diary, 1943-1951*, p. 281.
[26]*Regis College Self-Study 1950-1960*, pp. 76-77.
[27]*Op. cit.*, p. 79.

student and club activities. The general assembly should meet once a month and the students were to be encouraged to attend and make their opinions known. Officers, elected by their peers, constituted the executive board; these men were commissioned to carry out the will of the students expressed in the general assembly. A faculty representative appointed by the president of the college was directed to attend the meetings of the assembly and the executive board. It was his duty to act as an adviser and to approve all expenditures of funds allocated for the expenses of the student senate.[28] This reorganization had been long overdue. It worked with better than reasonable success once it was in operation. Given the circumstances of change and the development of a different concept of discipline, it was also deemed necessary to update the disciplinary practices. Matters pertaining to discipline were removed from the jurisdiction of the academic dean and entrusted to a dean of students and a committee of not fewer than three nor more than five faculty members, all appointed by the president. This committee, chaired by the dean of students, was to review cases of the more serious infractions of the regulations and submit its recommendations to the president who reserved the right to make final decisions in questions of suspension or expulsion from the school. A member of the executive board of the student senate was invited to attend such hearings so that he could witness to the fairness of the proceedings.

Students responded to these new approaches and became more involved in the activities on the campus. Evidence that the tempo of student life was accelerating during the 1950's is seen in the new organizations that were established, such as the Ski Club, KREG radio, and the Italian, Booster and Denver clubs. The last two especially attested to a new spirit. The Booster Club had as its purpose to support all activities sponsored by any Regis organization. Its members encouraged the backing of athletic games with special emphasis on basketball. The members promoted the sale of tickets and encouraged organized cheering at the games. The Denver club was organized to unite students of the metropolitan area and encourage involvement in all school activities. The members adopted the special project of organizing ways and means of meeting incoming freshmen and providing transportation to the campus. Moreover, they pledged themselves to help the new students during the difficult period of adjustment to college life.[29] The willingness of Denver students to participate in these activities was long overdue. In the past most of the local students had appeared on campus for classes and departed as soon as possible. In fact there were two almost

---

[28]*Op. cit.,* p. 80.
[29]*The Ranger,* 1959, p. 40.

separate components of the student body: boarders and day students, who were usually called "Day-Hops" or some less complimentary appellation. All things considered, there were plenty of opportunities for an enjoyable social life. The Presentation and Coronation balls became highlights of social life, rivaling even the Junior-Senior Prom.

Other organizations had academic connections, for example, the Regis College Playhouse, a dramatic club, and the Debating and Oratorical Society. Following a well-established Jesuit tradition, the college and high school continued to offer opportunities for students to develop their talents for acting on the stage. The record over the years in these endeavors was spotty because so much depended on the interest and abilities of those assigned to direct the performances. During Ryan's regime Andrew J. Deeman, who was assigned to the high school, directed a number of dramatic presentations that were well received by the academic community and its supporters in the city. The college debaters endeavored to keep the forensic tradition alive with varying degrees of success. One of the club's better years was 1958-1959, when Paul Horan, John Bruggeman, Thomas Scaglia, Allen Gerstner, and Dennis Gallagher, under the direction of moderator Charles F. Kruger, acquitted themselves with distinction when they participated in the University of Colorado Invitational Meet. The debaters were also successful in competition with the teams of the Air Force Academy and the then Omaha University. The Regis team competed in debates at Loyola University, Chicago, as part of a round-robin meet involving the top Jesuit colleges in the country.[30]

Interest in fraternities continued to occupy the attention of those who were looking for national affiliation. Shortly after Ryan became president, the Delta Sigma Commerce Club became the Gamma Sigma Chapter of Alpha Kappa Psi, a national fraternity dedicated "to further the individual welfare of its members; to foster scientific research in the fields of commerce, accounts, and finance."[31] That Delta Sigma qualified for national affiliation was a tribute to the dedication of Joseph A. Ryan, who had worked so earnestly to make accounting and business administration outstanding departments commanding the respect of certified public accountants.

Richard Ryan was interested in establishing a chapter of Alpha Sigma Nu, a national Jesuit honorary fraternity dedicated to promoting scholarship, loyalty and service. The president sent a memorandum to the members of the board of trustees on October 11, 1960, indicating that the matter be discussed in a forthcoming meeting. After some discussion the board concluded

---

[30]*The Ranger*, 1959, p. 48.
[31]*Catalogue 1960-1962*, pp. 17-18.

that more study was needed and postponed a final decision.[32] Subsequently, the necessary steps were taken to submit an application for affiliation, and six years later, in 1966, the fraternity was established.

Student spirit was sustained during the 1950's by the performance of the basketball team. Larry Varnell had achieved an enviable record before he resigned as coach to enter the business world. One of the more outstanding stars of Varnell's teams, Harvey E. Moore, was appointed head coach in 1953. Moore's teams continued to perform well, especially in the 1957-1958 season. Over the years the coaches had recruited these outstanding players: Tom Hitzelberger, Jim Butler, Bob Linnenberger, Terry Sheehy, Jerry Sherman, Howard Marshall, Ken Williams, Herb Millard, Paul Frey, Gary DeMarlie, and the sparkling Dennis Boone. The team seemed to be well on its way to national recognition. In the 1958-1959 season Regis won seven of its first eight games, one of the victories being over sixth-ranked Idaho State; but after this auspicious beginning the team lost ten of the remaining fifteen games, ending the season with a 12-11 record. Few coaches could survive such a reversal in the team's fortunes. Moore resigned and his assistant, Joe B. Hall, succeeded him as head coach. Perhaps it was unfortunate that the administration felt impelled at the same time to reassess its commitment to seek national recognition for its basketball teams because Joe Hall certainly had the qualities to make him an outstanding coach.[33] It became painfully clear to Ryan and his associates that a first-class basketball program was expensive. The response of the public after the fieldhouse was completed was disappointing and the athletic program became a financial burden. The trustees reviewed the entire problem in a series of meetings and decided to make some adjustments. Ryan wrote a memorandum on March 15, 1962, outlining certain steps that had to be taken to achieve the college's revised goal to concentrate on the improvement of the intramural athletic program and to adopt a more realistic policy regarding intercollegiate athletics. The first step to be taken was a declaration that the college would not strive for a nationally recognized basketball team. The second was to set guidelines for drawing up schedules. Coaches should contact schools of similar size to Regis in Colorado or adjacent states. By way of exception they could continue to schedule the Air Force Academy, University of Denver, and Colorado State University. Furthermore, the team could make only one long trip in any given season, either to the west coast or east no farther than Chicago.[34] The changes in the athletic policy were drastic,

---

[32]*Trustees' Meetings 1957-1963.*

[33]Joe Hall eventually became head coach at the University of Kentucky where he has achieved an enviable record.

[34]*Trustees Meetings, 1957-1963.*

especially in the matter of finances. Ryan stated that once the adjustments were made he would anticipate that the college would not spend more than $5,000 a year for the operation of intercollegiate basketball.[35] Joe Hall was understandably a disappointed man, though he made an effort to adjust to the new policies; but after a couple of years he resigned and eventually joined the coaching staff of the University of Kentucky.

A second program that did not measure up to earlier expectations was the evening division. When John Flanagan established the division in 1945 he envisioned a great future for the school. However, due to limited resources it was impossible for his successors to give the division the attention it deserved. After the transfer of the downtown division to the campus the courses continued to attract only a limited number of students. The departments of accounting and business administration furnished the best support for the evening division. Joseph A. Ryan, with the able assistance of John V. Coyne, kept the school alive. Teachers of the regular faculty were called upon to do double duty. Devices such as offering certificates and associate degrees attracted sufficient students to keep the division going. Some sturdy students managed over a period of years to gain their bachelor's degrees. The president did what he could to improve the evening school. In 1958 he appointed Fran A. Kiene as full-time director but even this attempt did not solve the enduring problems. Perhpas because of necessity, the evening division never met the expectations that were envisioned for it by John J. Flanagan. It would not have survived as long as it did if it had not been for the support it received from capable men who found time to teach a course or two after finishing a day's work in their offices; men like John A. Daly, Thomas J. McMahon, W. Barney Paul, Joseph Stephens, Joseph Sunderland, Elliot Wager, and Stephen M. Wagner. Finally, Edmund L. Mullen taught year after year; a gentleman of the old school, he gave much of his time and talent to support various projects sponsored by Regis.

Ryan was a man who faced up to reality and he realized that the time had come to admit that the effort to maintain the traditional Jesuit attitude toward classical studies had been less than effective. Regis paid lip service to the tradition by awarding the bachelor of arts degree only to students who had acquired sixteen or more credit hours in Latin. It became increasingly evident that only a few students were willing to meet this requirement. This matter was discussed by the board of trustees on February 16, 1959. The board voted in favor of keeping the Latin requirement for students who wished to work for a classical A.B. degree. However, the practice of awarding the bachelor of science degree to students who majored in such

---

[35]*Ibid*.

fields as English, history, philosophy and sociology was to be discontinued and these students were to receive the bachelor of arts degree even though they had not studied Latin.[36] Such a departure from Jesuit tradition had to be approved by authorities of the province; the approval was given. Ryan instructed the secretary of the board to include the following statement in the minutes:

> The Bachelor of Arts degree will be conferred on all students who have completed two years of a foreign language (or its equivalent) plus the other non-language requirements for majors in the fields of English, history, philosophy and sociology only.[37]

Another matter concerning degrees was this: Should the diplomas be printed in English instead of Latin? The dean, Mattione, favored the change to English and volunteered to investigate the cost of changing the format. Later the board voted that henceforth all diplomas would be printed in English.[38]

An important item on Ryan's *agenda* concerned the future of the high school. The trend in the country had been to separate the Jesuit high schools from the colleges and universities to the extent of finding a new location for the former with their own physical plant. The Jesuits preferred the high schools to have their own identity with a faculty and administration totally separate from the institution of higher learning. As early as 1955 Ryan proposed that the board of trustees vote in favor of increasing tuition in the high school from $150 to $180 a year and "that the accretion thus realized be earmarked for furture High School."[39] Ryan was preoccupied with his building program for the college but his interests ranged far afield. The minutes of a meeting of the trustees on September 20, 1958, record the terse statement "High School looking at property."[40] Less than a year and a half later, February 20, 1960, Ryan wrote to provincial Joseph A. Fisher that Regis had purchased sixty-odd acres in southeast Denver. The president was fortunate enough to have the able services of Milton Conway, a real estate agent, and the lawyer Martin C. Kelly, Ryan's assistant. Regis paid $5,000 down to effect the sale and agreed to pay $115,000 on April 10, 1960, when the warranty deed was delivered. The whole transaction was made possible by a loan of $55,000 from the Missouri Province.[41] To make sure that all of the legal technicalities were provided for, the board of trustees formed a corporation with the title Jesuit High School of Denver, Colorado. Articles

---

[36]*Trustees' Meetings, 1957-1963*, p. 5.

[37]*Op. cit.*, n.p.

[38]*Op. cit.*, p. 5.

[39]*Trustees' Meetings, 1935-1956*, p. 1925.

[40]*Trustees' Meetings, 1957-1963*, p. 4.

[41]M.P.A.

of incorporation were drawn up and notarized on April 4, 1960.[42] Due to unforseen circumstances a Jesuit high school in southeast Denver never became a reality. High hopes for a separate establishment were kept alive for some ten years and then finally abandoned.

The foregoing developments constituted one of the rare times that the president was actively involved with matters concerning the high school. It might be said that his attitude towards the affairs of that department was one of "salutary neglect." As a matter of fact there was no need for the president to be overly concerned because the administration of the high school was in the capable hands of James R. Eatough, principal from 1952 to 1968. Eatough, a graduate of Regis High, maintained the high standards set by his predecessors. Moreover, he actively promoted the expansion of the student body. In 1967 there were some 600 students in the school. The Jesuit system of sending scholastics to the high schools for a few years of teaching before they proceeded to the study of theology resulted in a continual turnover in the faculty. There were, however, competent Jesuit teachers who assured continuity: Francis F. Bakewell, Andrew J. Deeman, Aloysius S. Hahn, the perennial Stephen R. Krieger, Eugene L. Monnig, Joseph W. Poeckes, Eugene C. Renard, Joseph M. Sheehy, Ralph F. Taylor, and Arthur O. Verdieck. During Eatough's regime as principal he enlisted the help of some competent laymen who chose to stay with the school over a period of years: Rudy A. Breda (21), Guy Gibbs (19), Robert A. Guptil (14), Ken N. Jones (11), and Timothy Willard (11). Over the years these men guaranteed a quality education and the school continued to maintain high standards. Besides education as such, the reputation of the school in forensic activities was sustained and students performed with distinction in competition with their peers in the Rocky Mountain region.

After Clarence H. (Lou) Kellogg joined the faculty as Athletic Coach in 1937, Regis fielded good teams in football, basketball and baseball, which perennially remained in contention for championship titles; in fact, Regis and Mullen High tended to dominate the Parochial League in the major sports. With an expanding student body it became necessary to engage another teacher-coach to relieve some of the pressures that were building up on Kellogg. Guy Gibbs joined the faculty in 1957. Always the gentleman, Gibbs coached basketball teams that acquitted themselves with distinction and continued to dominate the league. It became clear that the league would have better balance if Regis and Mullen were excluded, and in 1966 these two schools played their last games as members. They faced the prospect of playing as independents or of joining some league. The first alternative was

---

[42]*Trustees' Meetings, 1957-1963.*

out of the question because it was too expensive. The second was difficult because existing leagues were not willing to admit private schools. In 1967 the Colorado High School Athletic Association changed its policy and Regis applied for admittance to the Skyline League. In March the superintendents of the Adams County high schools visited the Regis campus. They were satisfied with the qualifications of the school, and in April 1967 Regis was admitted to the league.[43]

When Ryan became president he was determined to improve the Regis public image and to encourage greater involvement on the part of the Jesuits in the affairs of the Denver community. His immediate predecessors had been aware of the need for better public relations but internal preoccupations prevented them from achieving notable success for their efforts. Ryan entered this field of endeavor with imagination and determination. He realized that there was a need for competent personable laymen to act as liaison between the school and the public. Consequently he engaged the services of David Hoene in the capacity of assistant to the president. The college hosted a public reception for Hoene to give him an opportunity to meet people. This was a move in the right direction. Regis, however, was not successful in keeping men of talent for very long periods. There was quite a turnover of the personnel who were connected with the administration. One of the more notable assistants to the president was Martin C. Kelly, a lawyer who was very knowledgeable about business affairs and who worked very closely with Ryan. In time it was clear that the president was modernizing his whole administration. Olga Curtis, a writer for the "Empire Magazine" of the *Denver Post,* wrote that Regis had begun to try some of the business ideas that other colleges had taken for granted such as hiring a public relations man, recruiting for students, and launching a public drive for building funds.[44]

The pattern of administration became clear during the early 1960's with the appointment of several directors: Donald K. Ryckman for development, George J. Reinert for public relations, James C. Haberer for admissions, John A. Flanagan for placement. Two departments were a matter of great concern to the president: the department of public information and the business office. The former position had been activated by former president John J. Flanagan when he engaged the services of Ed Williams on March 10, 1947. After a few years Williams was succeeded by Regis graduate John J. O'Hayre. Three years later Jack Sherlock succeeded; he was followed by Richard J. Connor. Finally, some continuity was assured when Philip E.

---

[43]*Diary 1961-1968,* p. 240.
[44]"Empire Magazine" The *Denver Post,* March 12, 1967.

Gauthier joined the staff. All these men were competent and helped immeasurably in bringing the college and high school to the attention of the civic community. Publications such as *The Roll Call* and *Regis Roundup Magazine* kept the lines of communication open between the administration, the academic community, the alumni, and the city. Gauthier had the longest tenure in this position and in his quiet, effective way succeeded in improving the public image of the institution. The effectiveness of the operation of the office of public information is clear from the amount of coverage given in the *Post, Rocky Mountain News,* and the *Register* during a twelve-month period beginning in May, 1964. It was obvious that Denver was becoming more aware of Regis. It is significant that the *Post* gave more column inches than the other two papers. A report to the trustees noted that "all of the space mentioned above was 'prime' space and cannot be purchased at any price."[45]

The second office that needed to be modernized was the business office. An expanding student body and plant demanded a more sophisticated accounting system and business management. The paternal days of Francis X. Hoefkens, with his assistants Mary Peck and Joe Price, were outmoded. A growing volume of business demanded a more professional approach to management. Just at the turn of the decade of 1960 Paul F. Dougherty was appointed business manager. Some three years later he was succeeded by Eugene A. Donohoue who was named director of business and finance. Donohoue had graduated from the college with a major in history and then decided to round out his education by studying accounting and business administration. He brought to the office considerable business acumen, something that was definitely needed in the complex dealings with the agencies of the United States government regarding loans for the building program and the supervision of the National Defense Student Loans. Ryan and his staff became more realistic in dealing with budgets and annual audits. In fact, there was notable improvement in the development of fiscal responsibility.

Ryan was determined to become involved in the public life of the city of Denver and to persuade the political and business leaders to become involved in the activities of Regis. The civic leaders welcomed his overtures and asked Ryan to serve on the Denver Planning Board. The committee that made the arrangements for the inauguration of Mayor Will F. Nicholson invited the president of Regis to deliver the invocation. In 1965 serious floods caused considerable damage in the city and adjacent territory; Regis offered its facilities for the help of flood victims. The American National

---

[45]*Trustees' Meetings, 1966-1971.*

Red Cross issued a citation in grateful appreciation for outstanding cooperation on the part of the school. Greater involvement in the civic Mile High
Fund produced good results.

The academic life of the college was enriched by the introduction of the
fall and spring convocations, organized by Harry E. Hoewischer and Edward L. Maginnis. A lecture series was initiated; learned professors and
distinguished men from various fields were invited to the campus to speak.
Awards ceremonies called attention to the notable academic achievements of
students.

Ryan succeeded in attracting greater support from alumni, parents, and
friends when in 1958 he established an organization known as The Regis
Directors. The objectives of the members of this group were to encourage
proportionate giving to the established financial support programs of the
college, to encourage financial support from other sectors, and to give each
director a broad familiarity with Regis' past accomplishments, present
programs, and future goals.[46] The success of this venture was pinpointed at
the annual Directors' dinner on January 8, 1966, in the announcement that in
1965 membership had reached an all-time high of 636. Members had
contributed $165,021 for an average gift of $259.[47]

High on Ryan's list of priorities was his determination to get businessmen
of Denver involved in the affairs of the college. As early as 1957 he informed
the trustees that he was studying the question of forming a board of lay
trustees. The minutes of a meeting held on December 26 record with the
usual conciseness, "thirty-five men (get names). Purpose: to have them
interpret what we are doing for Denver, interest them and more (not fund
raisers)."[48] Subsequent to this meeting Ryan was immersed in many matters
concerned with administration and building and seemingly did not seriously
pursue the project of forming such a board. Almost three years later, October
11, 1960, he informed the board that he proposed to make a recommendation
to higher authority that a distinction should be made between the house
consultors and the board of trustees because the matters that concerned the
former were sufficiently different to justify the organization of a separate
board. Consequently, he intended to bring the matter to the attention of the
provincial and hoped that he would have the consensus of the board.[49]
Somewhat later, January 28, 1962, the president presented a questionnaire
from the provincial's office regarding the possibility of establishing a sepa-

---

[46]*Regis College Report, January, 1966.*
[47]*Ibid.*
[48]*Trustees' Meetings, 1957-1963,* p. 3.
[49]*Op. cit.*

rate board of trustees including laymen.[50] Unfortunately, the answers to the questions are not available.

Ryan was not to be deterred; if he could not have laymen on his board of trustees he would find a solution by way of compromise. He proceeded to enlist lay advisers who were willing to serve on a President's Council. In 1961 he established a board of laymen to advise the staff of the college, make the purposes and work of the college better known to the community, and interpret to the college the needs and views of the community. Ryan appointed distinguished members of the civic community to serve on the council: Max Brooks, President of the Central Bank and Trust Company; Emmett Dignan, President of the Colorado Business Development Corporation; George Kolowich, President of the Denver-Chicago Trucking Company; Frank B. McGlone, M.D., Physician; Stephen L. R. McNichols, Governor of the State of Colorado and a graduate of Regis College; J. Kernan Weckbaugh, Chairman of the Board of the First National Bank of Englewood.[51] A year later he added William T. Blackburn, partner in Vaughey, Vaughey and Blackburn; Roger D. Knight, Jr., Chairman of the Board of Denver U.S. National Bank; John R. Moran, Sr., Attorney, partner in Moran, Reidy and Voorhes; and John F. Sweeney, President of B. K. Sweeney Company. It is difficult to assess the effectiveness of the council but it is clear from its membership that Ryan achieved great exposure to the Denver community.

Ryan's crowning achievement in public reltions was the inauguration in 1958 of Regis Week. Starting with a modest debut, it developed into an outstanding social event of the spring season. As usual, a terse statement recorded in the minutes of the board of trustees for February 2 noted in barest outline that the week of April 28 to May 4 was to be designated as Regis Week, featuring an academic symposium and a banquet culminating in the granting of awards to outstanding citizens of Colorado who manifested or had manifested integrity in ideals, concern for their fellowmen and service to mankind.[52] Ryan and his advisers decided that the awards should be distinctive and checked into history to find a distinguishing title that would not be trite. They chose one from classical Rome—*Civis Princeps* (First Citizen). A local sculptor, William Joseph, a graduate of Regis High School, was commissioned to design and execute medals to be awarded to the recipients.[53] Ryan and the members of his committee were very generous in the

---

[50]*Op. cit.*, n.p.

[51]*Catalogue, 1962-1963*, p. 5.

[52]*Trustees' Meetings, 1957-1963*, p. 3.

[53]Shortly before the first awards ceremony the Jesuit reputation as defenders of the classics was in jeopardy. The press releases about the award used the words *Cives Princeps*. The Jesuit

number of designated "First Citizens" in the first annual ceremony; seventeen medals were awarded, some to outstanding citizens of Colorado long since dead. In subsequent years the committee was more restrictive and, except for 1959 when there were four recipients, they gave three awards each year. In addition to conferring the medal on distinguished citizens, Regis recognized an outstanding institution in Colorado whose contributions to the state and nation were considered to be significant. During Ryan's regime the medals were given to forty-eight individuals and nine institutions. The list of those receiving this honor constitutues a *Who's Who* in the history of the state of Colorado. Extreme care was exercised in the selection of individuals to be honored. Names were submitted by a nominating committee and scrutinized by a screening committee; the final selection was made by a panel of five former recipients.[54]

A second feature of Regis Week was a civic conference hosted by the college providing a forum for the discussion of problems of interest to the business community of Denver. To facilitate participation of the downtown community some of the conferences were held at the Brown Palace Hotel. Two of the more notable of these sessions were those of 1963 and 1965. The former was co-sponsored by the Downtown Denver Master Plan Committee. Over 300 business and civic leaders attended to discuss a master plan for downtown Denver. The keynote speaker was Arthur Naftalin, then mayor of Minneapolis.[55] Many business leaders attended the sessions and were impressed at the involvement of Regis in the affairs of the city as well as its concern for the Denver of the future. The second conference was co-sponsored by the Denver Planning Board. Over 250 business, civic and government leaders attended. The conference had as its theme "Focus on Denver's Future" and it concentrated on the objectives for the city's new comprehensive plan and included a discussion on some type of metropolitan government. Senator Harrison A. Williams, Jr., of New Jersey was the featured speaker. Denver Mayor Tom Currigan expressed appreciation of the contributions of Regis in sponsoring these conferences and concluded,

> Certainly no one will deny the fact that Regis College's desire to "render service as a vehicle for civic progress and improvement through its abiding interest in civic affairs" is a statement from an institution that very clearly recognizes its responsibilities and obliga-

---

Latinist John J. Jolin placed a call to Joseph's studio only to learn that the sculptor could not be disturbed because he was working on the medals. Persistence was rewarded and Joseph corrected the mistake and spared the Jesuits embarrassment.

[54]The author is indebted to Mary O'Donnell, director of public relations, who researched this subject and published it in the program for the year 1974.

[55]*Regis Roundup*, August 1963, pp. 7-10.

tions to the community in which it resides.[56]

Shortly after the inauguration of the annual Regis Week, the students decided that they should take part in the week's events. They helped in various capacities in the preparations necessary for staging the programs. The highlight for the students was Ranger Day—a day of fun and games. The day's schedule, under the direction of the student senate, provided for contests and various kinds of competition, plenty to eat and drink, an evening barbecue, and—the climax of the day—a dance. The day was so popular with the students that it survived the many changes that since have made Regis Week a fond memory for friends of the college and high school.

Further evidence that Ryan was willing to become more involved in the civic and educational communities is found in his cooperation with the presidents or chancellors of the other independent colleges and universities in the region. In 1965 Colorado College of Colorado Springs, the University of Denver, Loretto Heights College, Colorado Woman's College, and Regis were incorporated as The Colorado Association of Independent Colleges and Universities. The purposes of CAICU were to foster and implement cooperation among the member institutions for the improvement of educational opportunities, to cooperate with all institutions of higher education, governmental agencies, and other interested groups and parties for the advancement of higher education, and to provide a unified voice for an effective communication regarding independent higher education in the State of Colorado.[57] The prospects for such cooperation were bright in 1965, but, unfortunately, were never fully realized. Another venture that did not materialize was the acquisition of Westminster School of Law. When the authorities of the school offered to transfer its assets to Regis College, Ryan made an investigation in depth of the possibility of acquiring the school. After consultation with the faculty and interested friends of Regis, he concluded that the college "cannot afford the responsibility of administering and operating a School of Law which would reflect the credit on the present Westminster School of Law or Regis College itself."[58]

Somehow Ryan found time to promote more improvements in the appearance of the campus. He made arrangement to have the cemetery relocated and the area north and east of the fieldhouse relandscaped. Ever since the days of Pantanella every Jesuit who died in Denver was buried in a cemetery located northeast of the main building. Over the years Brother Ben Tovani, with the help of Joseph A. Ryan, kept the cemetery in good

---

[56]*Regis Roundup,* August 1965, p. 8.
[57]Copy of the certificate of incorporation, *Trustees' Meetings, 1963-1965.*
[58]R.C.A.

condition. As these dedicated men grew older the graves were neglected. In time neglect led to deterioration and the activities of children in the neighborhood resulted in what amounted to desecration of the graves. Ryan quietly polled some of the older Jesuits on the question of moving the graves to Mount Olivet and found out that there were no major objections. He negotiated with the archdiocesan authorities about the feasibility of the project of transferring the remains to the Catholic cemetery. The director of Mount Olivet, Msgr. James P. Flanagan, a former student of the college and a loyal friend of the Jesuits, facilitated the arrangements for the transfer. In due time the Jesuits had an excellent location in which to bury their dead. Msgr. Flanagan deserves to rank with the outstanding benefactors of Regis, for without him the transfer would have been more complicated.

A second undertaking was the relandscaping of the area north and east of the fieldhouse. The old lake which had served as a terminus for the irrigation ditches had become a liability and an eyesore. The area was filled with dirt from the site of the fieldhouse and planted to grass. The land to the east was transformed into baseball, soccer, and intramural fields. South of the field, on higher ground east of the fieldhouse, tennis courts were laid out according to required specifications. Al Knoll supervised these transformations with dispatch. Somehow he managed to obtain the funds necessary to install a watering system that assured the pleasant, almost park-like appearance of the area.

The property east of the stadium to Federal Boulevard had posed problems down through the years since it had been acquired in 1924. The efforts to farm this land had ended in failure. Ryan was determined to make practical use of this real estate. He commissioned Martin C. Kelly, assistant to the president, to investigate various alternatives of making some practical use of the land that would make it revenue producing. Kelly, a very knowledgeable man of business, made a study of the problem in depth. He recommended that the college build a complex that would include a medical center, housing for senior citizens, and apartments for members of the faculty. It was an ambitious project. The question of financing such an undertaking was challenging; in the event, the matter had to be abandoned. Kelly kept his options open and was rewarded in 1964 when agents for the Northwest Land and Development Company showed some interest in leasing eleven and one-half acres of the property at Federal Boulevard and West 50th Avenue. The matter was presented to the board of trustees in a meeting on October 23, 1964. After Kelly explained the proposition, the board agreed to approve the leasing of the property. The minutes recorded:

> As a result of the negotiations and upon recommendation, Regis College, this 23rd day of October, entered into a ground lease with said

company, a Colorado partnership, wherein the college leased approximately 11 and 1/2 acres of its property at West 50th Avenue and Federal Boulevard to said company for a term commencing no later than 180 days after October 23, 1964, and ending 23 years thereafter.[59]
It was agreed that the lease was contingent on two conditions: Regis was to make arrangements for the rezoning of the property, and the company was to negotiate a sub-lease with S. S. Kresge Company.[60] All these problems were solved and a formal press release was authorized for January 30, 1965.

Ryan had charted new courses for the college while he depended upon Eatough to keep the high school true to its standards of imparting quality education. The needs of the college required greater concentration especially regarding the problem of maintaining an enrollment that would assure sufficient income to make it possible for the administration to meet its pressing financial obligations. During the summer of 1967 more and more attention was given to the question of making the college coeducational. To do so would not mean a complete break with the past because the evening division had been coeducational from the time of its inception. Moreover, young religious from the Marycrest convent had regularly attended classes. In a meeting of the board of trustees on August 3, 1967, the question of coeducation was discussed and the board decided that the president should summon representatives of the president's council, the student body, the faculty, and other interested persons to meet with the trustees to consider the question of Regis becoming a coeducational institution.[61] The minutes of this meeting are not available but the result of the deliberations must have been favorable because the board decided on September 26, 1967, that "Regis College officially declare itself a coeducational institution beginning in the fall of 1968."[62] All concerned personnel were aware of the problems that would have to be solved to assure a smooth transition. An unforseen factor delayed the preparations; Ryan, who had overextended himself in administering the many projects he had initiated, became ill and was taken to the hospital on October 19, 1967. After routine examinations the doctor ordered Ryan to take a complete rest for a few weeks. After further observation, the doctor recommended that Ryan be given a leave of absence. The trustees elected Frederick T. Daly acting president. Daly addressed himself to administering the affairs of the college and high school with preciseness and decision. High on his list of priorities was the continuation of the studies

---

[59]*Trustees' Meetings, 1963-1965.*
[60]*Ibid.*
[61]*Trustees' Meetings, 1966-1971.*
[62]*Op. cit.*

regarding the adjustments that had to be made to prepare for coeds who might apply for admission as boarding students. Daly addressed a memorandum to the dean of students, Robert F. Houlihan, requesting information as soon as possible concerning the housing of coeds on the campus. The communication also notified Houlihan that steps had to be taken immediately to engage a qualified woman as associate dean of students.[63] Other steps were taken to investigate every facet connected with the change. The committee was divided into subcommittees for future planning, housing, curriculum, and extra-curricular activities.[64] All concerned worked well and directed the transition with a minimum of turmoil. Some of the seniors and juniors resented having to yield their rooms in Carroll Hall to the coeds but there was no serious agitation. Mary Constance Keough, a very competent person, was engaged as associate dean of students. Some alumni and friends were surprised that the transition was achieved without trauma, and in due time the students adjusted to the situation and accepted the presence of coeds as the normal condition on the college scene.

Ryan returned on December 6, 1967, but soon discovered that his superiors had decided that he had worn himself out during his term of fourteen years. On December 21st the community learned that Louis G. Mattione, former dean of the college, would succeed Ryan as president of Regis High School and College. Ryan left an institution which he had transformed as no one of his predecessors had done. His legacy included six new buildings, a thoroughly reorganized and expanded administration, a reasonably efficient business office, a viable public relations department, and an excellent public information agency. He had tapped resources for funds by establishing the Directors Program and he improved alumni giving. The campus had become a showplace, thanks to the expertise of Brother Al Knoll who had kept pace with the building program and had enhanced the appearance of the areas adjacent to the new buildings by his superb choice of shrubs, trees and flowers.

Ryan's accomplishments were so plentiful that it is nigh impossible to record them. Two, however, should be mentioned because they were the first steps in the direction of changing the relationship between the Jesuit community and the institution. The first step concerned finances. Traditionally the financial status of the college and high school was known to a very few people and it seems that even they did not know all the facts. In the course of time, as the obligations of the institution to the federal government increased, it was necessary to determine the extent of the liability of the

---

[63]On file in President's Office.
[64]*Ibid.*

constituents of the Regis community. This realization is reflected in the minutes of the board for November 20, 1965, which record: "It is now evident that Regis must set up separate books for: 1) the Jesuit community; 2) the college; 3) the High School. This will of necessity be beneficial as is required for proper accounting in all areas."[65] The second significant move was made in order to relieve Ryan of some of his responsibilities by appointing a superior of the Jesuit community who would be responsible for the administration of the affairs of the community. He would, however, be a dependent superior; the president-rector would retain all authority concerning the academic life of the college and high school and the right to approve of any Jesuit's public appearance to deliver a lecture or make an address.[66] After all the preliminaries had been worked out, Thomas J. Sheehy was appointed superior of the Jesuits, effective on August 15, 1961.

Time will afford a better opportunity to make a complete assessment of Ryan's administration but a few words are in order. It is evident that he made a major impact on the development of the college and high school. It was to be expected that a forceful, decisive man would irritate some people. Because of his uncompromising stand in negotiations he lost some very capable men. There was a great contrast between his dealings with the public where he was eminently successful and his relations with the faculty and staff. The measure of his success in the former category is found in the honors that were conferred upon him. He received honorary Doctor of Laws degrees from the University of Colorado and the University of Denver. The Downtown Denver Improvement Association named him an honorary citizen of downtown Denver. A scroll from Pope John XXIII bestowed the Apostolic blessing upon Ryan's first ten years' tenure at Regis. The author of the summary of the president's first decade of service concluded:

> Under his guidance the College has grown in stature as an educational institution, as a citizen of Colorado and as a leading contributor to the betterment of the Denver metropolitan area.[67]

It is not possible to evaluate the contributions of the many men and women who assisted Ryan in achieving his many goals. Some few should be mentioned because they could be so easily overlooked, for example, the lay brothers, John J. Renk, John B. Szczesniak and Herbert A. Bussen. Brother Renk did yeoman service as infirmarian and supervisor of the bookstore. He also had two notable hobbies both of which brought favorable publicity to Regis: he had outstanding collections of butterflies and sea shells. Brothers

---

[65]*Op. cit.*
[66]M.P.A.
[67]*Regis Roundup,* August, 1963, pp. 14-15.

Szczesniak and Bussen were in charge of the receiving room and the distribution of the mail. They kept pace with the demands that were made of them by an expanding student body, faculty, and staff. Two Jesuit priests, Bernard J. McMahon and Louis A. Bloomer, made notable contributions. Father McMahon started a second career after teaching for thirty-six years at St. Mary of the Lake Seminary, Mundelein, Illinois. He taught philosophy for a few years and became a valuable asset to the Jesuit community. Louis Bloomer had joined the faculty in 1943. For years he taught English and speech in the college. He made some valuable contacts with influential people in the community and numbered among his friends Mrs. Louise Coors Porter who donated her mountain estate to Regis. This excellent facility provided a place of rest and recreation for the Jesuits until it was sold to obtain funds to help lighten the financial burden of the school. With the support of capable men and women, Ryan had accomplished much in fourteen years. When he left Denver to assume less onerous duties at Marquette University he departed with the knowledge that he deserved accolades for work well done.

Chapter 7

Transition to
the Second Hundred Years

1968-1977

Louis G. Mattione assumed the responsibility of guiding the destinies of Regis College and High School at an exciting and challenging time. A number of colleges had passed through crises, most of them instigated by students who were questioning policies and procedures that had been taken for granted in academic institutions throughout the land. Change, amounting to revolution in some instances, was the watchword of the sixties. It was a difficult time for any Jesuit to become the chief administrative officer of a growing institution. Mattione returned to Denver a well-seasoned man. The experience of twelve years in the office of dean of the college had given him a thorough knowledge of the plant, the faculty, and the composition of the student body. During the eight years of his absence he had been busy as a teacher and administrator. After he left Regis in 1960 he taught at Chaplain Kapaun Memorial High School in Wichita for a year. He was then assigned to Rockhurst High School in Kansas City, Missouri, at a time when the president of Rockhurst, Maurice E. VanAckeren, had undertaken to finance the building of a new high school in a different part of the city. Mattione was appointed president-rector of the new school. After a term of six years at Rockhurst High School he was appointed to succeed Ryan.

Mattione had the good fortune to experience a smooth transfer to his new responsibilities. Ryan gave him invaluable assistance during the month of February by explaining the financial condition of Regis and introducing him to the supporters of the college and high school. Some four hundred professional and business men, including the governor of the state and the mayor of Denver, attended a public luncheon in the Brown Palace arranged to introduce the new Regis president. When he assumed office on March 1, 1968, Mattione had to fill some vacancies on his staff created by the resignations of George J. Reinert and Thomas J. Regan. The former had been director of college relations, the latter, acting director of alumni relations. Mattione appointed Andrew J. Martelon to succeed Reinert. Martelon, an experienced businessman, was well known in the Denver community and throughout the state. He had been president of a printing firm, and as a very active member of the Knights of Columbus he held the highest offices in that fraternal organization in Colorado. As a graduate of the college, he was familiar with the problems and the aspirations of the institution. The president chose

William R. Matt, another graduate of the college, to direct alumni relations. Other positions that had to be filled were a director of the evening division and summer school and a librarian. Mattione appointed George Williams to the former and Dennis D. North to the latter. Williams, who had been engaged as an admissions counselor in 1967, was given the charge to develop programs for the evening division and summer school; North took over the responsibility of directing the recently dedicated Dayton Memorial Library and developing its resources.

The president realized that there was a need for planning for the future. His predecessor had established a college planning committee; Mattione made it a permanent committee and commissioned its members to supervise all phases of operation and to establish goals. Members of the committee were recruited from the administration, faculty and student body; Martelon succeeded Donald L. Salmon of the department of history and political science as college planning chairman.[1]

One of the more significant changes in the new administration developed in the relations between the president and the members of the board of trustees. Ryan had considered the trustees as advisers and expected them to agree with his decisions. Mattione's style was different; he wanted board members to have a greater part in the decision-making process. There is a definite change in the recorded minutes of the meetings of the board under Mattione and it is obvious that the deliberations were more than consultative. From time to time the members considered adding laymen to the board. In March, 1969, students asked to have a representative with the right to vote, but the trustees voted against this proposal with the reservation that "this does not reject the presence of such a student representative on special occasions or in the future, when conditions change."[2]

It is a tribute to Mattione's open-mindedness that he invited two of the more forceful Jesuit members of the faculty to serve on the board, Edward L. Maginnis and Frederick T. Daly. Neither of these men was known for his reticence. The former was elected vice-chairman and secretary. It is not surprising that soon after they took their places on the board someone moved that the board meet at designated times twice a month.[3] Serious consideration was given to inviting Jesuits from other colleges to serve on the Regis board. Mattione stated in a report on the state of the college delivered at a luncheon in 1971:

In the future the Board of Trustees will be reorganized under a new

---

[1]*Regis Roundup*, February 1969, p. 5.
[2]*Trustees' Meetings*, 1966-1971.
[3]*Op. cit.*

constitution and by-laws which will initially alter its composition to include Jesuits from outside the Regis community. Later expansion will include laymen and women.[4]

Without a doubt, the board of trustees had come a long way in three years.

After Richard Ryan left Regis, the dean of the college, Harry R. Klocker, indicated that he wished to resign. This happened at a time when Jesuit obedience was being reexamined and there was talk among some Jesuits about the "principle of attraction," that is, that Jesuits should have a part in the decision regarding the apostolate to which they would be assigned. Concurrently, Jesuit colleges were adopting the method of setting up search committees to select from a list of applicants the men who would fill vacated administrative posts. At the same time a rumor reached Regis that provincial Gerald R. Sheahan had decided to assign Eugene E. Grollmes, who had recently received his doctor of philosophy degree in education from Boston College, to succeed Klocker. The latter demurred at this procedure and urged Mattione to invite Grollmes to submit his credentials as a candidate for the position of dean to a committee of faculty members and students appointed by the board of trustees; if the committee decided not to recommend Grollmes it should be instructed to identify someone else who might qualify for the position.[5] The trustees discussed the question at length; they eventually agreed with Mattione's conclusion that Grollmes be appointed dean but that in the future the procedure recommended by Klocker be followed.[6]

Grollmes attacked with enthusiasm the problems which confronted him. It took a little while for him to get acquainted with his faculty. This was no easy task because the number of teachers had been increased until there was a total of eighty-two full-time and thirty-three part-time professors. Fourteen full-time laypersons had been added in 1970, a fact that called attention to a drastic change that had developed during the sixties, namely, the decreasing number of Jesuits available for assignment. In 1971-1972 there were twenty Jesuits compared to sixty-two laypersons; eighteen of the latter were women.[7] Grollmes, fresh from his doctoral studies, initiated another self-study. He urged the department chairpersons to enlist their colleagues in drawing up a plan that would set goals for the succeeding ten years. The dean urged the faculty to be bold and imaginative in planning for the future (the favorite slogan was "blue-sky it"). When the plans were submitted, the president announced that the proposals regarding programs, personnel, and

---

[4]*Regis Roundup,* April 1971, p. 3.
[5]*Trustees' Meetings,* 1966-1971.
[6]*Op. cit.*
[7]*Catalogue,* 1971-1972, pp. 7-15.

physical needs over the next ten years called for an outlay of $18.5 million.[8]
This was an exhilarating but unrealistic exercise. It took some time for
Grollmes to adjust to the challenges that faced him as academic dean and it
was difficult for him to establish a proper rapport with some of the members
of the faculty.

The faculty received special recognition under the Mattione regime with
the inauguration of the Faculty Lecturer Award. Since the introduction of the
spring convocation in Ryan's time, the authorities found it difficult to
identify and obtain speakers for the occasion. Someone suggested that a
faculty member be chosen to lecture at the convocation and that the one
selected be given an award in recognition of his or her performance as a
dedicated teacher. Full-time faculty members were eligible for the award.
Names were to be submitted to the members of the Committee on Rank and
Tenure and the Committee on Research. The designated professor was
requested to deliver a formal address at the spring honors convocation on a
subject of his or her choice. The event became annual and the award was
coveted by the professor selected by the committees and approved by the
president. The recipients were: Harold L. Stansell, S.J., 1969; John V.
Coyne, 1970; Clyde Currie, 1971; Alice O'S. Fehrenbach, 1972; Edward L.
Maginnis, S.J., 1973; Harry E. Hoewischer, S.J., 1974; Thomas J. Steele,
S.J., 1975; Ronald S. Brockway, 1976; Frederick T. Daly, S.J., 1977.

The period of the late sixties and earlier seventies was a difficult time for
college administrators. Students were becoming more vocal. Edward J.
Power summed the new spirit up when he wrote:

In the 1960's, the forgotten man in Catholic higher education—the
student—began to assert himself. First he assaulted and then demolished the doctrine of *in loco parentis;* next he challenged the right of
college officers to conduct the college's business without the benefit of
his counsel.[9]

Regis students were not as vigorous as their peers in other schools in
challenging the administrators and the established disciplinary code, but
they were determined to be heard. The students won approval of their request
to have a representative on the more important committees; however, they
were denied representation at meetings of the board of trustees except on
special occasions when matters of immediate concern to students were
discussed.

Another evidence of the changing times is found in the decision of the
board of trustees to abolish all mandatory religious practices and to substitute

[8]*Regis Roundup,* April 1971, p. 3.
[9]*Op. cit.,* p. 412.

a more adequate program of religious activities on a voluntary basis.[10] This matter had been submitted to the members of the board by the college chaplain, William E. Olszewski, who had discussed the matter with the Religious Life Committee and the dean of students, Robert F. Houlihan. The authorities had been frustrated in their efforts to enforce attendance at religious exercises and to convince students that they should make a three-day retreat.

The students won another concession when, in due time, the board approved their request to install a bar on campus for the sale of 3.2% beer. Drinking of alcoholic beverages had been a perennial problem down through the years. Rather severe penalties had been established to discourage students from drinking on campus. But it seemed to be a losing cause. When John Budinger, accompanied by a committee of fellow students, appeared before the board and presented the students' request for a bar on campus, the trustees were receptive but cautious. The board "voted unanimously to withhold approval for the initiation of the action until specific regulations governing the operation can be drawn up and agreed to by administrative and student body officials."[11] In time, when all problems had been resolved and a license obtained, the student-operated bar was opened and given the puzzling name "Belial."

No college administrator in the late sixties could ignore the problems of minorities. A number of students with Spanish surnames but few black students had enrolled at the college, excepting of course a number of basketball players over the years since the Second World War. For various reasons Catholic colleges did not have an enviable record in recruiting black students,[12] and Regis was no exception. Ryan broke with the policies of the past when he appointed Clyde Currie assistant professor of biology in 1966. A few years later a committee on human relations was established and Currie was appointed chairman. On January 11, 1969, this committee recommended that the president add a person from a minority group to assist the director of admissions, Philip R. Flanigan, in the recruiting of minority group students. A second recommendation was that twelve full-tuition grants-in-aid be set aside for students from minority groups. The committee asked, furthermore, that all members of the Regis community be informed of the reality of racism and prejudice and encouraged to commit themselves to work for better human relations.[13] On May 16, 1969, the board unanimously

---

[10]*Trustees' Meetings,* 1966-1971.

[11]*Op. cit.*

[12]*Power, op. cit.,* p. 437.

[13]*Trustees' Meetings,* 1966-1971.

approved a proposal that $12,000 be set aside for grants-in-aid to students from minority groups until March 1, 1970.[14]

These efforts to show awareness of the need to do something about minorities did not forestall a demonstration on the campus. On March 19, 1970, some fifty college students accompanied by several members of the faculty confronted the president in his office and presented him with a list of "demands." Mattione told the students that their petitions would be given consideration. Some students kept agitating and it was decided that a forum should be provided for the airing of their grievances. An open meeting was arranged to be held in the fieldhouse with the board of trustees present. Between 250-300 students and faculty members attended and held an open and candid discussion of complaints. A larger segment of the student body presented a statement asserting that the protesters were not representative of the student body. In the course of a few days the "demands" of the initial group had become "suggestions." Some of these requests had been submitted to the board by the Committee on Human Relations; others were obviously manifestations of the prevailing climate which reflected student aspirations for more freedom and a relaxation of academic requirements. For example, the students asked for a reduction of the required credit-hours in theology and philosophy, expansion of pass/no-pass system, and elimination of the "cut system." In time agitation subsided and campus life returned to its normal course. Mattione attributed the relatively peaceful settlement to the "willingness of all concerned to work within the system."[15]

In 1970 some changes in the administrative staff took place. Jesuit superiors gave Robert F. Houlihan a new assignment, and, for the first time in its history, the college selected a layman, L. Morgan Lavin, for the office of dean of students. The choice of Lavin was the result of a search conducted by a special committee established for that purpose. Lavin had served as dean of students at Loyola College, Baltimore, and at John Carroll University. Another significant appointment was that of Jerome B. Coll to the office of special assistant to the president. Father Coll came to Regis after serving as dean and vice-president at St. Joseph's College, Philadelphia. A third appointment, that of William W. Williams, revealed the beginning of a new approach to providing for the religious needs of the students; Williams was named coordinator of religious activities, replacing William E. Olszewski. Two dedicated secretaries retired from their positions in 1970, Mrs. Ann Kalbaugh, who had served in the athletic and admissions offices for eleven years, and Mrs. Mary Peck, who had served in various offices for

---

[14]*Op. cit.*
[15]*Regis Roundup,* July 1970, p. 5.

nearly forty years. Mattione honored the two women at a luncheon and presented mementoes to both in appreciation of their many years of service.

One of the major preoccupations of the president and board of trustees was the question of building another dormitory. There was no unanimity among the trustees on this problem. The matter was discussed as early as January, 1969, when the board agreed that preparations should be initiated to apply for a government loan and commissioned Frederick T. Daly to take charge of procedures.[16] Eight months later, on September 11, the proposal was discussed at great length. Four days later the trustees met with the staff of the dean of students' office together with Andrew J. Martelon, director of college relations, Philip R. Flanigan, director of admissions, Eugene A. Donohoue, director of business and finance, and Randy Roth, president of the student body. Mr. Donohoue made an excellent presentation dealing with the implications of obtaining a government loan for such a project. The minutes reflect a serious consideration of all the facets of the proposal. On September 17, 1969, the board passed a resolution authorizing Mattione and Maginnis the board secretary "to apply to the Department of Housing and Urban Development for a loan in the amount of $950,000 to assist in financing the construction of a new three-story dormitory to provide housing for 217 women students."[17] When the application was submitted the officials of HUD raised objections; they showed concern about the number of vacancies in the existing dormitories. At the time there were 117 unoccupied spaces in the three residences. Donohoue argued that this was a temporary situation and that there was definitely a need for a separate dormitory for women students.[18] Then there are no references to this matter in the minutes of the board for a year. Finally, the trustees met with Robert Borella of HUD, general contractor, Emil Gimeno, and Manuel Salinas of the Department of Justice Community Relations Services on February 23, 1971, to discuss the procedures of considering bids on the building project.[19] A month later Daly reported to the trustees that bids had been turned in, and on April 5 the board empowered the president of the college to award the contract in the amount of $1,108,933 to Webco Construction of Lakewood for the construction of the dormitory. Ground was broken in April, 1971.[20]

Mattione's most pressing preoccupation throughout his incumbency was

---

[16]*Trustees' Meetings,* 1966-1971.

[17]*Trustees' Meetings,* 1966-1971.

[18]*Op. cit.*

[19]*Op. cit.*

[20]John Otto of HUD expedited matters leading to the final arrangement with the Federal Government. Mr. Otto had attended classes in the evening division of the college and earned his degree from Regis.

that of working on a plan for building a high school. Ryan had taken a few tentative steps in this direction when he had ordered that some tuition money be set aside for this purpose and purchased property in southeast Denver as a site. In time, the value of the property on Havana Street increased dramatically, and before Ryan left Regis he proposed that the land be sold and the money used to construct a building on the Regis campus. After Mattione assumed the responsibility of governing the two divisions, he explored the possibilities of establishing the high school as a separate entity. During his first year there was some delay in formulating plans because the provincial transferred James Eatough to Wichita and the new principal, David L. Hartenbach, needed time to familiarize himself with his responsibilities.

During the period from September, 1969, to June, 1971, the minutes of the board of trustees reflect the fact that questions regarding a separate high school with its own plant and administration were a major concern of the board. It would serve no useful purpose to pursue those discussions in detail; however, a summary of the deliberations concerning the problems of choice of site, recruitment of manpower, and financing may be of some interest.

In choosing a site it was quite clear that there was no intention of adhering to Ryan's first plan of relocating the school in southeast Denver. It was evidently more practical to construct a new plant on the Regis property. The college engaged the Haldeman-Lonco Associates, an architectural firm, to assign an engineer the task of making a feasibility study of a possible site for a new plant. The engineer, W. Don Nesbet, proposed three potential sites: Federal Boulevard, 50th Avenue at the stadium, and the northeast corner at Lowell Boulevard. Mr. Nesbet made his report to the trustees in a meeting held on May 4, 1971; since there were so many other problems to be considered, especially finances, the board did not make a choice at that meeting.[21] In the meantime Hartenbach had considered the possibility of purchasing the ten-year-old building of Mapleton High School which had been put up for sale.

After checking on this lead, the Regis principal reported to the board that the building was in disrepair and not flexible enough for the purposes he had in mind for Regis.[22] The second alternative was that Regis consider taking over Cathedral High School, but after discussion the board rejected this solution.

As the discussions progressed it became increasingly clear that any solution to the question of establishing a separate entity had to include a consideration of available manpower. Through the years Regis had counted

---

[21]*Trustees' Meetings,* 1966-1971.
[22]*Op. cit.*

on a regular supply of young Jesuits who were assigned to the faculty by the provincial of the Missouri Province. This source began to dry up dramatically in the late sixties, and it was obvious that financial plans for a new school would have to include lay teachers' salaries at current scales. Without a considerable endowment it would be difficult for the high school to survive as a separate entity.

The most complicated problem confronting the trustees was that of finding enough money to finance the project of building a new high school. There was no hope that the corporation could secure a loan from the federal government for such an undertaking. A second potential source, the Archdiocese of Denver, was so burdened with financial problems that it was not possible for recently installed Archbishop James V. Casey to support a major fund-raising project. Monsignor William H. Jones of the Archdiocesan board of education was invited to meet with Provincial Gerald R. Sheahan and the Regis board of trustees to explore the possibility of financial support from the Archdiocese. Monsignor Jones could give encouragement but was not in a position to make any promises of financial aid. In the course of the discussions about finances it became apparent that a solution might be found in the sale of the Havana Street property and the Fraser villa. The provincial had asked Mattione to send him accurate figures on the value of these properties by November 1, 1969.[23] Estimates were made with the help of Thomas A. Waters, businessman, and Milton Conway, realtor, former Regis students. When the board met on November 12, 1969, the members discussed six options that had been suggested by the provincial: close the high school; build on Federal Boulevard; take over Cathedral, Holy Family, or Mullen; or operate Mullen jointly with the Christian Brothers.[24] The trustees concluded that the second option was the only possible one.

The question of a new high school was a matter of great concern for the trustees in successive meetings. As discussions progressed it became increasingly clear that a decision had to be made regarding the separate incorporation of the high school. It was also obvious that there would have to be a division of assets. The provincial of the Missouri Province was so interested in finding a solution for this problem that he brought his consultors to Denver along with John W. Padberg and Charles F. McDermott as resource persons to meet with the Regis board of trustees on December 23, 1969. After lengthy discussion the province consultors recommended that the board find the answer to two questions; "a) how much would the present Regis Corporation pay to buy out the High School Corporation for its

---

[23]*Op. cit.*
[24]*Op. cit.*

equitable share in the present assets of the existing Regis Corporation? b) what kind of help would the college give the high school to raise the balance?"[25] The provincial requested answers to these questions by January 30, 1970. The board proceeded with dispatch and agreed to establish a committee of five men to work out an equitable maximum and minimum statement of division of assets. Ralph F. Taylor and Arthur O. Verdieck were chosen to represent the high school, William T. Miller and John P. Teeling the college. John W. Padberg of St. Louis University was selected as a referee to help work out an equitable settlement of the assets. After an intensive review of the possessions of the corporation the committee submitted its recommendations to the board of trustees. The board considered the report at great length and finally agreed that the college would give the high school approximately thirty acres of land and $2,000,000 for a new high school.[26] The college hoped that it could realize that sum of money from the sale of the Havana Street and Fraser properties. A month later, on February 17, Hartenbach received approval from the provincial to work out a plan for a new building. The trustees, furthermore, planned to launch a concerted fund-raising campaign using the slogan "Jesuit Education in Denver," and they engaged the Brakeley Corporation for this purpose.

In the following months a committee worked out the details for the proposed building. The committee was chaired by the president and included James H. Baker, successor to Hartenbach as principal, Guy H. Gibbs, assistant principal, and Jesuit faculty members Arthur O. Verdieck and Elmer J. Carroll. The proposal was sent to the provincial who forwarded it to Jesuit General Pedro Arrupe. The latter wrote to Provincial Sheahan and asked some searching questions, concluding, "I ask that you explain more clearly how the high school hopes to meet its annual budget deficit, what the new building will cost, and where the faculty intend to reside; only then can I bestow my approval upon this enterprising and laudable proposal."[27] The questions were answered to the general's satisfaction and Mattione informed the board of trustees in a meeting on November 10, 1970, that Rome approved the construction of a new high school on condition that there would be a balanced budget and no capital debt.[28] At this juncture the provincial assigned to the Regis community Gregory H. Jacobsmeyer, who had recently supervised the building of DeSmet High School in St. Louis, as special consultant to the building committee "to advise it [the committee] for cost

---

[25]*Op. cit.*
[26]*Op. cit.*
[27]M.P.A.
[28]*Ibid.*

especially in those areas of building where technical expertise is required."[29]

Mattione, in his usual decisive way, proceeded to obtain the necessary money and on April 21, 1970, he asked the board to approve the sale of the Havana Street property to JAM, Inc. and the trustees voted unanimously in favor of the transaction. Finding a purchaser for the Fraser property was not as successful and many Jesuits began to have misgivings about giving up the property donated by the Cozens family. Furthermore, serious consideration had been given to a major fund-raising campaign. Jerome Coll, special assistant to the president, and Mr. Lucien Escallier reported to the board on February 23, 1971, that a ten-year campaign to raise $10,000,000 was feasible. In the light of future developments it is interesting to note their recommendations:

In order to bring this about the development office must be restructured. Emphasis is to be placed on a coordinated college/high school effort involving salesmen for both parts of the Regis community. A more effective public information program must be developed. Regis' family picture must be stretched out to the community. The President's role is envisioned as critical and the annual fund must be improved substantially in order to form a basis of giving experience to Regis from its various publics.[30]

In the meantime a change had been made affecting the relationship of the Jesuit community with the corporation. During Ryan's regime a superior dependent upon the president had governed the Jesuits relieving Ryan of some of his responsibilities. Thomas J. Sheehy, Bernard S. Karst and Robert J. O'Sullivan had served in that capacity. In February, 1971, the general of the Society of Jesus appointed John P. Teeling rector of the Jesuit community and in April the provincial wrote to Mattione informing him that the time had come to divide the Regis corporation into three separate entities: college, high school, and Jesuit community. The provincial concluded, "I hope that during my forthcoming joint meeting with the trustees and the Rector and his consultors on Monday, May 17, we shall be able to make definite decisions about a high school corporation and Board of Trustees, and that we shall set reasonable target dates for making the Jesuit community a separate corporation and for making the Board of Trustees a larger and more diversified body."[31] Sheahan met with representatives of the Jesuit community on May

---

[29]*Trustees' Minutes,* 1966-1971.
[30]*Op. cit.*
[31]*Op. cit.*

17. There was frank and lengthy discussion of the matters included on the Provincial's agenda.

On May 17, 1971, Louis G. Mattione submitted his resignation. He had accepted the office with reluctance and administered the affairs of the college and high school during a very critical period of three years and four months. He charted a new course and prepared for future developments by making more effective use of the board of trustees in seeking a solution to such problems as the building of a new high school and making adequate provision for the coeds on campus. Mattione possessed an openness to suggestions and was very accessible to faculty, students, and staff. Impatient with protocol and lengthy discussions, he preferred to make decisions and get on with the business of keeping the college and high school operating on a day-to-day basis. Pressing problems kept him so occupied that he delegated to others the task of keeping the image of college and high school alive in the civic community.

The academic life of the college went through some notable changes during Mattione's administration, changes that reflect the trend toward liberalization of requirements. Many departments had required that seniors pass an oral comprehensive examination in their major field as a requisite for graduation. During the sixties there was some agitation against this requirement and the faculty submitted a recommendation that this practice be discontinued. The trustees discussed the matter on May 6, 1969, and voted to approve the request of the faculty.[32] The trustees also approved a pass/no-pass policy for most electives with the proviso that it be studied for a two-year period and a report submitted to the board. Students had been challenging the school's policy of requiring fifteen hours of philosophy so vehemently that the trustees took the matter under consideration and voted to reduce the requirement to six hours.[33] Given the hectic activities during the spring of 1971, it is not surprising that Mattione asked to be relieved of the burdens of administration to make way for a fresh approach to the complex problems of discovering sources of funds for building a new high school and restructuring the Regis corporation.

Three weeks after Mattione tendered his resignation, to take effect on July 1, Provincial Sheahan met with the board of trustees. He informed the members that he realized that in the changing climate of opinion in Jesuit educational circles provincials should no longer appoint presidents of colleges or universities; they should be selected by a search committee appointed by local authorities. Sheahan explained to the trustees that because

---

[32]*Op. cit.*
[33]*Op. cit.*

of the complexity of the current problems confronting the Regis community he had decided, after consultation, to recommend that Thomas James Casey be approved by the board to serve as acting president for one year. After some discussion the trustees voted to offer the presidency to Casey. They also deemed it advisable that each member of the board submit his resignation to be effective on July 1, 1971. The resignations of James Baker and William Miller were refused, those of Frederick Daly and Edward Maginnis were approved. The trustees then invited Arthur Verdieck and Harold Stansell to become members of the board with terms beginning on July 1. The provincial then suggested that the acting president proceed to set up a search committee to identify a permanent president, to reopen the question of the high school in the light of a decrease in manpower and a rise in building costs, and, finally, to undertake the task of reorganizing the corporate structure of Regis College and Regis High School.[34]

Thomas James Casey, a man of wide and varied experience, was a native of Massachusetts. After earning his bachelor's degree at Boston College, he entered the armed forces and went through basic training at Lowry Field, Denver, then served with the Air Corps in the southwest Pacific until the end of hostilities. When the war was over, Casey returned to Denver and enrolled in Westminster Law School, since amalgamated into the University of Denver; having earned his degree, he began a career as a lawyer working in the firm of Holland and Hart. In 1952 he left the firm and entered the Missouri Province of the Society of Jesus to study for the priesthood, completing the course in ten years and being ordained by Richard Cardinal Cushing, Archbishop of Boston. Casey's religious superiors, wishing to capitalize on his legal training, sent him to the University of Chicago to study for a Master's degree in business administration with a major in hospital administration; he was then appointed assistant to John J. Flanagan, executive director of the Catholic Hospital Association, and shortly thereafter succeeded Flanagan in that office. In 1970 provincial Gerald R. Sheahan assigned Casey to his staff as supervisor of Jesuits engaged in the pastoral and social apostolates. When Mattione resigned as president of Regis, the provincial asked Casey to accept an appointment as interim president of the college and high school. Sheahan met with the Board of Trustees on June 12, 1971, and recommended that they elect Casey to serve as president for one year. After frank discussion of all the aspects of the proposal, the trustees voted to approve the selection of Thomas James Casey as the twenty-first president of Regis; in the course of the discussion with the trustees, Sheahan stated that the new president should address himself to the task of finding

---

[34]*Op. cit.*

solutions to three major problems: deciding the future of Regis High School, the revision of the corporate structure of the institution, and the establishment of a search committee to identify a permanent president.[35]

Before he left office Mattione had undertaken the project of realizing a million dollars from the sale of the property in southeast Denver and another million for the land in Fraser; the money was to be earmarked for building a new plant for the high school. Casey reviewed the record of the initial transactions regarding the Havana property and reported to the trustees on July 1 that the closing date for the purchase agreement had been extended to September 15, 1971, at which time Regis would receive the first payment. The rest of the money would be paid over a period of ten years.[36] In reviewing the records concerning the Fraser property, Casey discovered that there were complications. A potential purchaser had been identified but problems of zoning and water rights had to be solved. Moreover, there was a growing concern regarding the interests of the Jesuits in the property; some maintained that the Cozens family had deeded the property to the Jesuits as members of a religious community and not to the college as a corporation. Casey informed the trustees that he would study the problems, consult with attorneys, and make his recommendations to the board.[37] It became increasingly clear that the high school would not get a new plant in the near future; in fact, the architects for the proposed building, Haldeman-Lonco Associates, submitted their bill "in accordance with the provisions of the recently terminated contract for the construction of a new high school building."[38]

The second problem that needed immediate attention, the revision of the corporate structure, had been under consideration for some time. Ryan and Mattione had worked on the project but did not finish a final draft. Casey received a mandate from the provincial who reminded the president of the necessity of a revision since the Jesuit community was moving toward separate incorporation, following the example of Jesuit colleges and universities throughout the country. Casey addressed himself to the task of revising the constitution with commendable thoroughness. He sought the assistance of Anthony F. Zarlengo, a prominent lawyer, who helped him to draft amendments to the articles of incorporation. The amended document was shown to John P. Teeling and his consultors and to provincial Gerald R. Sheahan, who recommended that it be submitted to the general of the Society of Jesus and his American advisers, Vincent T. O'Keefe and Harold O. Small, all of whom approved the amendments. The document was ratified

---

[35]*Op. cit.*
[36]*Minutes, July 1, 1971*, p. 2.
[37]*Ibid.*
[38]*Minutes, Dec. 9, 1971*, p. 1.

by the trustees and then submitted to the members of the Jesuit community who, after considerable discussion, accepted the revised document. The major revisions made in the articles of incorporation were a change in name from Regis College to The Regis Educational Corporation, provision for the enlargement of the board of trustees enabling Jesuits from outside the Regis community and eventually lay persons to serve on the board, and restriction of membership in the corporation to the members of the Board of Trustees.[39] Finally the way was prepared for the expansion of the board and the separate incorporation of the Jesuit community.

In the meantime the acting president had taken steps to identify a successor. He contacted other Jesuit institutions and asked for information concerning the procedures that had been adopted to find a qualified Jesuit to succeed him in the office of president. He followed the suggestions given in answer to his questions and, after consultation with the trustees, established a search committee to consider applications and make recommendations. The committee chaired by Francis J. Ozog (chemistry), included Alice Fehrenbach (psychology), John L. Flood (business administration), Harry R. Klocker (philosophy), Thomas J. Steele (English), Martin C. Kelly, (Denver businessman and member of the Board of Regents), and John M. Lamb (president of the student senate executive board). Under the competent leadership of Dr. Ozog, the committee initiated a search for a president in September. After numerous meetings during which applications were screened, the field was reduced to three applicants. The committee submitted its recommendations to the board of trustees on February 2, 1972. The board commended the members of the committee for its accomplishment in meeting the deadline that had been set. After considerable discussion of the strengths and weaknesses of the candidates, the board decided to invite David M. Clarke to visit the campus and to meet the trustees and other appropriate corporate officers.[40] Clarke was willing to accept the challenge and the board voted to offer him the presidency of Regis College and High School.

Casey had been a busy man during his year of incumbency. He had to suspend plans for building a new plant for the high school. His legal instinct saved the corporation from being embarrassed over the transactions leading to the sale of the property in southeast Denver, and he wisely suspended

---

[39]The constitution of 1893 stipulated that "all the priests of the Society of Jesus residing and domiciled in said College shall be members, and eligible to office in the Corporation." Some Jesuits took a dim view of the amendment changing this provision and restricting membership in the corporation to members of the board. It took a great deal of effort on the part of the president to gain the necessary two-thirds vote of the total membership required by the Constitution of 1893 to win approval of the amendment.

[40]*Minutes, February 7, 1972.*

negotiations for the sale of the Fraser property. After considerable planning he prepared the way for a new era for the board of trustees as directors of The Regis Educational Corporation. With considerable help from a search committee he found a man to succeed him in the office of president.

During Casey's short regime life on campus was reasonably orderly and the students quite content. The presence of coeds became part of the normal scene. The young ladies did not hesitate to participate in campus activities, in fact, a first was attained when Penny Dempsey was elected president of the executive board of the student senate in February, 1972. Under the able administration of Clarence H. Kellogg, who had transferred from the high school to the college in 1966 to become athletic director, students could participate in intercollegiate or intramural sports. Those who were more athletically inclined could compete in interscholastic soccer, swimming, skiing, tennis, golf, baseball and basketball. Membership in the Rocky Mountain Athletic Conference facilitated the scheduling of games with schools having a comparable number of students. There was, moreover, greater participation in intramurals; the bulletin for 1970-1971 recorded that the program involved over fifty percent of the student body in a wide range of sports.[41]

Casey had little time to give to the development of faculty during his year as acting president. He did, however, take steps to add some capable men to the staff of the administration. In December 1971, he proposed to engage Thomas A. Emmet to study the future of the educational program of Regis High School and its relation to the college. In reviewing his qualifications, Casey referred to Emmet's experience as an educational consultant and as dean of men, dean of the evening college of arts and sciences, and assistant academic vice president of the University of Detroit. The trustees voted:

> to approve Emmet as special assistant to the president, to conduct a
> study and prepare recommendations to the Board of Trustees toward
> effecting greater integration of Regis' secondary and higher education
> programs and more efficient utilization of resources and facilities.[42]

The appointment of George T. Burns to the position of executive director for development manifested a growing awareness of the need for better coordination of all aspects of fund development, public relations, and alumni programs. Burns, a personable man, had sixteen years experience working on the staffs of several colleges; eventually he established his own consulting firm. A third significant step was the promotion of Lawrence W. Durance, Jr., to the position of director of alumni program planning.

---

[41]*Bulletin for 1970-1971*, p. 25.
[42]*Regis Roundup*, Spring of 1972, p. 6.

Durance had joined the staff in December, 1969, and was aware of the challenge of his new responsibility for the development and implementation of all programs for the alumni.

During Casey's year as president the last link between Regis and the former New Mexico-Colorado Mission was broken. On December 25, 1971, Bernard J. Murray died at the age of eighty-two. He had attended old Sacred Heart College before he entered the Society of Jesus. He served at Regis as principal of the high school, recruiter, counselor, and spiritual director. He never seemed to be at home in the classroom but had proved invaluable as a recruiter for Regis in Nebraska, Wyoming, and Colorado, especially during the critical years of the depression. His Irish wit endeared him to many and won lasting friends for the school. During his declining years he counseled students and young Jesuits. Few could match his love for Regis. Anyone interested in the history of the school must of necessity appreciate the dedication of this man who preserved the knowledge of the past and helped to perpetuate a feeling of appreciation for the work of the Jesuits from the province of Naples.[43]

David M. Clarke became the twenty-second president of Regis on August 1, 1972, the first president in the history of the school who held the office by virtue of a vote by the members of the Board of Trustees. The new president had impressive credentials: he earned his doctorate in physical chemistry at Northwestern University and gained experience in administration as academic vice president at Gonzaga University and, later, provost and academic vice president at the College of St. Francis, Joliet. He was a member of the boards of trustees of Loyola University in Chicago and Holy Cross College. The day after Clarke assumed the presidency, the trustees met, elected him a member of the board, and then chose Thomas James Casey as chairman.[44]

During the summer of 1972 some members of the college faculty took steps to form the Regis Educational Association. They distributed circulars explaining their objectives. The message was not well received by some faculty members who responded by initiating a movement to establish a chapter of the American Association of University Professors on the campus. By the time the semester was well under way it was clear that the faculty was fairly evenly divided between the two associations. At this juncture the

---

[43]Dick Connor, a former publicity director of Regis, wrote an interesting appreciation on ''B.J.'' for the *Regis Roundup,* October, 1971, pp. 11-12.

[44]As one approaches the contemporary scene it becomes increasingly difficult to maintain a proper perspective. Consequently, it seems prudent to record the more important developments that took place in the final five years of the first hundred, events that marked the beginning of a new era for the college and high school.

officials of the National Labor Relations Board became involved. After conferring with the interested parties, the NLRB decided that there should be an election; the ballot presented three options: REA, AAUP, No Agent. The voting was so close that the officials of the board ordered another election to be held on January 24, 1973. After the results of that election were tabulated, it was announced that the supporters of AAUP had won. Henceforth, the officers and agents of the Regis chapter of AAUP would undertake collective bargaining with the representatives of the college administration.

A second significant development under Clarke was the expansion of the board of trustees. Casey had prepared the way and his successor took steps toward implementing the plan of identifying and inviting qualified prospects. The president was under constraint to keep a majority of Jesuits on the board and sent his first invitations to three distinguished members of the Society of Jesus: James J. Hennesey, Associate Professor, Jesuit School of Theology at Berkeley; Paul C. Reinert, President, St. Louis University; and John H. Reinke, President, Loyola Academy, Wilmette. These were excellent choices and, fortunately, the three men agreed to serve and joined the board at its September, 1973, meeting. In the meantime, Robert J. Starratt had succeeded James H. Baker as principal of Regis High School and became an *ex officio* member of the board; Baker was invited to continue to serve. An expanded board became a better board. Under Casey's direction as chairman it was clear that the board was becoming more professional. The meetings were scheduled and held at designated times, the minutes were recorded in a more presentable manner, and it became obvious that the emphasis in directing the affairs of the institution was shifting from the president of the corporation to the board of trustees. There was a growing realization of the need for fiscal responsibility, and the president kept the board informed about the steps he was taking to achieve this. He engaged the firm of Frantzreb, Pray, Ferner and Thompson as consultants, and established a corporate finance group to act as advisers in matters financial with the special charge to give advice regarding the balancing of the budget. Earlier he had asked the board to approve the appointment of James W. Robertson as director of corporate services.

It is fortunate that Clarke strengthened the corporate structure because it enabled him and the board to meet the challenge of making difficult decisions about repairing Main Hall, building a facility for the high school, and relocating the members of the Jesuit community. A special meeting of the Board of Trustees was called for April 20-21, 1974, to discuss these matters and make the necessary decisions regarding them. The principal of the high school, R. J. Starratt, forcefully presented his case for a new high school and the rector of the Jesuit community, John P. Teeling, reported on the possibility of renovating Carroll Hall and making it a residence for the Jesuits. The trustees considered these matters and asked probing questions. Finally, after much intense discussion it was moved that the board authorize the construction of Phase I of the high school and the attendant renovation of Main Hall. The trustees further authorized the renovation of Carroll Hall and relocation of the Jesuit community. The board charged the corporate finance group to recommend the most effective method of financing the projects.[45]

After these difficult decisions had been made, Clarke and Casey took steps to add more members to the board. In due time five Jesuits were added and the way was clear for inviting lay persons to serve. Invitations were sent to Max G. Brooks, Annabelle Deline, Walter F. Imhoff, Joseph P. McConaty and John R. Moran, Jr. offering them positions on the Board. All accepted and were elected at the meeting of the trustees on October 4, 1975. Ryan's dream of having lay participation on the board of trustees had finally become a reality. One further significant step was taken in February, 1976, when John R.Moran,Jr.,a Denver lawyer,was elected chairman of the board.

With a strong board supporting him, Clarke worked with determination to find solutions to the many problems that faced the institution in the seventies. Some important decisions had to be made regarding the high school. One important matter concerning the division was the necessity of establishing stability in the administration. After the seventeen years (1951-1968) of Eatough's regime as principal there was a succession of short-term administrators. Clarke sought to remedy this by appointing a headmaster to be the chief operating officer of the high school. This matter was presented to the board of trustees in May, 1975, and the board approved the appointment of Sherwood T. Boian for this office. During the early seventies notable changes were made in the high school curriculum. A modular approach to scheduling provided greater flexibility for students following a course of studies. A separate office was established, making it possible for the officials of the high school to plan development and promotion and to organize the alumni. Arthur O. Verdieck, S.J., became assistant to the headmaster for alumni and community relations; and Timothy Willard was designated as assistant to the headmaster. The long tradition of excellence in forensics was maintained under the direction of William E. Becker, S.J. Students competed in the programs sponsored by the National Forensic League; David Miller placed first in the nation in impromptu speaking at the University of Pittsburg in 1973, and three years later James Attridge won first place in the National Forensic Tournament held at the Air Force Academy.[46]

---

[45]*Minutes, April 20-21, 1974*, pp. 7-9.
[46]Memorandum from W. E. Becker.

The college had a similar problem regarding stability. Grollmes resigned as dean in 1973. Under the circumstances Clarke did not have time to institute a search for a new dean; he appointed the ever-reliable John V. Coyne as director of faculty academic services to administer the business of the dean's office during the interregnum, then named a search committee to find a new dean. The committee recommended Edward J. Lynch of the California province and the trustees offered him the position. Lynch resigned after two years, and Clarke appointed Franciscan Father David J. McBriar as acting dean while another search was conducted. After the qualifications of the applicants had been assessed, the position was offered to Michael J. Sheeran, S.J., who had recently joined the college faculty.

Two significant innovations were introduced, one in 1975, the other in the following year. The first was the addition of a lawyer to the administrative staff. At the time that this matter was presented to the trustees, many searching questions were asked. Finally, the trustees voted to approve the position of legal counsel for the corporation with the understanding that there be a review of the performance of the lawyer after a year and a consideration of the necessity for continuing the position.[47] The president appointed A. Thomas Elliott to this position and in February, 1976, named him executive secretary to the board of trustees. The second innovation involved a reorganization of the corporate structure prompted by the increasing importance of continuing education.[48] Clarke appointed a presidential panel to study the existing structure and make recommendations for updating the same. The members of the panel realized that the corporation should recognize the importance of the office of continuing education. Under the able direction of Donald L. Salmon and the assistance of Frederick T. Daly, S.J., that office was growing in stature. The panel recommended that continuing education be given equal status with the high school and the college and that the office of provost be established. The provost would have the duty of overseeing the academic programs of the three divisions. When this proposal was presented to the board of trustees in October, 1976, some of the members of the board asked searching questions but, after thorough discussion, the board approved the appointment of David J. McBriar, O.F.M., as the first provost in the history of the corporation.

President Clarke found it necessary to reduce the size of the faculty in an effort to meet the requirements of budgetary responsibility. Under his

---

[47]*Minutes, December 12-13,* p. 11.

[48]Donald L. Salmon resigned his position as chairman of the Department of History and joined the administrative staff. He was responsible for developing the continuing education program.

leadership and that of the board of trustees a new era in the relations between the high school and college was initiated. Some faculty members taught in both divisions and high school students shared the use of some of the facilities of the corporation. The high school flourished and attracted a great number of students until the limitations of space demanded the stabilization of enrollment. The college authorities had to cope with a decline in the number of students but, fortunately, the decline stabilized as the school approached the end of the first hundred years. As Regis prepared to celebrate its centenary the high school and college appear, by all the signs, to be ready to continue the best of their cherished traditions into another century.

Chapter 8

Alumni

One of the facets of the American educational experience has been the formation of alumni associations. Graduates of colleges and universities were, more or less willingly, persuaded to organize into groups that offered an opportunity to foster continuing friendships that had been formed during the years of study as well as to give moral and financial support for Alma Mater. The former students of the College of the Sacred Heart formed such an association in 1900 and elected as officers for the following year James S. McGinnis, president, John W. Bucher, first vice-president, Thomas F. Murphy, second vice-president, and J. Hervey Nichols, secretary and treasurer.[1] There is no available evidence of the effectiveness of the alumni during the early years of the existence of the organization; in fact there seemed to be a great deal of uncertainty about the need for such an association. During the years a pattern is discernible—a period of enthusiasm in fostering a lively alumni association followed by a period of neglect. After the first attempt to involve the alumni in 1900 proved to be ineffective, the association was revived and reorganized in 1908. The catalogues for the years 1912 through 1914 do not have a reference to the group. The revival in 1915 deserves mention because in that year the alumni elected as their president John J. Sullivan, who was to become a successful businessman. Sullivan, a graduate of 1915, kept a lively interest in the development of the school for the better part of the century. Another active member, John P. Akolt (1911), the president of the association in 1917, was to contribute inestimable services in giving legal counsel to the presidents and the trustees through more than five decades.

The record for the first twenty years of the association was not impressive, perhaps due to there being few projects that would constitute a challenge for the alumni. A self-contained community made up entirely of Jesuits who were committed to the business of imparting a quality education to young men was not overly concerned about the public image of the school in the Denver community. The students, however, felt a need to foster continuing loyalty to Alma Mater. When the school paper was revived in 1919 the editor and his associates published alumni notes to help former students to keep

---

[1]*Catalogue 1899-1900*, p. 47.

informed about the careers of their former classmates.

The dissolution of the New Mexico-Colorado mission and the arrival of Robert M. Kelley as president inaugurated a new phase in the involvement of the alumni in the activities of the school. Alumni participated in the preparations for the introduction of the new president to the Denver community. Kelley intended to instill new life in the organization and to use it more effectively in his efforts to expand the facilities of the school. The catalogue for the year 1920-1921 recorded that there were a thousand members in the association and stated that they were to be given a "large share of the labor of building a greater Regis College."[2] The president counted on the support of former students when he launched his drive for funds to finance his building program. In the event, he realized that the alumni gave him moral and vocal assistance but were not able to help him achieve his financial goal. The results of the fund-raising campaign were less than spectacular, and a disappointed Kelley seems to have abandoned his plan to build an active alumni association. The catalogues have very brief statements for the years 1925 to 1933 referring to the organization and no reference at all from 1934 to 1962. Former students, however, were not inactive during those years; they did as much as was possible to help the college and high school during the critical periods of the depression by participating in the "Save Regis" campaign. The college was not unmindful of its students during the Second World War. The president sanctioned the publication of the *Alumni Magazine* even though the school had to operate on a very limited budget. When John J. Flanagan conducted a quiet campaign to help liquidate the debt, he received support from the alumni. In 1946 Flanagan appointed Thomas E. Kelly moderator of a newly formed group including both graduates and non-graduate friends of Regis. Some four years later thirteen individuals decided to revive the alumni association and pledged themselves to recuit more members by the time of the next scheduled meeting. In 1950 the members of the Alpha Delta Gamma fraternity assumed the responsibility of publishing the *Alumni Review* and solicited names and addresses of former students. The response was good; some six hundred addresses were recorded. The success of the basketball team in the fifties revived the interests of a number of the alumni.

A new era in the history of the alumni was initiated by Richard F. Ryan, who was determined to bring Regis into the mainstream of public life by initiating programs of public and alumni relations, publicity, and development. Ryan benefited from an opportunity that had not been available to his

---

[2]*Catalogue 1920-1921*, p. 56. The task of compiling a list of alumni was facilitated because the catalogues up to 1919 published lists of graduates since 1890.

predecessors, the chance to share in an exchange of ideas with Jesuit presidents and their staffs of colleges and universities in the Midwest regarding the many problems with which they had to cope. Enlightened by what he learned during the sessions, Ryan took steps to make better use of his meager staff. A Regis Club had been organized on April 26, 1954, with the objective of establishing a better relationship between the college and former students and alumni. In subsequent years the number of graduates increased and a greater percentage of them came from states other than Colorado; the president and his staff adjusted to the changing pattern by making the Regis Club, which had been established in 1954, into a national organization.[3] Evidence of growing interest in alumni is found in the *Regis Roundup* which in 1959 published an advertisement for a director of alumni relations of expanded alumni and related programs.[4]

In a few years the efforts to instill new life in the alumni association showed results. The catalogue for 1962-1963 recorded that there were approximately three thousand members of the National Regis Club with active chapters in Washington, D.C., Chicago, Milwaukee, St. Louis, Wichita, Pueblo, Los Angeles, and San Francisco. Many members of the club participated as well by contributing to the Alumni Fund, which brought in more than $100,000 for the college's development program.[5]

Ryan and his staff had established a viable alumni association, and his successor, Louis G. Mattione, took steps to make it even more effective. In 1968 Mattione appointed Michael D. Groshek, a graduate of 1953, chairman of a special study committee whose basic function was to formulate recommendations for reorganization of the alumni association.[6] Groshek invited active alumni from a number of cities in the country to participate in the work of the committee. The response was impressive. The committee developed a questionnaire and contacted alumni throughout the United States, soliciting their responses to the questions proposed. Daniel M. McNeill and Father Edward H. Wintergalen recorded and analyzed the responses of the six hundred alumni who replied. The results of this venture enabled the members of the committee to get down to the serious business of reorganizing the association and planning for the future. The committee met at the college on January 16 and 17, 1970, and after serious discussion about the structure, activities, and objectives of the alumni association, submitted a report to the president on its findings and made recommendations for the future. The

---

[3]The author is indebted to the anonymous writer of a report submitted to President Mattione in April 1970 for much of this material.

[4]*Regis Roundup,* Summer 1959, p. 15.

[5]*Catalogue 1962-1963,* p. 101.

[6]*Regis Roundup,* February 1969, p. 13.

major subjects of the final report were: alumni representation on the board of trustees and on the administrative committees of the college; adoption of a constitution and bylaws; promotion of continuing communication with alumni; and continuing involvement of the alumni board in cultivating annual gifts.[7] A considerable amount of enthusiasm was generated by this experience and new vistas opened up for a greater participation by alumni in the affairs of the college. In the next year, 1971, the board of directors of the association selected Edwin J. Feulner, a graduate of 1963, as president for the year 1971-1972. He was the first non-Denver president in the history of the alumni organization. The future seemed full of promise but the financial crisis of 1971 forestalled the realization of the hoped-for goals. Unfortunately, it was difficult to guarantee continuity in the office of alumni relations. The turnover of the alumni directors precluded long-range planning. But a number of events involving the alumni, such as the annual picnic and golf tournament, met with at least moderate success, and the alumni news published in the *Regis Roundup* kept the alumni informed about the accomplishments of former classmates.

No alumni association could continue long in existence without showing some interest in the careers of graduates and others who, without graduating, had spent some time in the halls of Alma Mater. It is difficult to determine how much influence a school had on its students, but most, if not all, schools claim a share in the success of its former students. When administrators appeal to the public for financial support they often strengthen their case by publishing a list of successful alumni. David M. Clarke directed the staff of the Development office to prepare a Case Statement for the college in 1975. The authors of the statement, relying on the research of Paul Q. Riederer, stated that the college numbered among its alumni 250 physicians, 100 dentists, 300 lawyers, 1700 businessmen, 400 accountants, 200 educators and 500 teachers.[8] There were, moreover, a goodly number of former students serving as priests in the archdiocese of Denver and various religious orders, especially the Society of Jesus. Some former students achieved notable success in public life. For example, Charles F. Brannan, who attended the college for three semesters, served as Secretary of Agriculture in the cabinet of President Harry S. Truman from 1949 to 1953; Edward C. Day, a graduate of the college, was elected to the Colorado Supreme Court in 1956; Stephen L. R. McNichols was Governor of the State of Colorado from 1957 to 1963; Joseph M. Montoya, who attended the college from 1931 to

---

[7]Report submitted to President Mattione, April 1970. This report is in the files of the director of alumni relations.

[8]*Case Statement*, 1975, p. 5.

1934, served as United States Senator for New Mexico; and Dennis J. Gallagher, a graduate of the class of 1961, has represented his constituents in the state legislature and the state senate of Colorado. The Church has also been served well. Regis counts four bishops among her alumni: Bernard J. Sullivan, S.J., missionary bishop of Patna; Hubert M. Newell of Cheyenne; and two auxiliary bishops of Denver, George R. Evans of Regis High School and Richard C. Hanifen of the high school and college.[9] Among the many former Regis students who entered the profession of educational administration three have especially distinguished themselves. Paul C. and Carl M. Reinert are both graduates of Regis High School; the former was president of St. Louis University from 1949 to 1973 and chancellor since 1973; the latter was president of Creighton University and has continued as vice president in charge of development. George C. Roche, III, a graduate of the high school and college, is president of Hillsdale College in Michigan. It is impossible to name all the alumni who have been successful in the medical, dental, and legal professions and the considerable number who have been active in business in various cities in the country. A few former students have served with distinction as judges. The Society of Jesus benefited from the services of a number of Regis men who entered the order, especially Daniel H. Conway, Leo F. Weber, and James W. Naughton. Conway and Weber each served as the major superior of all the Jesuits in the Missouri Province; Naughton was Secretary General of the order and has been attached to the administrative center of the Society for three decades.

Presidents and their staffs concentrated on developing a more effective alumni association for the college and neglected to promote a similar organization for the high school. Theodore J. Schulte, teacher and spiritual counselor, endeavored to keep in contact with alumni of the high school but did not receive much support from the administration. When the high school began to achieve its own identity in the seventies, James H. Baker undertook to establish an effective alumni organization for his division. Baker organized the task of assembling a roster of high school alumni. In time the lay teacher Tim Willard, with the able assistance of Arthur O. Verdieck, S.J., succeeded in assembling an updated directory for the alumni. Willard and Verdieck instituted a series of class reunions and solicited the support of former students for projects to benefit the high school. When Robert J. Starratt became principal he introduced an auction to be conducted each spring the proceeds of which were set aside for the needs of the high school. After the death of Edward F. Maguire, a graduate of the high school, Brother

---

[9]John J. Brown, a member of the former mission and president of the college and high school, was appointed first bishop of El Paso but resigned before being ordained a bishop.

Joseph Gockel established the Father Maguire Scholarship Fund to give financial aid to needy students. The highlight of the developing program of high school alumni relations was the testimonial dinner honoring Stephen R. Krieger, mathematics teacher, and Bernard S. Karst, former principal, which was served in the Grand Ballroom of the Brown Palace Hotel on January 31, 1973. The response of the alumni was excellent. The event was graced by the presence of Bishop George R. Evans and the astronaut John C. Sweigert. The two honorees received many letters of appreciation. This event was a fitting climax to the earlier efforts to revitalize the alumni association of Regis High School.

As Regis moves through the seventies there is reason for optimism for the future of developing alumni participation in the plans for the high school and college. Tim Willard, with the able assistance of Arthur O. Verdieck, S.J., hopefully will direct the alumni of the high school to even greater achievements. The college has reason to expect improved alumni relations because Paul Max, a 1969 graduate of the college and former student body president, has been appointed to direct all alumni activities of the college. The second century of the high school and college should witness a more effective and enduring relationship between Regis and men and women grateful for the quality education they received there and fond of remembering the years, the events, and the friends they associate with the name of Regis.

Bibliographical Notes

A number of standard histories of New Mexico and Colorado proved helpful in furnishing background for understanding the region in which the Neapolitan Jesuits carried on their missionary activity. *The Far Southwest 1846-1912* (W. W. Norton and Company, Inc., New York, 1970) by Howard Roberts Lamar and *The Great American Desert* (University of Nebraska Press, Lincoln, 1975) were very useful. Paul Horgan's *Lamy of Santa Fe* (Farrar, Straus and Giroux, New York, 1975) is an excellent biography of the bishop who brought the Jesuits to New Mexico but he has little to say about the work of the Jesuits in New Mexico. Frederick G. Bohme wrote his doctoral dissertation on the history of the Italians in New Mexico and included material on the work of the Jesuits in Las Vegas College with some good accounts of the activities of Father Donato Gasparri, *A History of the Italians in New Mexico* (Arno Press, New York, 1975). There is an old but good account of the Church in Rev. James H. Defouri's *Historical Sketch of the Catholic Church in New Mexico* (McCormick Brothers, San Francisco, 1887). Giuseppe M. Sorrentino, S.J., wrote a short history of the Mission in *Dalle Montagne Rocciose al Rio Bravo* (Casa Editrice Federico & Ardia, Napoli, n.d.). Sister M. Lilliana Owens. S.L., edited the "Diary of the Mission of New Mexico, May 27, 1867-October 18, 1874," the first part of which is an account of the journey the Jesuits made in the company of Bishop Lamy from New York to Santa Fe. This Diary is published in *Jesuit Beginnings in New Mexico 1867-1882* (Revista Catolica Press, El Paso, 1950). A very helpful work is the typescript copy of Ferdinand M. Troy's *Historia Missionis Novi Mexici et Coloradi*. There are good accounts of Jesuit Activities during the early years of the Mission in *Woodstock Letters* (Woodstock, Maryland) and the *Lettere Edificanti della Provincia Napoletana,* Serie 1-17, 1874-1930. Refreshing incidents related to experiences with the Jesuits were recorded in Sister Blandina Segale's *At the End of the Santa Fe Trail* (The Columbian Press, Columbus, 1932).

In time the Neapolitans came into contact with Joseph P. Machebeuf who was responsible for the Church in Colorado. In 1882 the bishop persuaded Dominic Pantanella to establish a school in Morrison. The bishop's biographer, W. J. Howlett, gave useful information about the development of the Church in Colorado in *The Life of the Right Reverend Joseph P. Machebeuf,*

D.D. (The Franklin Press, Pueblo, 1908). The bishop donated property and a building in Morrison to the Jesuits. Sam Arnold wrote an interesting account concerning Morrison, *The View from Mt. Morrison, The Story of a Colorado Town* (The Fur Press, Denver, 1974). The story of Sacred Heart College in Morrison was narrated by Francis X. Kowald (Typescript Copy in Regis College Archives). Father Kowald wrote his story some fifty years after his experiences as a young teacher in the school. The most helpful work covering the early years is the unpublished master's thesis of Edward R. Vollmar, S.J., *History of the Jesuit Colleges of New Mexico and Colorado 1867-1919* (St. Louis University, 1938). One of the college's presidents merited a full-scale biography written by Sister M. Lilliana Owens, S.L., *Most Reverend Anthony J. Schuler, S.J., D.D.* (Revista Catolica Press, El Paso, Texas, 1953).

Many books have been written about Catholic education; three were very helpful in the writing of this history: *The Jesuits and Education* by William J. McGucken (The Bruce Publishing Company, Milwaukee, 1932); Edward J. Power, *Catholic Higher Education* in *America a History* (Prentice-Hall, Inc., Englewood Cliffs, N.J., 1972); Msgr. William H. Jones, *The History of Catholic Education in the State of Colorado* (The Catholic University of America Press, Washington, D.C., 1955). A fourth work was useful for comparison of the college with other institutions in the state, Michael McGiffert, *The Higher Learning in Colorado, An Historical Study, 1860-1940* (Sage Books, Denver, 1964). Three histories of other Jesuit institutions provided many helpful hints: Raphael N. Hamilton, *The Story of Marquette University* (The Marquette University Press, Milwaukee, 1953), John B. McGloin, *Jesuits by the Golden Gate* (University of San Francisco, 1972), William B. Faherty, *Better the Dream* (St. Louis University, 1968). Ruth E. Wiberg's *Rediscovering Northwest Denver* (Bradford Printing Company, Denver, 1976) is an excellent work on the area in which the college and high school are located.

Daily newspapers, *The Denver Post* and *The Rocky Mountain News,* and the weekly *Denver Catholic Register* recorded many events of the school's history. Pertinent information was found in the college and high school publications *The Highlander, The Brown and Gold, The Regis Roundup, The Ranger* (the college annual), *The Raider Review, The Raider* (the high school annual) and *The Alumni Raider*. Catalogues, diaries, and minutes of the Board of Trustees were indispensable. Archives in Rome, Naples, St. Louis, and Denver yielded much relevant material.

Index

A.A.U.P., 185, 214, 221, 222
Adamson, W., 9
Albuquerque, N.M., 2, 3, 5, 6, 8
Akolt, John P., 79, 227
Alpha Delta Gamma Fraternity, 170
Alpha Kappa Psi, 188
Alpha Sigma Nu, 188
Alumni, 79, 227
Anderledy, Anton, 45, 48
Antonelli, Phil, 159, 171
Anthony, Sister M. Antonia, 184
Arnold, Sam, 26
Arrupe, Pedro, 181
Arthuis, Joseph, 27
A.S.T.P., 149, 150
Athletic Association, 17, 57, 96, 97
Athletic Program, 96
Attridge, James, 223
Axtell, Samuel B., 14, 15, 16

Baker, James H., 214, 217, 222, 231
Bailey, D. C., 86, 91, 92
Bailey, Charles M. (Mrs.), 66
Bailey, Claude, 66
Bailey, Everett S., 92
Bakewell, Francis F., 192
Baldassarre, Raphael A., 6, 7, 8, 9
Bannon, John F., 100
Barnabo, Alessandro, 2
Barnett, Kollie, 163
Barry, Edward D., 46, 47, 48, 57, 81
Barry, Emmett, 83
Barrett, H. M., 81
Basketball, 158, 159
Basketball de-emphasis, 189, 190
Bazaar, 152
Bechtolt, George E., 159, 184
Becker, William E., 223
Beckx, Pieter, 2, 7
Belgian Jesuits, 154, 155
Benson, William S., 93
Bernalillo, N.M., 2
Berney, Pete, 159
Beta Chapter (Delta Sigma), 171
Bertram, A. M., 38
Bertram, Augustine J., 58
Bianchi, Raphael, 1
Bianchi, Joseph B., 88
Bilgery, Conrad, 117, 150, 183
Bischofberger, Ferman, 112
Blackburn, William T., 180, 196
Bloomer, Louis A., 150, 160, 203
Boffa, D., 50
Boian, Sherwood T., 223

Bonfils, Frederick G., 102
Bonnet, Christian L., 176
Boone, Dennis, 189
Booster Club, 187
Borgerding, John, 170
Boyle, Jerome R., 108
Brannan, Charles F., 230
Breda, Rudy A., 192
Breen, Aloysius A., 94-100, 102
Brockway, Ronald A., 208
Brothers of the Christian Schools, 1, 3, 8, 9
Brooks, Max, 196, 223
Brooks, Peter A., 112-115, 148, 151, 157
Brown & Gold, 71, 80, 81, 82, 84, 89, 90, 91, 97
Brown, John J., 46, 62-68, 71, 72, 74, 76, 88, 94, 172
Brown, Lawrence A., 88
Brown, Leo C., 114, 147
Brucker, Aloysius, 80
Bruggeman, John, 188
Bucher, John W., 227
Buchtel, Henry A., 84
Buddy, Charles F., 112
Budinger, John, 209
Burke, Michael J., 152
Burns, George T., 220
Burns, Bob, 159
Burrowes, Alexander J., 73, 74
Bussen, Herbert A., 202, 203
Buswell, Charles A., 181
Butler, Jim, 189
"Buzz Boys", 159
Byrne, Robert F., 29, 36, 37
Byrne, Vincent, 46

Campbell, Frank, 112
Carey, Thomas, 100
Carroll, Elmer J., 214
Carroll Hall, 87, 96, 118, 149
Carroll, John, 87
Carrozzini, Vitus, 5
Casey, James V., 213
Casey, Thomas James, 217-221, 223
Caso, Prisco, 1
Casolaroi, Januarius, 74
Cassell, M., 61
Castelan, Gilbert M., 181
Catholic Educational Assn., 70, 71
Celanga, Manuel, 26, 27, 35
Chisolm, Theodore A., 52
Cella, Joseph J., 100, 112
Cemetery, removal of, 198
Cervantes, Lucius F., 168, 183
Chappuis, Charles, 27
Civis Princeps (First Citizen), 196
Clair, Sophia, 172
Classical course, 18, 31, 66

Clarke, David M., 219, 221-230
Co-education, 200, 201
Coll, Jerome B., 210, 215
College of Sacred Heart, 49
College of Santa Fe, 3
Colorado Springs, 36
Commercial course, 18, 32, 38, 45, 58, 92
Commerce and finance, 92, 99
Connor, Richard J., 193
Constitution of 1887, 42
Conway, Daniel H., 166, 231
Conway, Edward A., 114, 147, 150
Core curriculum changes, 216
Cordoba, John N., 34
Cottrell, George F., 102
Coudert, Joseph, 22
Coursey, Jerry, 159, 170
Coursey, Patrick, 180
Coyne, John V., 159, 176, 184, 208, 224
Cozens, William, 101, 147
Cross, Arthur C., 115
Crowe, John V., 170
Curran, Con, 170
Curriculum, 17, 18, 31, 37, 71
Currigan, Martin D., 79
Currie, Clyde, 208, 209

Daly, Frederick T., 176, 180, 185, 200, 206, 208, 211, 217, 224
Daly, Gene (Dennis), 170
Daly, John A., 190
Damen, Arnold, 64
Dawson, Eugene A., 181
Day, Edward C., 230
Dayton, Elizabeth, 179
Deane, Inigo, 26, 27, 30
Debt reduction, 117, 153
Deeman, Andrew J., 188, 192
Deline, Anabelle, 223
DeLorenzo, Frank, 171
Delta Sigma Chi, 93
DeMarlie, Gary, 189
Denver Club, 187
Dermody, Thomas, 83
Desaulniers, Joseph, 102
De Smet Hall, 179
De Valera, Eamon, 71
Dignan, Emmett J., 173, 196
Diana, Guilios, 88
Discipline, 19
Diss, William, 171
Distler, Paul F., 156, 161, 162, 168
Dominquez, Joseph, 26, 27, 35
Donnellan, John T., 55
Donnelly, Joseph P., 114, 147
Donoghue, Stephen, 99

Donohoue, Eugene A., 185, 194, 211
Dooling, Joseph, 55
Doran, Thaomas A., 100
D'Orsi, Raphael, 58
Dougherty, Paul F., 194
Downey, Joseph V., 117, 150, 172
Dramatics, 52, 53, 91, 188
Druding, Robert, 170
Driscoll, John J., 98, 101, 103
Durance, Lawrence W., 220, 221

Eatough, James R., 168, 192
Education in New Mexico, 13
Ellerby, Alfred E., 180
Elliott, A. Thomas, 224
Elocution, 52
Emmet, Thomas A., 220
Enrollment, 100
Escallier, Lucien, 215
Estrada, Michael, 55
Evans, George R., 231
Evans, John, 26, 27
Evening Division, 92, 101, 155, 171, 190

Faculty, 57, 184
Faherty, William B., 168, 183
Farrell, Francis J., 98, 99
Fede, Lawrence, 9
Fehrenbach, Alice O'S., 208, 219
Ferrante, Francisco, 2
Ferrari, Enrique, 59
Feulner, Edwin J., 230
Field House, 177, 178
Figgins, Jessie D., 117
Finances, 60, 61, 62, 63
Fisher, Joseph A., 191
Fisher, Robert E., 158, 159
Fitzgerald, William J., 64
Flanagan, James P., 199
Flanagan, John A., 193
Flanagan, John J., 118, 147-160, 166, 228
Flanigan, Phillip R., 209, 211
Flood, John L., 219
Floyd, Daniel J., 79
Floyd, Leo F., 79
Football, 90, 96, 97, 98, 108, 109
Ford Foundation, 177
Forstall, Armand W., 32, 50, 78, 79, 100, 115, 116
Fraser, 213, 218
Frazier, Earl, 79
Frey, Paul, 189
Froebes, Phillip, 183
Frye, William P., 16
Fund raising
    "Save Regis Campaign", 104
    Greater Regis, 112, 113
    Drive for Loyola Hall, 164, 180
War Bonds, 151, 152

Gallagher, Dennis, 188, 231

Gargaro, Lucille, 171
Garibaldi, Giuseppe, 2
Gasparri, Donato M., 2-20
Gauthier, Phillip E., 193
Gebken, Bob, 170
Gentile, Aloysius, 20, 25-27, 36, 42, 45
Gerleman, Hugo, 173
Gerstner, Allen, 188
Ghosh, Stanley, 181
Gibbons, James, 29, 34, 62
Gibbons, John J., 150, 156, 182
Gibbs, Guy, 192, 214
Gildea, P. F., 54
Girard, Augustus, 50
Glennon, John J., 161
Gockel, Joseph, 232
Golden Jubilee (1938), 112
Gonzales, Joseph J., 159
Gorman, Michael A., 91
Graiff, Orestes, 172, 175
Greater Regis Assn., 85
Gribben, John, 185
Griffith, Martin T., 173
Grollmes, Eugene E., 207, 208
Groshek, Michael D., 229
Guida, John B., 41-43, 60, 61
Guptil, Robert A., 192
Gustavson, R. G., 181
Gymnasium, 68

Haberer, James C., 193
Hackett, Glenn L., 88
Hahn, Aloysius S., 173, 192
Hall, Joe B., 189
Hall, Stanley, 180
Hanifen, Edward A., 151
Hanifen, Richard C., 231
Hanlon, Louis C., 176
Hannon, James, 168
Hartenbach, David L., 212, 214
Hecken, Henry P., 183
Heffley, Bryce, 159
Herbers, Joseph A., 103, 104, 105
Hennesey, James J., 222
Highlander, The, 51-54, 58, 61, 71, 77
High School, 38, 69, 70, 71, 81, 82, 95, 96, 100, 110, 114, 115, 161, 162, 163, 168
    Havana Property, 191, 212
Hindelang, Michael L., 173
Hitzelberger, Tom, 189
Hoefkens, Frances X., 98, 105, 164, 167
Hoene, David, 176, 193
Hoenmeyer, A. H., 99
Hoewischer, Harry E., 185, 195, 208
Holt, Marmaduke, 179
Holy Family College, 5, 6
Horan, Paul, 188
Horan, William P., 84
Horine, Samuel H., 106, 107, 109
Horstman, Ignatius, 84

Houlihan, Robert F., 185, 201, 208
Hughes, Michael J., 10-20
Husmann, Robert, 180, 181
Hyde, Eldridge, 58

Imhoff, Walter F., 180, 223

Jacobsmeyer, Gregory H., 214
Jesuits in New Mexico (incorporation), 1, 2, 3
Johnson, Edward L., 61
Johnson, Edwin S., 148
Johnston James A., 55
Jollain, Japhet, 94
Jones, John Paul, 180
Jones, Ken N., 192
Jones, William H., 213
Joseph, William, 196

Kalbaugh, Ann, 210
Karst, Bernard S., 106, 110, 115, 147, 152, 155, 170, 185, 186, 215, 232
Keenoy, Francis P., 99
Keenoy, Louis T., 150, 173
Kellogg, Clarence H., 111, 174, 192, 220
Kelley, Robert M., 77-89, 91, 95, 105-118, 151, 228
Kelly, Francis M., 112
Kelly, Martin C., 185, 191, 193, 199, 219
Kelly, Thomas E., 156, 157, 228
Kenrick, Peter, 24
Kessler, Eugene H., 156
Keough, Mary C., 201
Kiene, Fran A., 190
Kilpatrick, John, 159
Klocker, Harry R., 207, 219
Knight, Rodger D. Jr., 196
Knights of Columbus, 91
Knoll, A. Albert, 169, 181, 199
Knudson, Clarence, 150
K-Mart, 199, 200
Kolowich, George, 196
Kowald, Francis, 27, 28, 31, 34, 37, 43, 44, 50, 63, 75, 76
Kramer, George N., 88
Krieger, Stephen R., 152, 173, 192, 232
Krueger, Charles F., 183, 188

Lafayette—South Side Bank, 86, 96, 108
La Junta, N.M., 3
Lamar, Howard, 14, 15, 24
Lamb, John M., 219
Lambda Tau Club, 93
La Motte, Frank A., 88
Lamy, Jean Baptiste, 1, 2, 3, 24, 129
Laughlin, Ann, 184
Las Vegas College, 6-12, 16
Las Vegas, N.M., 3-9
Lavin, L. Morgan, 210
Lay Advisory Board, 109

Lay Brothers, 19
Ledochowski, Wlodmir, 73, 107
Levings, William S., 116
Linenbrink, Sr. M. Cecilia, 184
Linnenberger, Bob, 189
Loans, 46
Loffreda, Joseph, 111
Lopez, Francisco, 8, 13
Lonergan, William, 50, 52, 58, 67
Lord, Daniel A., 111
Loretto Sisters, 1, 3, 8, 14
Lowery, Robert J., 67, 68
Luckenbach, Harry L., 79
Lynch, Bernard, 164
Lynch, Edward S., 224
Lyons, John F., 224

McBriar, David J. (OFM), 224
McCallin, Joseph A., 150
McCarthy, Raphael C., 102-160, 175
McConaty, Joseph P., 223
McCrary, Irvin J., 83
McCullum, John A., 34
McDermott, Charles E., 213
McEnery, M. J., 79
McGinnis, James A., 227
McGlone, Frank B., 196
McGreevy, Mike, 170
McKenney, Thomas K., 168
McMahon, Bernard J., 203
McMahon, Thomas J., 190
McMenamin, Hugh L., 84, 103, 104
McNamara, Thomas A., 90
McNeill, Daniel M., 229
McNichols, Stephen L. R., 191, 230
Machebeuf, Joseph P., 20, 21, 24, 25, 29, 30, 36, 37, 41, 53, 96
Magevney, Hugh, 32, 33, 49, 50, 51, 57, 61
Mackenzie, Donald M., 166
Maginnis, Edward L., 195, 206, 208, 211, 217
Maguire, Adrian, 100, 109
Maguire, Edward F., 231, 232
Maher, Zacheus J., 107, 110, 111, 114, 115, 117, 148, 151, 152, 155
Mahoney, Florence J., 147
Malecek, Francis J., 186
Maloney, David M., 181
Mallon, Wilfred, 155, 165, 166
Mandalari, Alphonsus, 56
Manning, Henry J., 83, 86
Manzanares, F. A., 22
Marra, Joseph M., 5, 17, 19, 22, 36, 42, 45, 48, 59, 60, 62, 64, 68
Marcellino, P. A., 17
Marshall, Howard, 189
Martelon, Andy, 170, 205, 206, 211

Martin, Luis, 60
Martinez, Jese, 3
Mattione, Louis G., 166, 168, 183, 201, 205, 218, 229
Matz, Nicholas C., 29, 42, 45, 53, 54, 64, 95
Max, Paul, 232
Mazzella, Camillus, 7, 12
Meehan, Emmett 176
Mentag, Joseph, 100
Miege, John Baptist, 24
M'Ilhenney, H. D., 9
Millard, Herb, 189
Miller, David, 223
Miller, William T., 214, 217
Milliken, Eugene, 147
Minasi, Anthony, 9
Mission dissolved, 73, 74
Monnig, Eugene L., 192
Montoya, Joseph M., 230
Moore, Harvey E., 158, 159, 189
Mora, New Mexico, 9
Moran, John R. Sr., 196
Moran, John R. Jr., 223
Morrison, George M., 26
Mother's Club, 100
Mullen, Catherine S., 102
Mullen, Edmund L., 99, 111, 190
Mullen, John K., 67, 84, 85, 102
Mullen, Raymond H., 86
Mungret College, 46
Murlini, George, 84
Murphy, John K., 100
Murphy, Thomas F., 227
Murray, Bernard J., 90, 95, 112, 115, 150, 168, 182, 221
Mueller, Dolores, 171

Naughton, James W., 181, 231
Naples Province, 1, 2, 4, 8
Neary, Joseph, 83
Newell, Hubert M., 173, 181, 231
New Mexico-Colorado Mission, 1 ff
Nichols, J. Hervey, 55, 227
Nicholson, Will F., 194
North Central Assn., 81, 82, 87, 88, 104-107, 113-118, 153, 155, 162, 165, 166
North, Dennis, 206
Notarianni, Aldo G., 160
Nugent, T. J., 20

O'Brien, Jack, 171
O'Bryan, J. Gratton, 56
O'Connor, Alice, 101, 171
O'Connell, Daniel, 106, 107
O'Connell Hall, 176
O'Connell, John, 102, 103, 108, 153, 154
O'Connor, James, 29
Odenbach, Frederick L., 78
O'Donnell, T. J., 67
O'Hayre, John J., 193
Olszewski, William E., 209

Ong, Walter J., 147
O'Ryan, William, 103, 112
O'Sullivan, Robert J., 147, 215
Otto, John, 211
Owens, Sr. Lilliana, 65
Ozog, Francis J., 168, 184, 219

Padberg, John W., 213, 214
Pantanella, Dominic, 20, 21, 25-82, 167
Paul, W. Barney, 99, 190
Paulot, Charles, 116
Peck, Mary (Ryan), 171, 210
Perrin, L. K., 43, 44, 47
Personè, Charles, 29
Personè, Salvatore, 7-9, 13, 19-21, 36, 48
Petry, Dick, 159
Phelan, J., 164
Phelan, Joseph, 50, 52
Pinkard, James W., 181
Pinto, Charles, 3, 34, 41, 61
Poeckes, Joseph W., 173, 192
Policio, Cornelius, 41
Polski, John L., 89
Powers, Don, 170
Power, Edward J., 32
Porter, Louise Coors, 203
President's Council, 196
Price, Adelaide, 161, 171
Price, Joseph, 194

Quintana, Pedro (Eddie Mack), 98, 100
Quirk, John J., 171, 183, 186

Radio (KREG), 187
Ranger (year book), 98, 99
Ranger Day, 198
Rangers, 90
Raverdy, John B., 24
Rayhawk, Arthur, 83
Razzer Club, 93
Red Rocks (Park), 35
Reedy, Bill, 170
Refinancing, 96, 106-108
Regan, Thomas J., 205
Regis College Building and Endowment Association, 82, 83
Regis Chapel, 164
Regis Directors, 195
Regis Educational Association, 219, 221, 222
Regis Library Association, 113
Regis Men's Club, 111
Regis Review Service, 113
Regis Week, 196, 197
Reinert, Carl M., 231
Reinert, George J., 193, 205
Reinert, Paul C., 22, 231
Reinke, John J., 222
Renard, Eugene C., 192
Renk, John J., 202
Renaud, E. B., 116
Revista Catolica Press, 5, 6, 49, 59, 75
Riederer, Paul Q., 230

Ritch, William G.,   14, 15
Rice, James,   42
Robert, Stephen,   41, 42
Robertson, James W.,   222
Roche, George C., III,   231
Rossi, Alphonsus M.,   9
Roth, Randy,   211
Rotar, Peter A.,   184
Rourke, Eugene H.,   102
Rush, John A.,   68
Ryan, J. Clement,   183
Ryan, Joseph A.,   92, 95, 98,
   99, 101, 105, 117, 166, 168,
   171, 182, 188
Ryan, Richard F.,   175-203,
   228
Ryckman, Donald K.,   193

St. Ignatius School and Mis-
   sion,   42, 45, 56
St. Mary's Academy,   25
St. Mary's College,   9
St. Michael's College,   9
Salazar, A. A.,   30
Salmon, Donald L.,   206, 224
Salpointe, John B.,   22
Sandoval, Emmanuel,   113
Santa Fe Ring,   14, 15
Santa Fe Trail,   1, 9
Sauve, Henry,   27
Scaglia, Thomas,   188
Schimpf, John B.,   58
Schirber, Martin E. (O.S.B.),
   166
Schirmer, Godfrey,   85
Schmittling, Joseph,   112
Scholl, William J.,   102
School colors (college),   56
Schorie, George,   170
Schrempf, Marie,   171
Schuler, Anthony J.,   58, 64,
   65, 112, 160
Schulte, Theodore J.,   106,
   173, 231
Schwinn, Leonard (O.S.B.),
   112
Seep, A. H.,   85
Segale, Sister Blandina,   3, 4
Seidenstricker, Charles C.,
   113
Seismology,   77, 78
Self-Study, College,   185
Shafer, Floyd,   88, 90
Sheahan, Gerald R.,   213-218
Sheehan, Jim,   159
Sheehy, Joseph M.,   192
Sheehy, Terry,   189
Sheehy, Thomas J.,   202, 215
Sheeran, Michael J.,   224
Sherlock, Jack,   193

Sherman, Jerry,   189
Shook, Warren F.,   88
Sillstrop, Chuck,   170
Simon, Jerry,   159
Simon, Walter F.,   180
Singleton, Thomas F.,   183
Sisters of Charity of Cincin-
   nati,   1, 3
Ski Club,   187
Smith, Charles,   112
Smith, Willard L.,   149
Sobeck, Joseph F.,   100
Sommaruga, Achimme,   89
Sorrentino, Giuseppe M.,   3
Stackhouse, William J.,   150
Stadium,   91
Stanley, John P.,   105, 168
Stansell, Harold L.,   208, 217
Starratt, Robert J.,   222, 231
Statue of the Sacred Heart,   54,
   55
Stauffen, Ervin A.,   183
Steiner, William H.,   176
Stengele, Joe,   170
Steele, Thomas J.,   208, 219
Stephens, Joseph,   190
Stocking, Glen O.,   185
Students,   9, 10, 93, 100, 169
Student Center,   176
   expansion of,   179
Student Conclave,   89
Student Government (Senate)
   College,   100, 186, 187
Stubbs, Charles Jr.,   100
Sullivan, Bernard J.,   160,
   182, 231
Sullivan, John J.,   79, 85, 87,
   111, 112, 227
Sunderland, Joseph,   190
Sweeney, John F.,   196
Sweet, William E.,   86, 97
Sweigert, John C.,   232
Swift, H. J.,   62
Szczesniak, John B.,   202, 203

Taylor, Ralph F.,   192, 214
Taylor, T. Raber,   100
Teeling, John P.,   214, 215,
   218, 222
Thro, Linus J.,   179, 185
Tihen, J. Henry,   79, 84, 86,
   95, 96, 103
Tipton, George M.,   168, 183
Tiptonville, N.M.,   3
Toer, John E.,   85
Tomassini, Pascal   54
Tovani, Benjamin,   3, 5, 6, 7,
   74, 167, 168
Trame, Elmer J.,   183
Tromby, Vitus,   5

Troy, Ferdinand (Trojanech),
   5, 6, 12, 21
Trustees, Board of,   42, 62,
   195, 206, 207, 222, 223
Tuition,   2, 9, 11, 38, 71, 77,
   95, 172, 178
Tynan, Thomas J.,   111, 151

Uliano, Anthony M. (Brother
   Julian),   75, 182, 183

Valdes, J. A. S.,   30
Varnell, Larry L.,   158, 159,
   189
Van Valkenburg, Fred R.,
   159, 184
Vehr, Urban J.,   104, 112,
   157, 163, 164, 165, 181
Verdieck, Arthur O.,   159,
   183, 192, 214, 217, 223, 231
Verhoosel, Alphonse B.,   154,
   155
Vezza, Raphael,   1
Vidal, Henry C.,   35, 55
Vigilante, Livio,   1, 4, 19
Vollmar, Edward R.,   6, 47
Vollmer, Edward J. (O.S.B.),
   181

Wager, Elliot,   190
Wagner, Stephen M.,   190
Walker, John Brisben,   28, 42,
   47, 54
Wallace, Bob,   159
Wallace, Patrick,   26, 27, 35,
   50, 75
Walsh, Gerald P.,   98, 100,
   101
Walsh, John,   112
Walsh, Joseph J.,   79
Ward, Joseph T.,   102
Waters, Thomas A.,   159, 213
Watters, John T.,   58
Weckbaugh, J. Kernan,   196
Weber, Leo F.,   231
Willard, Timothy,   192, 223,
   231
Williams, Edwin A. T.,   157
Williams, George E.,   206
Williams, Ken,   189
Williams, William W.,   210
Wintergalen, Edward H.,   150,
   229
Works, George A.,   104, 105

Young, Thomas R.,   99

Zarlengo, Anthony F.,   218
Zuercher, Joseph P.,   153,
   155, 156, 162, 163, 164, 165

ABBREVIATIONS

BG., The Brown and Gold
CDPN., Catalogue of the Dispersed Province of Naples
CPM., Catalogue of the Missouri Province
CSH., Catalogue of the College
   of the Sacred Heart

DAB., Dictionary of American
   Biography
LVC Cat., Las Vegas College
   Catalogue
MPA., Missouri Province Arc-
   hives

PN Arch., Province of Naples
   Archives
RCA., Regis College Archives
SJA., Rome, Society of Jesus
   Archives, Rome
WL., Woodstock Letters